Strategies of Commitment

and Other Essays

THOMAS C. SCHELLING

Strategies of Commitment

and Other Essays

Harvard University Press
Cambridge, Massachusetts ▪ London, England

Printed in the United States of America

First Harvard University Press paperback edition, 2007

Library of Congress Cataloging-in-Publication Data

Schelling, Thomas C., 1921–
Strategies of commitment and other essays / Thomas C. Schelling.
p.   cm.
Includes bibliographical references and index.
ISBN-13 978-0-674-01929-4 (cloth: alk. paper)
ISBN-10 0-674-01929-6 (cloth: alk. paper)
·   ISBN-13 978-0-674-02567-7 (pbk.)
ISBN-10 0-674-02567-9 (pbk.)
1. Social choice.   2. Choice (Psychology)   3. Policy sciences.
4. Social problems.   I. Title.
HB846.8.S34 2006
320.6—dc22   2005052786

Contents

SOCIETY AND LIFE

■

ECONOMICS AND SOCIAL POLICY

■

WEAPONS AND WARFARE

■

SOCIAL DYNAMICS

■

DECISIONS OF THE HIGHEST ORDER

■

Preface

■ Two of my earliest preoccupations bracket the chapters of this new book. Almost fifty years ago, Harvard University Press published my book *Strategy of Conflict* (1960), a central theme of which was what I called "commitment." Commitment is central to promises and threats, to bargaining and negotiation, to deterrence and arms control, to contractual relations. I emphasized the paradox that commitment—to a relationship, to a promise or a threat, to a negotiating position—entails relinquishing some options, giving up choices, surrendering opportunities, binding oneself. And it works through shifting the expectations of some partner or adversary or even a stranger of how one will behave or react. The first chapter of this book consolidates several newer essays on that subject.

The final chapter celebrates the most important event that did not happen during the second half of the twentieth century: no nuclear weapons have been used since Nagasaki. An appendix to my 1960 book emphasized the *tradition* of nonuse, a then fifteen years' tradition based on a perception that nuclear weapons were generically different from any others. President Lyndon Johnson spoke in 1964 of the "nineteen peril-filled years" since any nation had loosed the atom against another. It is now over sixty peril-filled years, and no weapons used. Let us hope the tradition bears heavily on any nation, or on any organization, that may have or may acquire the weapons. The outcome, I am convinced, depends less on luck than on policy. In the event that, contrary to all hope and effort, nations like Iran and North Korea have acquired or do acquire nuclear weapons, we shall need institutions and policies that reinforce any reluctance to use them and help avoid actions that erode the inhibition.

My 1960 book contained four chapters concerned with nuclear war and its avoidance through arms control and careful strategy. For twenty-five years that was my main policy interest. I published two books on the subject.* For the past twenty years or so my main policy interest has been greenhouse gases, global warming, and climate change. The topics are completely diverse: nuclear fission versus infra-red absorption. But the two have much in common, both in the demands they make on diplomacy and in the kind of challenge they pose. Nuclear weapons required an unprecedented reorientation of military thinking that took some decades; the prospect of climatic changes greater than any that have occurred in the past ten thousand years will similarly require more than a decade or two to generate ideas on how to cope with this unavoidably global problem.

While there is no strategic opponent in the climate challenge—climate change cannot be deterred by threats or subdued by containment—there is an alliance problem that may be more challenging than the formation and evolution of the North Atlantic Treaty. For three or four decades the "tragedy of the commons," as coined by Garrett Hardin, the "logic of collective action," as coined by Mancur Olson, the "multiperson prisoner's dilemma," as coined (somewhat carelessly) by game theorists (it is not, strictly speaking, a *dilemma* but a predicament), and generally the "free-rider problem" have been a preoccupation of social scientists. The global atmosphere is the largest, and may prove to be the most challenging—or, at least, the second-most challenging after nuclear proliferation—and most long-lasting "common" we must learn to manage, "we" the six billion and more who meteorologically share the planet. Three essays in this volume focus on this concern.

Commitment I also found to be central to another area of strategy: the way people try to govern their own behavior. I hinted at that in the

---

*Thomas C. Schelling and Morton H. Halperin, *Strategy and Arms Control* (New York: Twentieth Century Fund, 1961); Schelling, *Arms and Influence* (New Haven, Conn.: Yale University Press, 1966).

1960 book but began to take it seriously when I was invited to join a committee of the National Academy of Sciences on Substance Abuse and Habitual Behavior in the 1970s. That committee acquainted me with professionals concerned with heroin, tobacco, alcohol, marijuana, gambling, and eating disorders, as well as with exercise regimes and other "lifestyle" endeavors. I had earlier considered commitment as central to influencing the behavior of others; it dawned on me that people attempting to control their own behavior often appeared to succeed when they managed to commit themselves to a regime of abstention or performance, treating themselves the way they might treat someone else. People often seemed to embody two selves, a "wayward" self and a "straight" self, the latter attempting to bring the former under control. How to subsume this kind of behavior under the rubric of rational choice, so central to economic theory, is a challenge. In the preface to my *Choice and Consequence* (1984) I said, regarding rational choice, "Like most economists I am attracted to this model, at least as a benchmark, because when it works we get a lot of output from minimal input using a standard piece of intellectual machinery," but added, "I have been intrigued by cases in which that model seems not to work well." Three essays here reflect that interest.

I went on to found an Institute for the Study of Smoking Behavior and Policy at Harvard University; one essay relates to that specific concern with smoking.

End-of-life decisions are a fascinating area of both interpersonal and intrapersonal strategy. They are also profoundly moral and can be politically explosive. In one of the essays included here, "Life, Liberty, or the Pursuit of Happiness," I originally said, "Everyone who reads this book recognizes the name Karen Ann Quinlan and most will read about more than one judicial decision on the subject within the year." I said that in 1988; as I write this preface in 2005, with Terri Schiavo's photo still in the papers, I view that comment as an understatement, and I have added Schiavo's name to that sentence for the benefit of younger readers.

In 1994 I was invited to give the commencement address to the graduates in economics of the University of California, Berkeley. It happened to be exactly the fiftieth anniversary of my own graduation from that same department. "What Do Economists Know?" is something I'd been trying to say to economists for a long time, and Berkeley gave me another opportunity to say it. I wanted to discuss the things known to be true by economists that are sometimes called "mere" accounting identities. Many of these crucial identities, so often demeaned as not "science" because not refutable hypotheses, would be dignified as "laws of conservation" in other disciplines.

"Why Does Economics Only Help with Easy Problems?" is slightly deceptively titled, but only slightly.

In the late 1970s a former student phoned from the Environmental Protection Agency and said he had some funds for external research that he'd lose if he didn't commit them by the end of the fiscal year. He wondered whether I'd like to commission some studies focusing on why economists are keen on bringing environmental issues within the purview of the price system. After all, nobody else is, not legislators, not environmental administrators, not environmental activists. Is it that economists grossly exaggerate the virtues of the price system in environmental protection, egregiously underestimate the difficulties of implementation, and are bemused by their theoretical constructs? Or have they just failed to get their message across? Is their audience perversely or irrationally predisposed against their ideas, or is there some other removable impediment to the initiation of wise policies?

I took his money and commissioned three case studies—on benzene, aircraft noise, and air pollution—and one interview study of attitudes. The book that resulted needed a careful exposition of the economic case for using the price system, and that was up to me; it is included here entitled "Prices as Regulatory Instruments." You will wish to know what conclusions the book reached; they are not in my piece, so I'll state two of them briefly. One: the pricing of emissions, whether by taxation or charges or what are now called "marketable rights" or "cap and trade" regimes, appeared feasible, effective, and superior to what came to be called "command and control." Two—a conclusion not anticipated by the authors or me—many of the benefits of pricing systems could be obtained by regulation if the regulatory standards were appropriately focused on benefits and costs. Criteria were what mattered, as much as mechanisms; a main advantage of pricing mechanisms was that they obliged quantitative attention to benefits and costs. And I must report that, in the twenty-five years since that study, attitudes in both Europe and the United States have shifted hugely in favor of prices as regulatory instruments for the environment.

"Research by Accident" relates a story I've never seen told. There are excellent histories of the development of nuclear energy and nuclear weapons, but none that I've seen tells this fascinating history of vitally important knowledge of weapon effects discovered over and over again literally by accident on the weapons test range. (And none mentions that a potential effect was anticipated in 1933 by a fictional jet-delivered atomic bomb exploded under water three hundred miles off the coast of Charleston—as a weapons test—producing a tsunami that caused the deaths of 90,000 people!) For readers who enjoyed *Dr. Strangelove* I've included a snippet of "Meteors, Mischief, and War" from the *Bulletin of Atomic Scientists.*

"Dynamic Models of Segregation" appeared in the first issue of the *Journal of Mathematical Sociology,* in 1971, an issue that hardly anybody can find. I've published abbreviated versions before; I wanted the full version to survive. What I did not know when I did the experiments with my twelve-year-old son using copper and zinc pennies was that I was doing what later became known as "agent-based computational models," or "agent-based computational economics." As a prologue to the chapter, I have included, at the price of a little repetition, a recent reflection on that experience that I was invited to compose for a volume on agent-based computational economics. In a similar spirit I include an essay on social mechanisms and social dynamics.

In *The Strategy of Conflict* I said in the preface, "The essays are a mixture of 'pure' and 'applied' research . . . In my own thinking, they have never been separate. Motivation for the purer theory came almost exclusively from preoccupation with (and fascination with) 'applied' problems; and the clarification of theoretical ideas was absolutely dependent on the identification of live examples. For reasons inherent either in the subject or in the author, the interaction of the two levels of theory has been continuous and intense."

That hasn't changed in forty-five years.

Strategies of Commitment

and Other Essays

Strategies of Commitment

■ I wrote about "commitment" almost fifty years ago (Schelling 1960, chap. 2), and some colleagues have conjectured that I originated the concept. That pleases me, but I must decline. I was scooped by at least 2,400 years. When Xenophon, pursued by Persians, halted against an almost impassable ravine, one of his generals expressed alarm that they would have no escape. Xenophon (1957, 136–137) reassured him: "As for the argument that . . . we are putting a difficult ravine in our rear just when we are going to fight, is not this really something that we ought to jump at? I should like the enemy to think it easy going in every direction for him to retreat; but we ought to learn from the very position in which we are placed that there is no safety for us except in victory."

Elsewhere, in similar circumstances, Xenophon notes that when retreat is impossible, no soldier need fear that while he is preoccupied with the enemy his companions in arms will desert him; the "commitment" is thus to each other, as well as toward the enemy.

I use "commitment" to mean becoming committed, bound, or obligated to some course of action or inaction or to some constraint on future action. It is relinquishing some options, eliminating some choices, surrendering some control over one's future behavior. And it is doing so deliberately, with a purpose. The purpose is to influence someone else's choices. Commitment does so by affecting that other's expectations of the committed one's behavior.

Commitment is pertinent to promises and threats, both overt and implicit, and to many bargaining tactics. "Take it or leave it" offers, for example, to be credible, require some commitment, and commitment may not be easy to arrange. A threat to take someone expensively to court to recover modest damages may not be credible, hence not persuasive, unless the person or organization making the threat can show a believable commitment.

THE THREAT

To threaten is to incur a commitment, and communicate it, to perform or forgo something to one's own (possibly grave) disadvantage that will inflict cost, damage, or pain on the party threatened if the threatened party does not comply, perform, or abstain as demanded in the threat. A threat, unlike a promise, is invariably conditional on behavior. Without the commitment and its persuasive communication, the threat lacks "credibility." If the threat succeeds it is not put into effect, and the only disadvantage to the threatener is whatever it may cost to incur the commitment and display it; if it fails, it is both costly and ineffectual. If a threat to strike, to resign, to retaliate, to sue, or to collide is successful, there is no costly strike, resignation, retaliation, suit, or collision.

Creating Commitment

The ways to commit to a threat, like the ways to commit to a promise, are many. Xenophon's device was simple: get in a geographical position where it is physically impossible, and manifestly so to your adversary, to do other than what you want your adversary to believe you must do whether you want to or not.

Legally, one files suit. Reputationally, one takes a public position. Physically, one gathers speed before an intersection. Emotionally, one becomes obsessed. Locationally, one occupies a position from which retreat is impossible ("burns bridges"). One can rely on a third party: "I'll be punished—divorced, fired, foreclosed, exposed, liquidated—if I don't." In the movie *Dr. Strangelove*, the doomsday machine was set to cover the world with lethal radioactivity automatically if its sensors detected some number of atomic bomb detonations in Soviet territory. In Europe, though NATO forces could not halt a Soviet advance, they were positioned where (it appeared, and was asserted that) they could not avoid triggering nuclear war if attacked from the east.

Of course, the commitment works only if the intended recipient knows of it and believes it. The Strangelove device was a faulty stratagem: it was kept secret, but couldn't deter any American attack unless it was known (and known to be impossible to "disconnect" at the last moment in the event of an attack).

An announcement that punishment will be forthcoming in the event of misbehavior, when that punishment, given the misbehavior, would be in the rational interest of the one making the announcement, may be thought of as a "warning," rather than a threat, or as a "reminder," or a "notification." (If one would obviously be motivated to sue for recovery, saying so is no threat but rather a possibly helpful message.) It is typically in the interest of both issuer and recipient that a warning be reliably issued and received. In contrast, it is not in the interest of the target of a threat that the threat be consummated, that is, that the (conditional) obligation be successfully incurred and communicated; and if it cannot be successfully communicated it cannot succeed and cannot serve a purpose.

A threat, like a promise, to be effective must be persuasive, and persuasiveness has two dimensions that may be called "potency" and "credibility." Potency refers to the (manifest) ability of the person making the promise or the threat to carry it out on a scale sufficient to make compliance attractive. Credibility refers to the correspondent's belief that what is promised or threatened will indeed be carried out. Commitment refers to credibility.

Credibility, however, extends beyond commitment: one may brandish an empty gun, pretending it is loaded. But to brandish an empty gun effectively one must pretend (bluff) two things: that it is loaded, and that one would dare to fire. Thus two kinds of bluff: potency and credibility.

Commitment sometimes lends itself to collective action. A good example is a strike fund. Some unions that have many locals recognize that all have an interest in each local's success in bargaining, that winning a strike benefits all, and that successfully threatening a strike is even better than winning one. Successfully threatening a strike is more than threatening just to go out on strike: it is threatening to stay out longer than management can afford, relative to whatever is in dispute.

And most locals are not on strike simultaneously. A common strike fund, or common commitment to help striking locals financially, serves three important purposes. It helps to maintain family income during a strike—all the other locals chipping in. It, in consequence, allows a local to strike longer if necessary, enhancing the likelihood of success. And, most critical, it puts the firm on notice that the strike will not be entirely or even mainly at the expense of the workers on strike. The "commitment" is institutionalized at the level of the international, not the local. Being thus committed to share one another's strike burdens is intended to reduce the aggregate burden by enhancing the local's commitment, and probably does.

The Probabilistic Threat

An intriguing mode of commitment can arise with a "probabilistic" threat. A probabilistic threat is one that the threatener "may" carry out, or maybe not, if the second party fails to comply. "Come one step nearer and I may shoot." The motive may be that what is threatened is of enormous size and cannot readily be scaled down, so that a probabilistic "fraction" of the threat is all one dares. Or a fractional probability of a large threat is sometimes more economical than the certainty of a smaller one: one chance in twenty of a thousand-dollar fine for parking at a hydrant may be more cost-effective than the certainty of a fifty-dollar fine.

But let's consider the threat so large that the threatener would shrink from carrying it out. This concept at first appears to be an oxymoron: if one retains the option to carry out or not to carry out what he or she manifestly prefers not to carry out in the event of noncompliance, how can the threat carry any credibility? Without commitment, what force can it have? With commitment, how can its fulfillment be escaped?

Interestingly, the concept has meaning, even in very familiar terms. The key is creating a situation in which, if compliance is not forthcoming, the (mutually) damaging consequence has a credible probability—maybe not easily estimated, but clearly perceptible and consequential—precisely because the outcome is not within the control of the threatener. The hypothetical mechanical model would be the roulette-wheel doomsday machine: attack our western border and we spin the wheel; if zero or double-zero comes up—two chances in thirty-eight—the world is destroyed, your world and ours.

Strategies of Commitment

Two questions. Why not just wire the world to be blown up for any such attack? That ought to deter, and if it deters, nobody gets blown up. And how do they know you won't disconnect the machine when the attack occurs, since they know you'd prefer not to be blown up?

To the first question there may be good answers. "They" may misunderstand what constitutes an attack; "they" may attack inadvertently, by mistake; "they" may lose control somewhere; "they" may even come to prefer suicide. As long as they are sane and in control, two chances in thirty-eight ought to deter them; if they are not sane and in control, any blunder leaves us a 36/38 chance of survival. The arithmetic makes sense.

The second question—why should they believe we would actually connect the infernal machine or, if we've shown them the connection, not disconnect it in the event?—may be unanswerable. It is like the cheap sign "traffic speed under continuous radar control": where is the proof that we actually bought the expensive radar equipment?

The commitment has to come from manifestly relinquishing control. A familiar example is tailgating. Nobody is intimidated by a tailgater until he—it is always a he—is close enough to be dangerous. An eighteen-inch distance is okay as long as nothing goes wrong; but at sixty-five miles an hour on a crowded beltway something can always go wrong. And if something goes wrong, lives are at stake. The tailgater has no more interest in a fatal crash than I do; he will use all his driving skill, if something goes wrong, to save us both. But we both know that all his driving skill may not suffice: there is some chance we will both end up dead. The other driver, by coming close, puts me on notice. If I want not to accommodate, I have to consider how long it will take my persistence to make him back off and whether that is longer than I want to risk it; I may sense that he believes I'll eventually change lanes and that he can hold out longer than I. "Buzzing" an airplane to make it change course or land invokes the same principle: getting close enough for a collision to be a live possibility is the "commitment."

The Cuban missile crisis, as revealed in the Kennedy audiotapes, was a perfect example. The president's decision to impose a naval blockade against Soviet vessels approaching Cuba was recognized to threaten the risk of nuclear war. Evidently nuclear war was the last thing either side wanted; evidently no outcome of the crisis could have been worse than nuclear war; evidently the president and his advisors believed the blockade to carry the possibility of a nuclear war that neither side would ever deliberately undertake; evidently they believed that things could get beyond control once the blockade was under way. They considered the risk tolerable for what was at stake; they hoped the Soviets would find it intolerable for what was at stake. The blockade itself was the (probabilistic) commitment.

An early version of this "threat that leaves something to chance" took place outside the gates of Troy some three thousand years ago, in a race with horse-drawn vehicles:

> The road here led through a gulley, and in one part the winter flood had broken down part of the road and made a hollow. Menelaos was driving in the middle of the road, hoping that no one would try to pass too close to his wheel, but Antilochos turned his horses out of the track and followed him a little to one side. This frightened Menelaos, and he shouted at him:
> "What reckless driving Antilochos! Hold in your horses. This place is narrow, soon you will have more room to pass. You will foul my car and destroy us both."
> But Antilochos only plied the whip and drove faster than ever, as if he did not hear. They raced about as far as the cast of a quoit . . . and then [Menelaos] fell behind: he let the horses go slow himself, for he was afraid that they might all collide in that narrow space and overturn the cars and fall in a struggling heap.

Antilochos won, though Homer says—somewhat ungenerously—"by trick, not by merit" (Rouse 1950, 273).

It was mentioned above that a threat is invariably conditional. To condemn someone to death is not a threat; to make certain actions punishable by death is a threat. Two qualifications are in order. One is that a threat may take the form of an unconditional commitment, the *consequences* of which are conditional on the target's behavior. I file unconditional suit for repossession, which the defendant can dismiss by depositing the back rent with the court. I keep a vicious dog in my yard, which the vagrant can evade by staying off my property. To threaten artillery bombardment against invasion of a demilitarized zone is conditional on the enemy's behavior; to deploy land mines is unconditional, but the consequences equally depend on the enemy's behavior. To gather enough momentum to make collision inevitable with anyone in my way is an unconditional commitment; but the effects depend on who gets in my way.

The other qualification was illustrated just above: the Cuban blockade was an unconditional commitment: escalation or subsidence was up to the Soviets. In some threats, like the blockade, the commitment takes the form of initiating the threatening action, creating the risk, or delivering punishment that threatens cumulative pain or damage. The threat of forcible eviction of delinquent tenants may not be credible; shutting off the utilities is gentler but effective.

Threatening a predatory price war, with the intention of eliminating a competitor, is likely to take the persuasive form of initiating it, costing both parties until one or the other gives up. Initiation contains an element of commitment—at least some demonstration of willingness to incur cost. If for reasons of differential staying power the predator's victory is a foregone conclusion and bound to gain more reward than the war will cost, the tactic is probably best viewed not as a threat but as a warning, one that the target is wise to heed. If war to the death would be disastrous for both, only a persuasive "commitment" may induce the target to prudently leave the field of battle. The reputation of a chain store used to provide that kind of commitment in small-town battles for the grocery market. Some of the ways a monopolist can use commitment tactics to deter entry by a competitor are in Kreps (1990) and in Baird, Gertner, and Picker (1994).

The Welcome Threat

In discussing promises below we shall ask, Could a promise be unwelcome? Here we may ask, Can a threat be welcome? Remember, a threat is a commitment, conditionally, to do harm to the one threatened, to coerce a behavior that would not voluntarily be chosen. The answer is—only momentarily—surprising: yes. A threat, or something very like a threat, can be welcome.

One may badly need, even desperately need, to make a credible promise where honor, self-esteem, reputation, piety, legal contract, third-party sponsors, and other possible sources of commitment are unavailable. Offering a suitable forfeit or hostage to the promisee is giving that party a "threat" over the promissor. The seamstress who hocks her sewing machine, the saxophonist who hocks his instrument, puts a "threat" in the hands of their financial benefactor; the pawnbroker is given the power to cut off their livelihoods if they do not fulfill their pledges, and so becomes willing to make the loan.

I put the pawnbroker's "threat" in quotation marks because it doesn't quite conform to my initial definition, "a commitment . . . to perform or forgo something to one's own (possibly grave) disadvantage." The pawnbroker needs no commitment to sell the saxophone; he'll sell it in his own interest and keep the proceeds if it is not redeemed on schedule. The promissor is on "warning," though it has the effect of a credible threat.

To contrive a genuine threat that is welcome, we can concoct a scenario—maybe Hitchcock could have used it—in which a young convicted felon cannot get a job: he can't be trusted not to rob the company. California passes a "three strikes and you're out" law, according to which conviction on a third felony results in life without benefit of parole, pardon, or early release for good behavior. Our protagonist proceeds to get himself arrested and convicted a second time. Upon release he promptly gets a job! He cannot risk another conviction, so he's obviously bound to stay clean. The state would be obligated to pursue him at whatever cost and keep him locked up at great expense for fifty years—medical care and all—whether or not he's still dangerous at age fifty, sixty, seventy, or beyond. The state is committed to fulfilling a hugely costly threat if the two-time felon misbehaves again; if the threat succeeds, it is costless, and the young man is subject to a welcome threat that guarantees his good behavior to whoever would like to employ him.

The difference between a threat and a promise—between coercion and compensation—sometimes depends on where a baseline is located. A California judge promised a destitute mother convicted of a crime that he would not sentence her to six months in prison if she would submit to sterilization. If the six months that he promised to excuse her from was the standard baseline, the proposal was an offer and a promise; if the baseline was probation, the judge made a threat.

A threat is sometimes achieved via a promise to a third party. In the 1950s the United States ratified a "mutual defense" treaty with the National government of the Republic of China. It was nominally for the

Strategies of Commitment

benefit of that government—we were not expected to be defended in return. But the obvious intent was to assure mainland China that America's worldwide reputation for meeting its defense commitments would henceforth depend on fulfilling, if necessary, its commitment to the defense of Taiwan.

THE PROMISE

In the movie *The Princess Bride,* the reluctant maiden is wed to the evil prince in a bumbling ceremony that is interrupted by an attack on the castle. In the confusion she meets the hero, whom she loves, and disconsolately confesses that all hope is lost, she is married. The hero, a young man who does not easily yield, demands of the maiden, "Did you say 'I do'?" After some reflection and some prodding by the young man, she is pretty sure that that part of the ceremony got omitted. "Then you are not married. You can't be, if you didn't say 'I do.'" That settled, they ride off together on white horses.

"I do" in a marriage ceremony is a "performative utterance," in the terminology of J. L. Austin (1952) and a "speech act" in the terminology of John R. Searle (1969). It is not merely the answer to a question. It is part of a formula that changes the legal and social status of the person and her relation to the man who also says "I do." (Consider that to answer "sure," or "hell yes," might be considered insufficiently solemn to consummate the ceremony.)

If you ask me whether I customarily wear socks of the same color and I respond "I do," my answer is not much of an act; it is merely a declarative sentence that communicates information. But if you ask me under oath whether on the night of the crime I was wearing socks of the same color, my response is a speech act, or performative utterance; it changes my status under the law in the event I am demonstrated to have lied. So is "I do," uttered with my hand on the Bible when I am sworn in to testify.

"I promise" is usually a speech act and intended as one. It is the act that we refer to as a promise. Linguistically one can say "I promise" without promising: "I promise my children rewards when I want them to be good." But when I make the promise to my children, it is an act. The verbalization "I promise," followed by a description of what is promised, is intended and interpreted as a way of incurring obligation to perform as promised, typically with sanctions of some sort to enforce the obligation.

The words "I promise" may not themselves be essential. "If you clean your room, I'll let you go to the movies" is understood as binding; even so, the verbal ceremony is such an expected part of the promise that the child may respond, "Promise?" It is one of the interesting asymmetries between threats and promises that the threat has no comparably ceremonial language: "Shut your mouth or I'll shut it for you," uttered in the presence of one's peers, may incur an obligation and be intended to, but adding "I threaten" adds nothing.

I find it useful to enlarge the concept of promise to include acts that are not primarily verbal that incur an obligation that can be appreciated by the second party. "If you lend me $100 I'll pay you back next week with interest" may lack credibility, even when accompanied by "I promise." But surrendering an electric guitar to the pawnshop can be thought of as a promissory act. The difference is in the nature of the sanction.

The purely verbal or ceremonial promise can place one's honor and self-respect on the line, and one's reputation for keeping promises. And if sworn on or in relation to a religious object, the promise can affect one's prospects in heaven and hell. Sometimes the reputation at stake is only one's reputation with the person to whom the promise is made: if the two of us can arrange our affairs successfully only by relying on each other's promises, keeping one promise may be a prerequisite for having the next one believed.

Among the pledges, forfeits, and vulnerabilities that someone may incur as assurance that a promise will be kept are hostages. Until that term lost its traditional definition through indiscriminate use in the last couple of decades—coming to mean any prisoner, captive, or victim of kidnapping—a hostage was "a person held as security for the fulfillment of certain terms," and in another dictionary, "a person held by one party in a conflict as a pledge that promises will be kept or terms met by the other party." Hostages have sometimes been freely given as pledges, sometimes taken to enforce a pledge. When Caesar's soldiers conquered unruly tribes in Gaul, they took children as hostages to enforce the good behavior of the remaining villagers. It was in the villagers' interest that the hostages be taken; the alternative, to ensure appropriate tranquility, would have been to kill all the men.

In fiction, the person who witnesses a serious crime may volunteer to be blinded to "promise" not to be a witness. He may reveal a horrid secret with which he can be blackmailed. Or he can even commit a crime in the presence of those to whom he wishes to promise silence, leaving evidence in their hands that they can use against him. In "Wet Saturday," a John Collier story produced on the old Alfred Hitchcock television series, the local priest, taking a shortcut home, stumbles on a girl's father dropping down the well the body of the man she just killed. The priest is given a choice: join the body down the well or leave his handprints on the murder weapon, which will be kept as security by the girl's father. The priest "promises" by grasping the axe handle firmly. (He should have insisted on sharing the axe handle with the girl's fingerprints or the father's; as it was he got badly cheated.)

Eunuchs, it has been said, used to get some of the best jobs because of what they could promise not to do.

And then there are promises that utilize the credibility of a third party. Someone can endorse your promissory note because that person's promise is good where yours is not. Bail bondsmen can afford to post bail against your returning for trial because they are skilled in the business of finding you if you don't show. And to promise reliable performance in a job, one gets recruited by a friend who already works there and whose own job will be in jeopardy if he recommends a recruit who proves unreliable.

Now that I have identified promises defined verbally and promissory acts of many kinds, let me call them all promises and state just what a promise is. A promise is the creation of a perceived obligation to do or to bring about what is promised. But that basic definition includes most of what we would call threats, so promises must be a subset. What distinguishes a promise, as an obligation, from a threat is mainly this: what is promised must appear to the one to whom the promise is made as being in the latter's interest. It is an obligation welcomed by the party to whom the promise is incurred. (Incurring an obligation to punish in the event of misbehavior we would call a threat.)

There are some exceptions, some borderline cases, and a few strange cases.

For instance, a promise of amnesty, or of partial forgiveness, is sometimes coupled with a threat of prosecution, perhaps in connection with tax delinquency, when without the promise the threat would be so ineffectual that it wouldn't be made and the delinquent would go free. After the victim has yielded to the threat, what was promised is desired, but the promise itself is not welcome in the context of the threat. A blackmailer has to be able to promise not to reveal the secret or to publish the picture, and to promise also not to keep coming back to be paid again and again; if the blackmailer cannot credibly promise, the victim gains nothing by paying and the blackmailer cannot make the sale. The blackmailer's keeping the promise once the victim has paid is in the victim's interest; the blackmailer's being able to make the promise is not.

Promising an act that I am committed to do anyway may be of value to the second party if, though I am fully committed, he or she is not convinced. Dropping someone in the wilds to spend a week fishing, and incurring a credible promise to return at the end of the week to pick the person up, may be more effective, for the sake of the bargain, than casually saying that I have my own reasons for returning at the end of the week.

What about "I promise I didn't do it"? The language of promises, especially among children, is often mobilized in support of the truth of what one alleges, not merely of a commitment one incurs. The same language can be used in support of a forecast of something that is not of one's doing, like an eclipse of the sun. Similarly, introducing my boss to a friend and "promising" that my friend is reliable is putting up a pledge in support of my judgment and veracity, or possibly my commitment to enforce my friend's good behavior.

I believe the language of promising in support of one's own veracity is close enough to the meaning of a promise to be included. If I had to include it in a formal definition, I would explain that "I promise I didn't do it" and "I promise the moon will eclipse the sun" are two-tiered. "I promise to speak the truth in my next sentence" can be coupled with "I didn't do it" or "the sun will be eclipsed." Thus the promise is to speak the truth, and for convenience the promise is simply incorporated into the statement that is promised to be true.

Another two-tiered promise is the guarantee. To guarantee a secondhand car is to promise that either the car will perform satisfactorily or restitution will be paid or the car repaired or replaced. Notice that a guarantee typically not only promises restitution but also conveys some extra assurance that the guaranteed performance will be forthcoming. That is, it supports the promise itself. To see this, consider two guarantees. The first: if your oil tank runs dry we will come instantly to fill it and give you a $100 rebate as compensation. Alternatively, we will donate $100 to the charity of your choice. Assuming that the promised rebate or donation is itself credible, either way there is a $100 penalty on nonperformance that makes it less likely the tank will run dry. Sears's guarantee to replace immediately a defective water heater is, because of the cost of installing a new one and carting away the old, powerful assurance that my heater is reliable. The guarantee (promise) is a demonstration of confidence.

Comparing promises with threats, there are some differences but also some connections. One difference is that promises that are contingent on some quid pro quo are usually costly only when they succeed and have to be kept, threats only when they fail and have to be carried out. A threat that appears excessive and disproportionate—get out of my way or I'll run over you—is not too large if it succeeds; it may be less credible if apparently disproportionate, but if it works it is as cheap as a smaller threat would have been. A promise that is too large pays more than the result is worth.

Promises can be conditional or unconditional, that is, contingent on something the second party is to perform or abstain from or bring about, or absolute and independent of the second party's behavior. Timing is important: if the second party's performance comes after the first promise has to be fulfilled, the first's promise must be conditioned on a promise in return, I promising to do for you today what has to be done today, on condition you promise me to do tomorrow what I need done tomorrow. In this case, both parties to the transaction have to be capable of making credible promises. At least, they do if you cannot witness my performance—whether or not I kept my part of the bargain—before your performance is due tomorrow. If you can observe my performance my promise is unnecessary and yours alone does the trick.

An important consideration is whether or not the second party, or any interested third party, will ever be able to tell whether or not the promise was kept. A promise to keep a secret, not to speak ill of a person, to keep the thermostat turned down in an apartment, to try hard to find a job, to brush one's teeth after every meal, or not to engage in espionage in a friendly country may suffer the peculiar difficulty that one may not be found out if the promise is broken. Indeed, the paradox is that in many of these cases the promise is needed only because what is promised cannot be monitored. If the child were to brush his teeth in the kitchen with a parent in the room, the sanction could be on the behavior itself, and not on the breaking of a promise.

Sometimes the promises are enforced by a deity from whom broken promises cannot be hidden. "Certain offenses which human law could not punish nor men detect were placed under divine sanction," according to H. D. F. Kitto (1951, 197). "Perjury is an offense which it may be impossible to prove; therefore it is one which is peculiarly abhorrent to the gods." This is a shrewd coupling of economics with deterrence: if divine intervention is scarce, economize it by exploiting the comparative advantage of the gods. If their intelligence system is better than that of the jurists, give them jurisdiction over the crimes that are hardest to detect. The broken promises that are hardest to detect may, like perjury, fall under their jurisdiction. But be careful not to go partners with anyone who does not share your gods.

Just as a threat can be a bluff, there are deceitful or disingenuous promises, although we have no name for them corresponding to "bluff." A particularly interesting "false promise" is promising, in return for a favor or good behavior, what one is fully motivated to do unconditionally, pretending that one would not otherwise do it. This tactic converts a promise to do something into a threat not to, possibly a bluff. "If you behave yourself I'll take you to the zoo this afternoon" implies "If you don't, I won't." There are now two possibilities in the event of bad behavior: no zoo, even though I originally looked forward to it and still would prefer it, but having made the promise conditional I am obliged to carry out the threat. Or zoo anyhow, and I was bluffing.

Legal contracts can be interpreted as reciprocal promises (Fried 1981). Among the legal privileges of corporations, two that are mentioned in textbooks are the right to sue and the "right" to be sued. I first wondered what was so good about being sued, but soon realized that the right to be sued is the power to make a promise: to borrow money, to enter a contract, to do business with someone who might be damaged.

And indeed a powerful technique for preventing certain transactions that are considered socially undesirable is to make promises unenforceable, to deny the right to be sued. Gambling debts, for example, are often made unenforceable by law, as are debts to loan sharks in some states, or any financial contract signed by someone under eighteen years of age. Many developing countries have "mechanics lien laws" specifying the kinds of tools and equipment that may not be placed in hock. Insurance companies cannot write a contract according to which they will pay your fines or maintain your wages while you serve a prison term.

And the secret ballot is intended not only to assure you your privacy but, being mandatory, to deny you any way to credibly promise your vote, either for compensation or under duress. (Whether the increasing use of mail ballots will be found to violate this fundamental principle of democracy is still to be seen.)

BARGAINING

Much bargaining is "distributive," over the sharing of a "surplus." The price one pays for the house, the claim one receives from the insurance company, the wage package agreed to by union and management, the settlement of a suit out of court, the loan a country gets from the International Monetary Fund, the allowance of a child in college, the salary in a new job—all eventually, if the job and the house and the loan don't fall through, are at a point within some range, wide or narrow, within which any point is a potential jointly beneficial bargain. Sometimes that range is quite uncertain: I know the most I'd pay for the house but not what the seller's lower limit is; the seller knows roughly his or her lower limit, at least momentarily, but not how much I'd be willing to pay. Sometimes we have a pretty good idea what that range is, and then we both know that there is something "indeterminate" about the outcome: one of us, and probably both of us, will eventually settle for a figure from which we'd have been willing to retreat to save the sale.

In such a potentially fluid situation it can be advantageous to place a credible limit on what one can be expected to concede. In the salary negotiation one would like to demand close to the maximum that the employer could contemplate—not so close as to risk going over the limit and being unable subsequently to back down. The employer would like to offer more, but only somewhat more, than the applicant's reservation price. Either party may seek a commitment—an "objective" basis for asserting that a certain figure is as low, or as high, as he can go. The dynamics may be complex: displaying commitment may take time, both parties may simultaneously seek commitment, one may want the option of softening and backing down if he or she seems to have gone too far, either may try to discredit the other's effort to establish commitment, and establishing the commitment may require both evidence and persuasion.

A classic textbook in labor–management relations (Walton and McKersie 1965) devotes an early chapter to commitment. The subheadings provide a useful outline:

Determining Appropriate Degree of Commitment
Communicating Party's Commitment
Making Party's Commitment Credible
Preventing Opponent from Becoming Committed
Enabling Opponent to Revise Commitments
Abandoning Party's Commitments

They say, "The purpose of commitment is to affect the choice of Opponent by influencing his perception of what Party intends to do. 'Commitment' refers to the act of pledging oneself to a course of action" (50).

A particularly notorious commitment tactic acquired a proper name, "Boulwarism." A succinct account is in the *MIT Dictionary of Modern Economics* (Pearce 1996): "In the US General Electric Company, however, it was once the practice to make a firm offer to the union and refuse to bargain thereafter. This approach to bargaining is named after Lemuel Boulware, a former GE vice-president for industrial relations. The practice has since been declared contrary to the legal requirement to bargain in good faith by the US National Labor Relations Board."

For interfirm bargaining an ingenious commitment device has been what came to be known as MFN contracting, the name coming from "most favored nation" tariff treatment. A company wishes to commit itself to a firm price—no haggling allowed. It offers each of its customers a contract according to which that customer will always receive the lowest price offered any customer, an "offer it can't refuse." Once the supplier is surrounded by MFN beneficiaries it cannot respond to any customer's demand for special treatment: "If I do it for you I have to do it for everybody else."

Governments, especially democratic governments, find it both important and difficult to commit themselves. Periodic free elections make pledges transient—never to impose price controls, never to run large budget deficits.

Commitment can sometimes be achieved by separation of authorities. The Congress can anticipate diplomatic negotiations with legislation or joint resolutions that circumscribe executive-branch options. Whether the "commitment" so produced serves well or ill, it usually not only weakens the negotiators' ability to maneuver but strengthens the negotiators' commitment, by visibly denying the flexibility that might be exploited by their negotiating partners. During 1949 the United States government tried to interest the Marshall Plan countries in the establishment of a European Payments Union, which was going to entail diverting some Marshall Plan funds into the project. The Europeans paid little attention, until the Congress wrote into the aid bill for 1950–51 a stipulation that $300 million of the total appropriated was available solely for endowment of a European Payments Union. Negotiation went smoothly after that.

PERSONAL CREDIBILITY

Just as there is a gamut of devices and techniques and arrangements by which persons may deliberately commit themselves, knowingly and consciously and deliberately getting committed in order to influence the behavior of others, for personal benefit or for the common good, so also is there a spectrum of personal traits, qualities, abilities, handicaps, compulsions, idiosyncrasies, and superstitions that allows them or helps them to become credibly committed, for better or for worse, through who and what they are rather than through what they deliberately do for the sake of commitment.

To illustrate. In Joseph Conrad's (1923) *Secret Agent,* anarchists plot to destroy Greenwich Observatory. They get their nitroglycerin from "the professor," a stunted little chemist. The authorities know who provides the stuff, but this little chemist walks the streets of London with immunity. A young man tied in with the Greenwich job is in wonderment: why, he asks, do the police not apprehend him? The "professor" answers that the police may not shoot him from a safe distance, for that would be a denial of the "bourgeois morality" that the anarchists want to discredit. And they dare not capture him physically because he always keeps some of the "stuff" on his person. He keeps his right hand in his trouser pocket holding a hollow ball at the end of a tube that reaches a container of nitroglycerin in his jacket. All he has to do is to press that little ball and anybody near will be blown to bits. The young man wonders why the police would ever believe anything so preposterous as that the "professor" would actually blow himself up. The stunted chemist's explanation is calm. "In the last instance it is character alone that makes for one's safety . . . I have the means to make myself deadly, but that by itself, you understand, is absolutely nothing in the way of protection. What is effective is the belief those people have in my will to use the means. That's their impression. It is absolute. Therefore I am deadly" (65–68).

Conrad intended that we believe the "professor" really would blow himself up. We can deduce that he's never been tested: if the police had laid hands on him and he hadn't immolated himself, they wouldn't be avoiding him now, and if they had laid hands on him and he had, they might have new respect for his spirit but he wouldn't be around for the Greenwich escapade. He could be bluffing. But he doesn't sound like it. And "the belief those people have in my will to use the means" is crucial. Rigging the nitroglycerin in his clothing is deliberate; being the kind of person he is is not.

I think we can call him "committed." But he didn't "commit himself." He just *is* committed. I once wrote a chapter entitled "The Art of Commitment" (Schelling 1966). It is about deliberately *getting* committed. That is different from *being* a committed person or *being* the kind of person who can incur believable commitments without external enforcement. We doubt that the professor got himself committed—incurred his commitment, arranged his commitment, negotiated his commitment. He didn't make himself the kind of person who would blow himself up rather than surrender. He just is that kind of person. We might diagnose pride, honor, obstinacy, destiny, identity; he might himself not know why he's that kind of person.

Sources of Commitment

We cannot tell—I cannot, anyway—whether he is "hard wired" biologically to be so obstinately determined, or has been conditioned by experience and surrounding culture. An interesting contrast, at the level of the group rather than the individual, is the "character" of the sixteenth-century Swiss, who acquired similar respect by the way they lost battles as well as by the way they sometimes won them: "The [Swiss] Confederates were able to reckon their reputation for obstinate and invincible courage as one of the chief causes which gave them political importance . . . It was no light matter to engage with an enemy who would not retire before any superiority in numbers, who was always ready for a fight, who would neither give nor take quarter" (Oman 1953, 96).

It is easy to see that the Swiss recognized the value of reputation—a reputation costly to acquire but invaluable once acquired—but also that a propensity for such behavior could become embedded in their culture and cease to be only strategically instrumental. The "professor" may have been uniquely genetically different from the rest of us, the sixteenth-century Swiss probably not.

An intriguing question is whether for human beings the value of being recognized as the kind of person who keeps his commitments purely on the basis of his own character and emotional makeup, not by rearranging incentives or external constraints, could be so valuable in interpersonal relations that those with a slight genetic proclivity to be that kind of person would enjoy enhanced reproductive success, and the genetic propensity would proliferate and become embedded in the species.

Being versus Becoming

I distinguish between being committed and becoming committed. Some people simply *are* trustworthy, trusting, vengeful, charitable, faithful, grudge-bearing, forgiving, vindictive, hot-tempered, stubborn, easygoing, brave, persevering; imbued with pride, honor, hatred, cruelty, or kindliness; passionately identified with tribe, race, language, gender, class; devoted to a deity, fearful of God, believing in a consequential afterlife, capable of calling on God as a witness ("cross my heart"). And often they are so recognized, at least by some. Many of these recognizable traits are likely advantageous on balance, although some may make a person vulnerable.

"Becoming" is the ability to adopt for the occasion the capacity for recognizable commitment. One who by nature turns the other cheek may be able to swear resistance and retaliation when it seems crucial; one who abhors violence may be able to threaten punishment; one who is known to be devious and selfish may be able to commit convincingly to loyalty or honesty when it most matters; one who is normally hard to arouse may become incensed when presented with certain challenges. "Becoming" committed probably is more strategic, that is, less a matter of an abiding character than of a rising to the occasion.

"Becoming" is apparently more optional than "being." A proclivity to lose my temper may be an occasional advantage, perhaps more often a disadvantage, in interpersonal relations. Being able to lose it when losing it would serve my purpose—to make threats credible, even unspoken threats—whether dealing with mischievous children or with adult antagonists, especially if I can keep my temper when losing it would not be advantageous, can have genuine instrumental value.

Becoming and being overlap. If I am devoted to a deity, or if I belong to a culture of honor, that requires fealty to any sworn obligation, I "become" committed only if I swear, but I "am" the kind of person who can swear credibly.

A Genetic Basis?

The evidence is overwhelming that there are people who are committed, and are recognized as committed, to certain performances. Less obvious is that genetic inheritance is a significant contributor. People can behave strategically, knowing, for example, the value of maintaining a reputation for good behavior; people can be dedicated to a deity that issues commandments; people can be reared in a culture that gives them little choice about some behaviors, whether truthful, vengeful, or self-sacrificing; and people can be biologically predisposed, in a visible way, to behave in ways that are advantageous if anticipated. Just as people wisely avoid disturbing a mother bear with cubs, they can wisely avoid antagonizing a large man who is known to be easily enraged.

Bluffing

Evolutionary theory suggests that if humans had acquired, because of the fitness advantage it conferred, a capacity for persuasive commitment, they may also have acquired a capacity for faking. And if faking becomes a significant capability, the species may as a result have also developed at least some capacity to detect falsity.

I conclude with the advice that Edward R. Murrow, dean of television commentators, gave to Daniel Schorr upon the latter's moving into Murrow's role: "The secret to success in television broadcasting is sincerity. If you can fake that, you've got it made."

APPENDIX: ALTRUISM, MEANNESS, AND OTHER POTENTIALLY STRATEGIC BEHAVIORS

Biologically, "altruism" poses the puzzle of how a genetically determined behavior that is apparently non–self-serving can favor its own inheritance. Several answers to this puzzle have been found. Equally intriguing is meanness—harmful behavior that serves no evident purpose yet costs something. An illustration was the boy at camp who publicly and viciously hit a "friend" in the mouth while the friend was taking a nap. The act was so threatening that the aggressor became the undisputed leader of his group.

The kinds of behavior I have in mind, of which favors and insults are merely examples, might be called "strategic." A behavior propensity is strategic if it influences others by affecting their expectations. Strategic behavior is ubiquitous in human society and often takes forms that have a paradoxical quality—eliminating options, impairing capabilities, incurring penalties or risks, making expensive demonstrations, destroying possessions, disarming oneself, and other apparently non–self-serving behaviors that are advantageous only in their *anticipation* by others.

To prove that I will not harm you I disarm myself; to keep you from kidnapping my children I have to be poor; to persuade you that I will never bear witness I have to go blind; to keep you from desiring me I have to make myself ugly; to persuade you I shall never retreat I have to be chained to my post. Each is a gratuitous impairment or sacrifice except for the influence it has on your behavior.

I have known since I was a child that bees can sting and that when they sting they die and that nevertheless they sting. Unable to explain to a bee that its stinging would merely hurt me but would kill it, I have behaved with great respect toward bees. Scores must have lived, because of my anticipation, for every one that died stinging me.

Meanness and altruism are not only alike, except for sign, but often indistinguishable. Punishing a wrongdoer can be a "public good" motivated as well by meanness as by public spirit. It is even a favor to the victim if it serves as warning, or instills discipline among victims. That boy who hit a sleeping friend became an instant leader: maybe they needed a leader.

Strategically there is no difference between behavioral and anatomical constraints. The bee's sting is behavioral; the cactus needle is inert; porcupine quills are both. Cactus is allowed to grow in gardens because it is, though potentially dangerous, very well behaved—it never chases people. Whether it is immobile or merely lethargic doesn't matter. The deterrent effect of being known to defend one's nest to the death will not depend on whether the predator perceives obstinacy, maternal loyalty, or physical incapacity to escape.

I close with a short sample of potentially strategic propensities. For brevity I state each as a declaration of a constraint or incapacity that would be costly if not believed but could be advantageous if believed. But let me clarify my motivation. My interest here is not in the possible genetic heritability of any human traits we might identify as strategically self-serving. It is the opposite, to see whether the richness of observable strategic behavior in people can provide hints to the biologists who study other creatures. The fact that people's strategic behavior appears to be conscious, even calculating, does not mean that such behavior has to be conscious and calculating to serve a purpose—rather, it may serve strategically, whether or not the creature has a "purpose."

Here is a small sample of strategic declarations; the reader can add dozens more of his or her own.

I'm harmless, and couldn't hurt you if I wanted to.

I attack anyone who comes near me.

I'll expose us both if you don't do what I ask.

If a predator spots us it will prefer me to you.

I can't run because I'm vulnerable with my back to you.

I'll destroy my property if you approach it.

I will not fight for my property, so you needn't kill me to get it.

If I do what you ask I'll be severely punished.

I hurt anyone who fails to help anyone who helps me.

If we fight it will have to be to the death.

I do not taste good.

You do not taste good.

REFERENCES

Austin, J. L. 1962. *How to Do Things with Words.* London: Oxford University Press.

Baird, Douglas G., Robert H. Gertner, and Randal C. Picker. 1994. *Game Theory and the Law.* Cambridge, Mass.: Harvard University Press.

Collier, John. 2003 [1949]. "Wet Saturday." In *Fancies and Goodnights.* New York: New York Review of Books.

Conrad, Joseph. 1923. *The Secret Agent.* New York: Doubleday, Page and Company.

Fried, Charles. 1981. *Contract as Promise.* Cambridge, Mass.: Harvard University Press.

Kitto, H. D. F. 1951. *The Greeks.* Baltimore: Penguin Books.

Kreps, David M. 1990. *Game Theory and Economic Modelling.* Oxford: Oxford University Press.

Oman, C. W. C. 1953. *The Art of War in the Middle Ages.* Ithaca, N.Y.: Cornell University Press.

Pearce, David W., ed. 1996. *The MIT Dictionary of Modern Economics.* 4th ed. Cambridge: MIT Press.

Rouse, W. H. D., trans. 1950. *The Iliad.* London: Mentor Books, 273.

Schelling, Thomas C. 1960. *The Strategy of Conflict.* Cambridge, Mass.: Harvard University Press.

——— 1966. "The Art of Commitment." In Schelling, *Arms and Influence,* 35–91. New Haven, Conn.: Yale University Press.

Searle, J. R. 1969. *Speech Acts*. Cambridge: Cambridge University Press.

Walton, Richard E., and Robert B. McKersie. 1965. *A Behavioral Theory of Labor Negotiations*. New York: McGraw-Hill Book Company.

Xenophon. 1957. *The Persian Expedition*, trans. Rex Warner, 236. Harmondsworth: Penguin Books.

Climate and Society

2

What Makes Greenhouse Sense?

■ We have had "global warming" for more than a decade, the hottest decade on record worldwide. Is this the "greenhouse effect" that scientists have been warning about, a response to increased carbon dioxide in the atmosphere, or is it some natural, rather than man-made, climatic change?

The Intergovernmental Panel on Climate Change (IPCC) has cautiously proposed a "discernible" human influence. The IPCC is a cautious body not disposed to outright conclusions; most of the several climate models do not predict the sudden increases in temperature of recent years. But something is going on. What does it tell us about the need to curtail, drastically, carbon emissions during the coming century?

The popular guessing game—do we see a greenhouse "signature," can we identify a clear "signal" in the "noise"?—is probably premature. The history of climate shows that sudden changes of global atmospheric temperature have occurred. There are random or chaotic influences on global climate; El Niño is an example, volcanic emissions are another. There are human influences besides greenhouse gases: aerosols of dust and, especially, sulfur emissions can block incoming sunlight; urbanization can produce "heat islands" that affect local temperature estimates. Finally, most of the globe is ocean. Relative to air the specific heat of water is great and the oceans act as a huge cooling reservoir that delays by probably decades the arrival of atmospheric warming. (The metaphor of "signal to noise" is inappropriate here: noise is random, while the problem here is that there are several competing "signals" to sort out.)

So the recent temperature record is unlikely to be conclusive on the cause of the warming. Greenhouse warming is not clearly established by the temperature record, nor is it in any way ruled out. We may see the greenhouse "signal" clearly in another decade or two. Meanwhile we have to rely on what science can tell us.

There are a few indisputable facts about the "greenhouse" phenomenon. One, well understood for more than a century, is that a high density of greenhouse gases, as on Venus, can cause surface temperatures many times the boiling point of water, while the absence of such gases, as on Mars, makes surface temperatures too low for water to exist in liquid form. (Distance from the sun makes a difference but cannot account for the gross disparity.) Earth is unique in our solar system for its temperature range, and greenhouse gases can be thanked.

Another well-understood fact is that carbon dioxide molecules absorb infra-red radiation. This is easily measured in the laboratory. Carbon dioxide is transparent to incoming sunlight; but as the earth, warmed by daylight sun, radiates energy back into space it does so in the infra-red part of the electromagnetic spectrum, and the carbon dioxide in the air absorbs some of the energy and gets warmer. If the daily absorption is not matched by radiation back into space, the earth gets warmer until the intensity of that outgoing thermal radiation matches the intensity of the incoming sunlight.

Citrus growers in California and Florida use smudge pots—ceramic tubes of burning crude oil—to produce, on a clear still night, a blanket of carbon dioxide that captures some of the heat radiating from the ground and keeps the fruit from freezing. (Actual greenhouses do not produce the "greenhouse effect"; they mainly trap the air that is warmed by contact with the ground that is warmed by the sun. We should have called it the "smudge pot effect.")

Carbon dioxide is only one of several gases that have that property. The most important one is water vapor, and part of the estimated enhancement of temperature is the positive feedback of warming on absolute global humidity.

I find the case for prospective greenhouse warming to be convincing. In large part the uncertainties are not about whether greenhouse warming is going to be real, but about the magnitude and speed of warming and about the variegated climatic effects—not just "warming," but all the changes in precipitation, humidity, sunlight and clouds, storms, and variations between night and day, summer and winter, polar regions and tropical, mountains and plains, and east and west coasts.

In the two major unspecialized scientific journals, *Science* and *Nature*, one has to go back a decade or two to find serious doubts about the basic science. Rarely is there such scientific consensus as there is on whether the greenhouse effect is real, even though it cannot yet be incontrovertibly detected in the recent climate record.

But the uncertainties are daunting. The best the IPCC can do—apparently the best anyone can do—is to give us a range of possible warming for any given increase in carbon dioxide. And the upper bound of that estimated range has been, for over twenty-five years, three times the lower bound—an enormous range of uncertainty.

On top of that are the uncertainties of what the changes in temperature will do to climates around the world, what those climate changes may do to the worlds we live in, and what peoples in different climates can do to adapt successfully.

■

As a policy issue this is a new subject. Just as nuclear weapons required an unprecedented reorientation of military thinking, a reorientation that took some decades, and modern terrorism has recently required a reorientation of homeland security thinking, a reorientation that is barely begun, the prospect of possible changes in climate greater than any that have occurred in the past ten thousand years has had only a decade or two to generate ideas on how to cope with this ineluctably global problem.

I will illustrate from personal experience. In the 1970s, during what was called the "energy crisis," I was a member of two panels, each consisting of twenty experts from economics, petroleum engineering, nuclear engineering, public health, international relations, environmental science, and other pertinent disciplines. One panel had to do with the likely future of nuclear energy and the other was concerned with the future of energy policy in the United States. Both produced reports, the first, *Nuclear Power: Issues and Choices* (Nuclear Policy Energy Study Group 1977), the second, *Energy: The Next Twenty Years* (Ford Foundation Study Group 1979). What could have been more pertinent to nuclear issues than the evident fact that nuclear fission produces no carbon dioxide? And what turned out to dominate energy and environmental disputes before the next twenty years had passed? And what did these two careful studies have to say about global warming? The nuclear book, out of four hundred pages, had two pages on carbon dioxide. The six-hundred-page energy book, oriented toward the coming two decades, had ten scattered references amounting to less than ten pages.

Thinking about warming and climate had not begun among "experts" concerned with energy policy, nor had it yet attracted concerted attention among scientists in the pertinent fields of atmospheric chemistry and physics, meteorology, oceanography, agronomy, marine biology, glaciology, ecology, or paleoclimatology.

By 1992 the largest intergovernmental conference ever assembled, with heads of state from more than a hundred nations including the United States, was focused on global environmental issues, with climate change at the center. In Rio de Janeiro the conference produced the "Framework Convention on Climate Change," promptly ratified by the United States.

Five years later, in Kyoto, a "protocol" to the Rio treaty was drafted (and signed by the United States), requiring very substantial reductions in CO_2 emissions for the developed countries over the next dozen years. It finally went into effect in February 2005, having been ratified as required by nations accounting for 55 percent of total world emissions of carbon dioxide. The Clinton administration let the Kyoto document languish for three years, and President Bush declared it unsuitable shortly after his inauguration. Russian ratification, which cleared the 55 percent threshold, was widely viewed as opportunistic, as the Russian economy's slump from 1990, the baseline from which reductions were to be measured, had made it likely that Russia would not need to restrict emissions and might even sell excess emission rights—dubbed "hot air" by commentators—to participating nations that could partially fulfill their obligations by such purchases.

While the Bush dismissal of "Kyoto" sounded harsh and unfriendly, compliance with what had been assented to in 1997 was almost certainly infeasible by 2001, nothing having been done to identify what policies, including new legislation, might be required to meet the U.S.

obligation. Whether Kyoto will turn out to be a "first step" in an international effort to cope with climate change remains unclear.

■

While the uncertainties about the magnitude of likely climate changes and their impact need not preclude precautionary steps to anticipate and to cope, they certainly preclude any definitive regime of obligatory limits on national emissions of carbon dioxide (and other greenhouse gases) for some decades to come. Ultimately what matters is not any annual emissions rate but what the limit should be on the concentration of greenhouse gases in the atmosphere, that is, on the cumulative emissions over all the decades to come minus what gets permanently absorbed in the oceans or somewhere else.

As mentioned earlier, the average temperature change for any given concentration is uncertain by at least a factor of three, that is, the upper estimate is at least three times the lower ("at least" because those estimates are not absolute bounds). So even if we knew what the limit should be on the change in average global temperature, which we do not, we could still be off by a factor of three in knowing the indicated concentration of greenhouse gases. And how much of the emitted CO_2 will be absorbed by the oceans is a further uncertainty; currently it appears that something like two-fifths is being absorbed somewhere—in the oceans, in vegetation, in the soil—but whether the oceans will be as ready to absorb the gas when the oceans themselves have higher surface concentrations is not confidently predicted.

A further complication, as far as quota regimes are concerned, is that whatever may be the ultimate limit on the total carbon in the atmosphere, the trajectory of emissions should almost certainly—and differently from country to country—continue to increase for at least some decades before leveling off and eventually turning sharply down. There are several reasons.

One reason is that better and cheaper technologies for mitigation will become available, the longer we wait, especially if we invest heavily in the improved technologies to make sure they become available when we need them. A second reason is that anything we can postpone for twenty years becomes drastically cheaper if we can invest the equivalent cost at 5 or 6 percent and invest the proceeds in mitigation twenty years from now. A third reason is that postponement avoids the scrapping of costly capital assets that have substantial lifetimes left, like plants that generate electricity. A fourth reason is that later generations will almost certainly enjoy higher incomes than ours and be better able to afford any costs of switching to new energy sources. A fifth reason is that we should have a better understanding, in each successive decade, of what and how much needs to be done to slow down the global warming.

Kyoto focused on near-term emissions. That probably made sense. There undoubtedly is, as the U.S. National Academy of Sciences reported a decade ago, some "low-hanging fruit" to be harvested—opportunities to reduce emissions significantly at little or no cost. They are mostly onetime opportunities, not indefinitely exploitable. These are things we know will eventually prove justified, and postponing them merely loses time.

A reasonable question is why, after more than a dozen years of intense investigation, the basic uncertainties about the magnitude of projected changes have not been reduced. Part of the answer is probably that no official body has been willing to commit itself to defending a quantitative challenge to the standing estimate. An important part is probably that climate science, like brain science or genetics, has turned out to be much more complex than was originally appreciated, early in the recent concern with global warming. Twenty-five years ago the oceans were modeled mainly as cooling reservoirs. Now ocean currents are seen as active participants in the circulation of heat, and that circulation depends on temperature and salinity at different depths and the turbulence on the surface due to winds. Clouds were formerly little understood, and unable to play an active role. Now clouds are understood to be reflectors of incoming radiation or absorbers of outgoing radiation depending on their altitude, density, droplet size, and geographical location. It was earlier known that particles of dust in the atmosphere, and especially of sulfur (historically from some volcanic eruptions), could significantly reflect incoming sunlight; but there were no reliable studies of the amounts in the air, their geographical distribution, or their residence time.

A major scientific coincidence has been the burgeoning availability of satellite reconnaissance of oceans, clouds, glaciers, forests, sea ice, airborne particles, and atmospheric temperatures that has paralleled the concern for climate change. With the cascade of new knowledge

32

has come new appreciation of the complexity of interactions among atmospheric, oceanic, and terrestrial phenomena, including human activity.

■

Without being able to forecast the speed or even the nature of climate change—"warming" is just a shorthand expression for what will motivate the changes—we can still try to foresee the kinds of impacts those changes may have. But here we must be careful: there is a strong temptation—I know because I have been suffering it for twenty-five years—to think of changes in climate as superimposed on life as we know it, or know of it. Climate change may become serious, if little or nothing is done about it, in the second half of this century and, even if substantial mitigating efforts are undertaken, toward the end of the century. To discern the likely effects we have to try to imagine the world as it may be in sixty, eighty, or a hundred years.

How do we do that? A possibility, just to acquire some perspective, may be to imagine how we might have reacted—"we" being our children's grandparents or great-grandparents—if, say, eighty years ago global warming and attendant climate changes of the kind now being discussed had been seriously considered. Several thoughts occur to me. One is that people in the United States, with "warming" on their minds, would have been more interested in milder winters than in hotter summers. A second is that, where summer was concerned, a major worry might have been mud. Automobile tires were skinny, hard as wood (with pressures of sixty pounds per square inch), and absolutely no good in mud. Bicycles were no good in mud, either, and walking was difficult. It might not have occurred to us (to them) that before the century was out the country would be paved almost solid.

Pursuing this line of thought we could ask, if the climate change so predicted in 1925 had actually occurred by now, how might a farm boy of that time who stayed on the farm and lived to the present reflect on the changes that had occurred during his lifetime? Would the change in climate stand out?

My guess is that the now-aged farmer would be more impressed with the disappearance of the horse; with the coming of electricity, telephone, and radio (let alone television); with hybrid corn, antibiotics, and pesticides; with still having most of his original teeth; and with having college-graduate grandchildren whom he could visit easily a thousand miles away. He might not notice milder winters: he has gloves and boots and parkas that didn't exist when he was a boy, his car has a heater, and, in case his road isn't plowed, he has snow tires (and air conditioning for the summer). His agricultural technology has changed so much he isn't sure what difference any change in climate may have caused in agricultural productivity.

Seventy years ago we didn't have electronics, radioisotopes, nuclear energy, antibiotics, genetics, satellites, or even plastics—it was all silk, rayon, isinglass, and celluloid. How do we possibly foresee seventy years from now?

Still, we can assert a few things with some confidence. Most production for markets in developed countries is substantially immune to climate. We can assemble automobiles, refine oil, transmit radio and television, do open-heart surgery and banking and insurance, perform symphonies, manufacture pharmaceuticals, teach classes, operate airlines, and hold golf tournaments in Massachusetts, Washington, Texas, Georgia, or Michigan, even in Alaska as far as climate is concerned. Only agriculture and animal husbandry, forestry, fisheries, and outdoor recreation are susceptible to climate in the United States and in most developed countries. Agriculture, forestry, and fisheries are no more than 3 percent of the U.S. gross domestic product. If the cost of producing raw food and lumber doubled over the next sixty or seventy years, it would reduce gross product by 3 percent while that same gross product doubled from ordinary productivity growth. We would double our per capita income in 2067 instead of 2065.

It is different for developing countries, many of whom depend on agriculture for a third or half of their gross product while as much as two-thirds of the population may depend on agriculture for a living. Although it is not certain that the likely changes in climate would everywhere be adverse to farming, at least in those countries people are potentially vulnerable in a way that we in America are not. Additionally there could be serious health consequences: many vector-borne diseases become more virulent in hotter climates, and their prevalence may extend further as subtropical climates become more tropical.

I conclude that most, nearly all, of the adverse effects of likely climate change will accrue to the descendants of those living today in what we call "developing countries" (not all of which are actually developing). First, that is where the people are, three-quarters of them today, seven-eighths of them by the end of the century. Second, they are vulnerable in ways that we are not. Third, they do not have the resources to cope, to adapt, or to defend against adverse weather and climate and what it may do to health and productivity. The nations least able to afford to do anything to abate forthcoming changes in climate are the nations with the most at stake (whether their leaders realize that or not).

To draw this comparison between today's developed and undeveloped in their vulnerability to potential climate change, however, is also to identify what is likely to be the best defense against changing climate: development. Consider health, malaria in particular. This disease kills more than a million people every year, a large proportion of them children. Malaria is no problem in the United States, Canada, or western Europe. Climate does not altogether explain the lack of malaria; malaria got its name in ancient Italy and was serious in the United States a century ago. It is now associated with the tropics.

But consider Singapore and Malaysia, two nations separated by a kilometer of seawater. Their climates are identical. There is virtually no malaria in Singapore; malaria is serious in Malaysia. If anyone living in Singapore does get malaria (by spending a weekend in Malaysia) he or she is probably in good health to begin with and gets the necessary medical care. Singapore, of course, has the advantage of being small and rich, so environmental measures can take care of any mosquitoes. But this is the point of the comparison: Singapore and Malaysia were identical not only in climate but in development forty years ago. Both have developed, but Singapore spectacularly. If Malaysia can reach, through a second forty years of development, where Singapore reached in its first forty years, it should no longer be at the mercy of the mosquito.

Measles kills a million children a year in poor countries, not in the well-to-do. Vaccine is a great help; but what the poor children in developing countries need most, to reduce the impact of measles, is adequate nutrition and freedom from debilitating chronic illness. For that they need development. With development, countries can afford sanitation and safe drinking water, not to mention a public-health infrastructure. The worst effects of deteriorating climate on health can be avoided if poor countries can become nonpoor in the coming half-century.

Health is just one area in which development can significantly offset the adverse effects of climate change. Development means higher incomes, which in turn mean individuals and governments better able to adapt to changes, and governments better able to participate in global efforts at mitigation. Development also means shifting away from subsistence agriculture and into productive activities less dependent on the weather.

■

A few years ago, two thousand American economists published a statement arguing that the nations of the world should adopt a rationing scheme under which every nation would be assigned a quota for carbon emissions, with strong sanctions for failing to meet quota obligations and with a trading system in which nations better able to come in under quota could "sell" unused emission rights to countries finding it more difficult to meet their quota obligations.

Few propositions appeal to economists more than that without clearly defined obligations backed up by the prospect of sanctions, international cooperation involving potential major sacrifices cannot be sustained, and that without trading rights any regime will be hopelessly inefficient.

I did not sign the statement. I am an economist who believes in the essentiality of incentives, in clearly defined obligations, and in the virtues of trading. I cannot imagine such a regime for carbon emissions. I have several reasons.

Any serious regime would have to allocate emission rights over many decades, not just a decade at a time but cumulatively. There is currently no possibility of reaching agreement on whether "acceptable" total emissions over the coming century should be 500 billion tons or 2,000 billion tons; in any event, what is ultimately acceptable will depend on the costs of moderating emissions, and these costs are also extremely uncertain.

Because any economical trajectory of annual emissions should grow for some decades before leveling off and declining severely thereafter, with different trajectories for different nations, it would be almost impossible to determine, during the first half-century or so, whether a nation was on target to meet its ultimate cumulative limit. (It would likely be just as hard for the nation itself to know, as for any monitoring secretariat or judicial review body.)

Any stringent regime would involve allocating emission rights worth many trillions of dollars among rich nations and poor, rapidly growing nations and more mature economies, and countries with fossil fuels and countries without. I see no possibility of any such compact being arrived at. If there were such quotas they would certainly have to be renegotiated periodically as estimates changed and as nations experienced greater and lesser difficulties. Any nation that "sold" part of its unused quota would clearly show that its original quota had been too generous.

Sanctions large enough to be effective deserve skepticism. Punishing poor countries will not be attractive; punishing rich countries, or large countries, or powerful countries will not be attractive. I can imagine the United States agreeing to quotas it believes it can live with and making serious efforts to live within the quotas; it is hard to imagine any international body or consortium of nations imposing sanctions on the United States, or the United States accepting severe sanctions.

Granting, for argument, the apparent logic that nations will not make sacrifices in the absence of sanctions, there is no historical example of any international regime that could impose penalties on a scale commensurate with the magnitude of global warming. (It is notable that the current most legally cohesive regime, the European Union—certainly stronger than any greenhouse regime that one could imagine—calls for severe penalties on any nation that runs a deficit greater than 3 percent of gross domestic product for three years running; in 2004 both France and Germany violated the rule, and nothing was expected to happen to those two nations, and nothing did happen.)

Nowhere are there any agreed criteria for allocating half a trillion tons, or a trillion or two trillion tons, of carbon dioxide emissions among almost two hundred nations. Undeveloped nations demand the right to "catch up" to the developed in carbon emissions per capita or per unit gross product. Some argue for uniform emissions per capita. All may see carbon quotas as partly cash equivalents, via trading for money, and indeed there have been proposals for allocating carbon quotas as "foreign aid" precisely to facilitate conversion of carbon quotas to cash. Any "democratic" allocation of quotas would require negotiation among nearly two hundred countries, some of whom are oil and gas producers that may object to any rationing. And how to penalize a poor country that fails to conform to its quota would require a judicial procedure to authorize sanctions and some enforcement mechanism, which would have to extract financial resources, embargo trade, restrict fossil fuel deliveries, or otherwise impose penalties or fuel restrictions. Nothing like this has ever existed and it is even hard to conceive.

The World Trade Organization (WTO) might appear to be a model or precedent. It does impose penalties for infractions of the trading rules and it has a judicial body to hear complaints and authorize sanctions. It has worked, but as a model it is not a good fit. WTO is essentially a system of detailed reciprocal undertakings; infractions tend to be bilateral, and specific as to commodities. Offended parties can undertake retaliation and make the punishment fit the crime (thus exercising the principle of reciprocity). Fulfilling or failing WTO commitments is piecemeal, not holistic. There is no overall target to which a WTO member is committed. In contrast, if a greenhouse-regime nation fails to meet its target, there is no particular offended partner to take the initiative and penalize the offender. There is no obvious formula to make the punishment fit the crime.

■

Is there any precedent, or model, of international cooperation on a scale equivalent to what a greenhouse regime might entail? The North Atlantic Treaty Organization (NATO) is my candidate. NATO, as an organization, grew out of the Marshall Plan, which itself is a model. The division of Marshall Plan aid was originally determined by the United States, the donor, after receiving tentative "plans" from Europe that amounted to more than was to be made available. Roughly five billion dollars was available for the initial period, April 1, 1948, to June 30, 1949. Funds had to be distributed among countries as disparate as the United Kingdom, Turkey, Norway, Italy, Iceland, and the rest—disparate in their prewar living standards, their wartime damage, their capacity for reconstruction, and their specific commodity needs. But through the Organization for European Economic Cooperation (OEEC, predecessor of the current OECD), the recipient nations were to negotiate later annual divisions of aid.

To that end, each country submitted detailed statements documenting its needs for hard currency during the coming fiscal year. They projected government expenditures, both civilian and military; private consumption, including rationed commodities like gasoline, meat, butter, and heating fuel; exports and imports by provenance and destination; feedstock requirements and projected growth in livestock populations; restoration of railroad beds and canals; housing repair and construction; machinery and equipment requirements; and finally, crucially, import requirements that had to be paid for in dollars. An ambitious effort by the secretariat of the OEEC standardized the accounts and definitions. ("National economic accounts" were new and unfamiliar to several governments.)

Then began a process of reciprocal multilateral scrutiny. Each government was represented by a team of senior officials. Each government team was examined and cross-examined by the other government teams; each defended its projections and demands for aid, revised its claims and defended anew. More aid for one country meant less for the rest.

There was never any formula. "Relevant criteria" developed. The parties did not quite reach agreement, but were close enough that two people, the secretary general of the OEEC and the representative of Belgium (which was not requesting any aid), offered a division that was promptly accepted. Of course, the U.S. government was insisting on agreement. Today there is no such "angel" behind greenhouse negotiations. Still, this precedent offers encouragement.

NATO went through the same process in 1951–52, the "burden-sharing exercise." The same people—by this time on a first-name basis—engaged in the same reciprocal scrutiny and cross-examination. Military contributions such as conscription and training; procurement of weapons, ammunition, and vehicles; and contributions of real estate for pipelines, maneuvers, and housing were now centrally involved. U.S. aid was still involved and was the pressure to reach agreement, which was almost attained. This time three people, including the U.S. representative, offered up a proposal that was immediately accepted. U.S. aid tapered off, but the procedures and the teamwork remained.

NATO, for which the Marshall Plan provided the congenial social infrastructure, is the only nonwartime institution in which so many countries cooperated over such high economic stakes. The procedures were not aesthetically satisfying: no formulae were developed, just a civilized procedure of argument and accommodation. Additionally, two of the participating nations, Italy from the outset and Germany soon after, were former enemies of the rest.

NATO nations undertook commitments, heavy commitments, arrived at through the process I have described, and generally met their commitments. There were no sanctions on nonperformance other than diplomatic argument. By any measure NATO was a success. The camaraderie and tradition of cooperation engendered by the Marshall Plan were immensely helpful. We have no such auspicious tradition to undergird the international greenhouse effort, but NATO is the only historical model I can find.

■

A striking difference between commitments under NATO, or under WTO, and commitments under the Kyoto Protocol (or almost any other greenhouse regimes that have been proposed) is the difference between commitment to actions and commitment to results. NATO governments argued over what they would actually do: raise troops, train and deploy them; procure vehicles, arms, and ammunition; submit to an international command structure; and, if it came to that, defend each other's territory as if it were their own.

The expected results were deterrence of attack or, if deterrence failed, defense. There was no way to measure how much added deterrence the Dutch contributed, or the Norwegians, or the British. The only way to assess how much the Dutch would, in the event, have contributed to slowing down a Soviet-bloc attack would be to count their troops and weapons. Essentially, "inputs" were visible and measurable; "outputs" in the form of deterrence or successful defense were conjectural, judgmental, not measurable.

As in NATO, commitments in the WTO are to what nations will do, or refrain from doing. There are no commitments to particular consequences. No WTO member nation is committed to imports of any sort from anywhere; it is committed only to actions, or abstentions, regarding tariffs and other restrictions, subsidies, and tax preferences.

In the Kyoto Protocol, commitments were not to actions but to results that were to be measured after a decade or more. A disadvantage is that no one can tell, until close to the target date, which nations are on course to meet their commitments. More important, nations undertaking results-based commitments are unlikely to have any reliable way of knowing what actions will be required, that is, what quantitative results will occur on what timetable for various actions. The Kyoto approach assumed without evident justification that governments actually knew how to reach ten- or fifteen-year emissions goals. (The energy crisis of the 1970s did not last long enough to reveal, for example, the long-run elasticity of demand for motor fuel, electricity, industrial heat, and so on.) A government that commits to actions at least knows what it is committed to, and its partners also know and can observe compliance. In contrast, a government that commits to the consequences of various actions on emissions can only hope that its estimates, or guesses, are on target, and so can its partners.

■

Comprehensive estimates of climate change are invariably gradual. This is mainly because climate-change models reflect, naturally, what is known about the behavior of climate; and what is not known, of course, is not known. Are there potential abrupt, large-scale transitions that can be realistically imagined? Are there potential catastrophes that should be gripping our attention?

Two have been seriously studied. One is the possible attenuation of the oceanic circulation involving the downward plunge of ocean-surface water in the northern Atlantic near the Arctic Circle and the corresponding northward surface flow of the Gulf Stream that warms western Europe. (Madrid shares its latitude with Cape Cod, Copenhagen with Hudson Bay.) There is some evidence that in earlier geological eras the Gulf Stream may not have existed, or was substantially attenuated. There are some estimates that global warming may influence the temperature and salinity of northern Atlantic waters and reduce the circulation on which the Gulf Stream depends. That could mean a severe cooling of western Europe as a result of global warming.

The other, more ominous, possibility relates to a body of ice known as the West Antarctic Ice Sheet. This is "grounded" ice, attached to Antarctica and secured by several islands, essentially an iceberg so thick that it rests on the bottom and extends a kilometer or more above sea level. If it should glaciate or otherwise move to sea, it would sink and raise the sea level drastically. (Floating ice, like the Arctic sea ice, does not affect sea level; the grounded ice would.) The estimate of potential sea-level rise is on the order of twenty feet. That would put major coastal cities, like New York or London, under water. They might be preserved with dikes—Amsterdam is about fourteen feet below sea level—but huge areas of nations like Bangladesh could not be protected. (Not only would the coastline of Bangladesh be prohibitively long to protect with levees but there would be no way for fresh water—already a source of severe flooding—to reach the sea.)

These are two phenomena that will need watching and study. Either, by the time it manifests itself, may be beyond prevention: the warming built into the system of greenhouse gases, delayed by the "thermal inertia" of the oceans—their capacity to delay the actual warming of the atmosphere—may be sufficient to continue the process.

■

An interesting policy option, probably only for the far future, gets remarkably little attention, possibly because it sounds too much like science fiction, possibly because it scares people who do not want it discussed. It has attracted the name "geo-engineering"—changing something about the earth. (Actually, with global warming, we are already geo-engineering, just not purposely.) The specific proposal would be to increase the earth's albedo, its reflection of incoming sunlight. It is now known, and somewhat measurable, that aerosols—fine solid or liquid particles in the atmosphere, especially those of sulfur—reflect sunlight. Volcano eruptions that put lots of sulfur in the atmosphere have famously had this effect. Today's pollution, especially industrial but also windblown dust and sand, is thought to be reflecting enough sunlight to mask somewhat the greenhouse effect.

Why not do this purposefully? one may ask. If we are putting things in the atmosphere, the various greenhouse gases that absorb outgoing radiation, why not put things in the atmosphere that reflect incoming radiation—just "preserve the balance"? We could not use sulfur, because it is too unhealthy for people and wildlife. Instead, we could spend a few decades experimenting to find something cheap and innocuous that could stay in the stratosphere long enough to be a partial solution to the greenhouse problem. The amount of incoming sunlight that would have to be kept out is small enough to be not noticeable. A report of the National Academy of Sciences mentioned the possibility a dozen years ago.

The idea has some attractions. It reduces the need to change the way people all over the world cook their meals, drive their cars, light and cool and warm their homes, grow their rice—rice paddies are a source of methane, a greenhouse gas—and produce their electricity. Instead of negotiating a complex regime of emission quotas, nations would negotiate shares in the costs of the program, a kind of negotiation with which they have had experience at least since the first UN budget. Diplomatically and administratively, it would drastically simplify the greenhouse issue. But for the time being this possibility is not visible on anybody's agenda. Research is certainly warranted at least into the possibilities for small-scale reversible experiments in case the greenhouse problem begins to appear diplomatically intractable some time in the decades to come.

■

What should be the role of developing countries, especially the major ones—China, India, Indonesia, Brazil, South Korea—but also more than a hundred others, some of them oil-exporting members of OPEC? The U.S. Senate overwhelmingly passed a resolution, in relation to the Kyoto treaty, calling for the full participation of the main developing countries in any treaty that the United States might join. Perhaps for some senators the resolution was a gentle way of disposing of the treaty. The developing nations were on record, unambiguously, as having no intention of participating. (A hundred of them actually ratified the Kyoto treaty, but their participation was ceremonial; the treaty excluded them from any obligation.)

Certainly the larger developing nations must eventually be brought into some form of cooperation to reduce emissions. China's emissions of carbon dioxide are already one-half the United States' and growing at a rate to surpass U.S. emissions in another two or three decades. Two motives make the Chinese uneager to join. A main motive is their correct perception that rapid development will reduce their vulnerability to climate, and suppressing energy use is likely to hinder development. Another is their view that the developed nations, especially the United States, having developed industrially through uninhibited exploitation of fossil fuels over the past century and a half, and now less in need of rapid further development to escape the dangers of climate change, should lead the way and demonstrate a serious commitment to emissions reduction. The Chinese probably do not yet perceive such leadership or commitment.

If western Europe, Japan, and the United States manage to demonstrate over the coming decade that they are serious about the climate issue, China, India, and others can probably be induced to take the subject seriously. At that time the wealthy nations can engage in planning how to help the developing world afford to join a global effort.

REFERENCES

Ford Foundation Study Group. 1979. *Energy: The Next Twenty Years.* Cambridge, Mass.: Ballinger.
Nuclear Energy Policy Study Group. 1977. *Nuclear Power: Issues and Choices.* Cambridge, Mass.: Ballinger.

3

The Economic Diplomacy of Geoengineering

■ In any discussion of geoengineering in the mid-1980s, before it had a name, part of the audience thought it crazy and most of the rest thought it dangerous. In 1992 the Electric Power Research Institute and the Scripps Institute of Oceanography hosted a conference that helped provide the subject some legitimacy, and the National Academy of Sciences report (NAS 1992) also helped make geoengineering a legitimate scientific concern. These sessions at the AAAS have helped pull the subject out of the closet, but not all the way.

When challenged on speaking to such an unmentionable subject, I used to defend myself by saying that nothing along these lines was going to happen for fifty years anyhow; that keeping silent today will not affect whether forty, fifty, or seventy years from now people who may despair of sufficiently reducing CO_2 emissions and who may be alarmed about global warming will get interested in direct intervention to change the radiation balance; that long after I am dead the subject may become pertinent.

But now I acknowledge two qualifications. One is that some of us may not take global warming quite so seriously if we believe it may eventually be susceptible to direct intervention. I confess I believe that it is as likely that we shall have benign, economical, effective direct intervention in the radiation balance fifty or seventy-five years from now as that we shall have benign, safe, convenient, economical alternatives to carbon fuels in that time. So I am subject to the charge that if I take geoengineering seriously it makes a difference to my attitude toward policy. But not a lot of difference.

The other qualification is that geoengineering was related, at these meetings of the AAAS, to the preservation of stratospheric ozone. If we did find a way directly either to introduce ozone into the stratosphere or to reduce chlorine or anything else that is destroying ozone, it could be pertinent immediately. Most discussion of geoengineering has been about climate change, not ozone.

Fifty years ago those of you who are my age hadn't the slightest idea that in the 1990s we would take carbon dioxide seriously. In the perspective of fifty years this is a brand new subject. That suggests that we do not know now what are going to be the candidates for geoengineering fifty years from now. We know about ozone depletion; we know about greenhouse gases. But I have no idea whether fifty years from now geoengineering will be focused on carbon dioxide and the radiation balance or something altogether different. The fact that it didn't occur to us fifty years ago, or to most of us twenty years ago, that CO_2 was going to be a problem suggests that demands for geoengineering twenty, forty, or sixty years from now may be related to things we haven't thought of yet. I do not know what they might be: El Niño, ocean currents, sea level canals, ocean food plantations.

Furthermore, fifty years ago we didn't have electronics, nuclear energy, radioisotopes, or satellites; we didn't even have plastics. (We were still in silk, rayon, and celluloid.) So when we talk about geoengineering the greenhouse problem we have to remember we are talking about technologies of intervention as they may be fifty years from now. The transistor has revolutionized the electronic highway that nobody had thought of fifty years ago. Maybe in fifty or seventy-five years we shall be harvesting so many crops from ocean plantations that fertilizing phytoplankton will seem a modest extension. What we are doing today is just getting a little practice in thinking about the subject, not really discussing what to do fifty years from now.

Geoengineering has been defined as altering the chemistry of the atmosphere. That is too brief a definition. Activities that change the albedo may prove interesting, and the chemistry and physics of the oceans may prove as interesting as the atmosphere as the decades go by.

I have given some thought to what we might mean by geoengineering. The term is a new one; I have two recent dictionaries in my office, neither contains the word. Geo means earth; but as the term has come to be used it appears to mean not just the earth, but the earth globally. If we learn to rearrange the tectonics of the San Andreas fault, that may not be 'geoengineering' because it is local or regional.

People who use the term also seem to have in mind something intentional. Otherwise we are geoengineering right now: burning fossil fuel changes the atmosphere's chemistry. To *reduce* fossil fuel combustion might be geoengineering because it is deliberately changing the chemistry of the atmosphere from what it was going to be, but evidently merely doing less of what we have been doing too much of does not count as geoengineering.

To build a sea level canal between the Gulf of Mexico and the Pacific Ocean for ship transit would not be geoengineering. There would be "geo" side effects, the intermingling of species that have always been ten thousand sea miles apart in waters of different temperature, salinity, and seasonal variability. It would be called geoengineering, I think, if we deliberately did it to interchange species. If we are slowly reducing the Arctic ice pack with global warming, that isn't geoengineering; but if we distributed carbon black to make the ice cover disappear more rapidly, that would be.

Most people probably don't think of planting trees as geoengineering. One reason for not considering afforestation to be geoengineering is that many people have a preference for dealing with causes rather than symptoms, and if the cause is defined as too much CO_2 the best thing is to produce less and the second best is to remove some. If the problem is defined instead as the radiation balance, people may think the problem is not just too much CO_2 but also too little sulphur aerosols, too little reflective cloud cover, too little albedo. But afforestation, because it is a familiar kind of offset to what is believed to be the source of the problem, doesn't need to be associated with science fiction.

Second, trees are not mysterious. If we increase photosynthesis in the ocean—put iron in the water around the Galapagos—people become uneasy. The ocean is opaque, the ocean is huge, and the ocean is mobile. If I plant a tree in Montana I'm pretty sure the tree will stay in Montana. But if I fertilize the ocean some clam may get larger and more mobile and proliferate and clog intake pipes. Trees have always been friendly; we celebrate Arbor Day, and children plant trees without geoengineering.

'Geoengineering' implies something unnatural. I would suppose, for example, that if the earth's atmosphere had always had a large amount of sulphur aerosols in the upper atmosphere and the aerosols increased and diminished from time to time and the carbon dioxide increased and diminished from time to time, and we began to have a greenhouse problem, it would be referred to as an imbalance in the ratio of the infrared-absorbing substances to the light-reflecting substances; reducing CO_2 and increasing the sulphur would both appear natural. If we put carbon black on the Arctic ice to make it disappear, that would be considered geoengineering; if we just let it disappear because of global warming, that is not geoengineering. If we learn to make it snow more in the Sierras and the Rockies to enhance the water supply of California and Colorado and improve the ski slopes in the winter, that is not geoengineering; if we learn to make it snow in Antarctica, in order to store water there to reduce the sea level, that is geoengineering.

The first thing to say about the economics of geoengineering compared with CO_2 abatement is that probably it totally transforms the greenhouse issue from an exceedingly complicated regulatory regime to a simple—not necessarily easy, but simple—problem in international cost sharing. I cannot be sure because we don't know just what geoengineering we are talking about fifty years from now; but if the subject is putting aerosols or objects in the stratosphere or in orbit, or fertilizing the oceans, these are what we can call 'exo-national' programs—programs not confined to national territories, not depending on the behavior of national populations, not requiring national regulations or incentives, and probably not at all dependent on universal participation. If we want to boost carbon black into the stratosphere we may do it from the decks of ships on the high seas.

In contrast, CO_2 abatement has to be very decentralized, very participatory, and very regulatory. It requires affecting the way people heat and cool their homes, cook, collect firewood, drive cars, consume energy-intensive aluminum, and produce steam for electricity and industrial use. Methane abatement involves how farmers feed their cattle and aerate their rice paddies. Carbon abatement depends on policies that many governments are incapable of implementing because they don't know how, or they haven't the resources, or they haven't the authority, or it is too expensive. But most of the direct geoengineering interventions that have been discussed involve just spending money. If you want to change the tuning of the carburetors of the jet aircraft that go through the stratosphere so that they will emit carbon black, you just pay them for it. If you want to send sulphur or carbon black into the stratosphere, you buy cheap sounding rockets or naval guns and purchase the substance to be lifted.

It may or may not be cheaper than reducing carbon fuels, but it is certainly way ahead in administrative simplicity. It will involve deciding *what* to do—carbon black, sulfur aerosols, ocean fertilizer; *how much* to do; and *who*'s to pay for it. (How much to do can be controversial. Some will say if we can do it cheaply we should offset back to the CO_2 concentration of 1875, others back to the concentration of 1995, others to some intermediate concentration; cost might be relevant to how much.)

But primarily the issue is who pays for it? And this is an old-fashioned issue; we have dealt with it before. We have had to decide how to share the cost of peacekeeping in Cambodia, the United Nations budget, subscriptions to the World Bank and the International Monetary Fund, postwar aid for relief and rehabilitation, and aid to Palestinians in the West Bank and Gaza. It isn't necessarily easy, but it is pretty uncomplicated compared with reducing carbon dioxide emissions.

Afforestation, which the National Academy report of 1992 classified as geoengineering, does of course depend on national territories. But planting trees, especially in areas where poaching for firewood is not likely, primarily requires spending money to acquire land, plant trees, and manage the forests. There is no reason why these costs need to be borne by the countries within whose borders the trees are planted. If the United States wanted to finance afforestation for greenhouse reasons, it should pick the most cost-effective locations, whether Siberia, Montana, South Carolina, or Australia.

The National Academy report, in assessing how much carbon dioxide could be sequestered in trees, analyzed prospects in the United States, probably because that is where it had data, and went on, I believe somewhat thoughtlessly, to compare the potential U.S. territorial sequestration with U.S. carbon dioxide emissions, apparently as if "we" could do "our share" of abatement by planting trees on "our" territory. But if the German government or the Japanese government wanted to plant trees as a contribution to greenhouse abatement, there is no good reason why they shouldn't be willing, and allowed, to plant trees in Montana or South Carolina and get "credit" for the money they spent. The host country may get some modest benefit (flood control?) or nuisance, and that could affect the competition in cost-effectiveness; but it seems unlikely that the United States would be credited with having done its share of abatement if it just turned out that America is full of good locations for cheap afforestation.

Although greenhouse geoengineering may prove expensive, the extant proposals would not be expensive in diplomatic tension and difficulty. One thing that can be said for geoengineering is that it immensely reduces the complicatedness of what nations have to do internally to cope with greenhouse problems and what nations have to do internationally to cope with greenhouse problems.

To avoid being thought too optimistic, I should admit that there can be international conflicts over some geoengineering. They may not show up with global warming and climate change; but an example that might meet the definition of geoengineering is intervening to control hurricanes, either reducing the ocean-surface characteristics that produce hurricanes or intervening in the formation of hurricanes. To Americans on the Gulf Coast, to the residents of the Caribbean and the Philippines, learning to suppress hurricanes is surely beyond controversy. But hurricanes provide essential rainfall in southern Mexico and southern China; hurricanes affect weather over a diameter of several thousand miles. I conclude that there may well be discovered some practical geoengineering interventions that are not only feasible and important but that can increase rather than reduce international tensions. I can imagine that fifty years from now when the Philippine Coast Guard cutter moves out to suppress a hurricane it meets a Chinese naval vessel armed with heavier firepower.

REFERENCES

National Academy of Sciences. 1992. *Policy Implications of Greenhouse Warming: Mitigation, Adaptation, and the Science Base.* Panel on Policy Implications of Greenhouse Warming, Committee on Science, Engineering, and Public Policy, National Academy Press, Washington, DC, pp. 433–464.

4

Intergenerational and International Discounting

■ Economists who deal with very-long-term policy issues, such as greenhouse gas emissions over the next century or two, are nearly unanimous in their opinion that future benefits that take the form of additions to future consumption need to be discounted to be commensurable with each other and with the consumption forgone earlier to produce those benefits. There is a near consensus among these economists that the appropriate discount rate should be conceptualized as consisting of two components.[1]

The first is pure time preference and, according to Fankhauser, deals with the impatience of consumers and reflects their inborn preference of immediate over postponed consumption.[2] The second component reflects the changing marginal utility of consumption with the passage of time, and is decomposed into a rate of growth of consumption per capita and an elasticity of marginal utility with respect to consumption. The two components—pure preference for early over later utility, and declining marginal utility with growing per capita consumption—are used to compare not only utility increments in the year, say, 2050 with costs incurred in 2000, but also utility increments in the year 2150 with increments in the year 2050.

Since this article argues that "discounting" is not the appropriate concept for dealing with the benefits of reduced greenhouse gas emissions in the distant future, it should be stated that this author finds traditional discounting perfectly appropriate for comparing costs and benefits of, for example, hazardous-waste cleanup, as with the U.S. Superfund program. In that kind of program, discounting with appropriate rates of interest is crucial to determining which sites are worth cleaning up, how much they should be cleaned up, and when or in what order of priority cleanup should occur. In that kind of program, those who pay the costs are saving and investing—forgoing some current consumption—in order to reap future benefits, along with their children and grandchildren. It makes sense to "optimize" the "investment portfolio" by reference to appropriate discount rates. The case is made that global greenhouse gas abatement is not like cleaning up one's own land for one's own benefit. *Costs* incurred for greenhouse gas abatement need to be discounted; *benefits* need an altogether different treatment.

PURE TIME PREFERENCE

Any time preference pertinent to discounting the long-term benefits of greenhouse gas abatement cannot have anything to do with impatience. The alleged inborn preference for earlier rather than later consumption is exclusively concerned with the consumer's impatience with respect to his or her *own* consumption.

I feel no impatience about an increment of consumption that will accrue to people whom I shall never know and who do not now exist in the year 2150, compared with an increment that will accrue to the people whom I shall never know and who do not now exist in the year 2100, or even in the year 2050. Reasons can be given for preferring a boost to consumption in 2025 to the same boost of consumption in 2075, but it is hard to see that it has anything to do with impatience and the inborn preference of immediate over postponed consumption. In 2025 my oldest son will be the age I am today and his brothers a little younger; with a little luck they will be alive and healthy and my grandchildren will be the ages that my children are today, and my great-grandchildren (whom I do not yet know) will have most of their lives ahead of them. Seventy-five years later they will all be strangers to me. My genes may be as plentiful in the population at that later date but they will be spread thinner. I probably would prefer the benefits to accrue to my own grandchildren rather than to their grandchildren, but when I remind myself that my grandchildren's happiness may depend on their perceived prospects for their own grandchildren, my "time preference" becomes attenuated.

Actually, time may serve as a measure of "distance." The people who are going to be living in 2150 may be considered "farther away" than the people who will be living in 2050. They will also be different in racial composition and geographical distribution from the people alive today. In redistributing income via transfer payments—providing foreign aid, contributing to charity, and so forth—people are expected to differentiate, and *do* differentiate, among recipient peoples according to several kinds of distance or proximity. One is geographical: Americans are expected to be more interested in their own cities than in distant ones, their own country rather than distant nations. Another is political: East Coast Americans are more interested in the people of Los Angeles than in the people of Quebec. Yet another is cultural: some people are closer in language, religion, and other kinds of heritage. Sheer familiarity seems to matter, and of course kinship does. Kinship distance has both horizontal and vertical dimensions; just as children are closer than grandchildren, children are closer than nieces and nephews. Time just happens to correlate with vertical distance.

The crucial point is that decisions to invest in greenhouse gas–emissions abatement for the benefit of future generations are not "saving" decisions"—not decisions about postponing one's own consumption—but are instead decisions about redistributing income, one's own income. To invest resources now in reduced greenhouse gas emissions is to transfer consumption from present-day people—whoever those people are who are making these sacrifices—for the benefit of people in the distant future. It is very much like making sacrifices now for people who are distant geographically or distant culturally. Deciding whether one cares more about the people who will be alive in 2150 than the people who will be alive in 2050 is a little like deciding whether one cares more about people in one continent than in another, or about English-speaking people more than people who speak other languages, or about those with whom one shares history and culture more than those who do not. People do have preferences about whom to help; the preferences show up in charitable giving, in foreign aid, in immigration policy, and in military intervention.

What is under consideration here is very much like a foreign aid program with some of the foreigners being descendants who live not on another continent but in another century.

MARGINAL UTILITY

The second component of the proposed discount rate is the rate of change over time of the marginal utility of consumption. The argument for including that component must be that in transferring or redistributing income, an important goal is to maximize the aggregate utility of consumption over time. The expectation is that, on average, the marginal utility of global consumption will decline over time as a result of rising consumption per capita. Resources invested now out of present incomes will benefit people in the future who are expected to be better off than those alive today—an unaccustomed direction for redistributing income!

Both within countries and among countries, civilized governments are expected to redistribute toward the poorer countries and toward the poorer elements of their own populations. The argument for transferring consumption from the poor to the rich, or from the decently well off to the much better off, would be that the resources transferred grow in the process, and grow so much that though the marginal utility of the recipient is lower than that of the donor, the magnitude that the gift achieves in transit more than compensates.

There is not much room for this idea in contemporary transfers. If a poor farmer has some poor soil and a richer farmer has rich soil, it could be argued that taking seed from the poor farmer and giving it to the rich farmer will so enhance the resulting crop that the somewhat utility-satiated rich farmer will gain more utility than the poor farmer loses. But that is just an argument for trade: the poor farmer is better off selling the seed to the rich farmer, and their joint utility is even higher. The ethical interest arises only if trade is not possible, as when society outfits an adventurer who will emigrate to the New World, become rich, and never be heard from again, or as public policy contemplates transferring consumption forward in time to people who have no way to reciprocate.

Depreciating the consumption of high-income future people makes sense; however, a fallacy must be avoided here. If average per capita income rises in every country for the next hundred years, and if the poorer populations grow more rapidly than the wealthier populations, and if most of the economic sacrifices in the interest of carbon abatement are borne by the countries that can best afford it, the transfers will tend to be from the well-to-do people of western Europe, North America, and Japan to the residents of what are now called the "developing" countries, who should be far better off a century from now than they are now. These people, though, may not be as well-off, during most of the intervening century, as those living today in western Europe, North America, and Japan.

In deciding how to value consumption increments over the coming century or two, consumption needs to be disaggregated according to the levels of per capita consumption at which they accrue. The optimization models err, on their own terms, in aggregating all future consumption and applying a uniform discount rate for declining marginal utility. Correctly, all increments in consumption should be valued at their own marginal utilities. In the optimization models, increments for poor people are discounted equally with increments for the rich; there is no adjustment for the fact that when Chinese per capita income has doubled and Chinese marginal utility may have been halved—using the popular but arbitrary logarithmic utility function—Chinese marginal utility will still be many times greater than that of the current populations most likely to pay for greenhouse gas abatement.

In neglecting to disaggregate, the optimization models assume that those who pay for abatement and those who benefit, or whose descendants benefit, are the same. Because all populations—all nations or regions—are assumed to enjoy increasing consumption per capita, and because investments in abatement precede the benefits, the benefiting populations are assumed to have higher consumption and lower marginal utilities than the populations that finance the abatement.

It can be expected, however, that for the first fifty years greenhouse abatement will be paid for by the countries that can afford it: the developed countries of western Europe, North America, Japan, and a few others. The beneficiaries of abatement will mainly be the descendants of those now living in the undeveloped countries, for several reasons explained below. Thus the consumption transfers will be from well-to-do countries that will mainly pay for abatement over the coming fifty years to the developing countries that, though probably progressively better off over the same time period, will have lower consumption levels fifty years from now than the current consumption levels of the developed countries. Benefits from abatement during the first fifty years will almost surely be negligible compared with benefits during the second fifty years. Thus the consumption transfers, despite the hoped-for uniformly (not uniform) positive growth in gross domestic product (GDP) per capita everywhere, will be generally from rich to poor—that is, from lower marginal utility to higher marginal utility. The implications are startling, but first it should be explained why the beneficiaries will mainly be the descendants of the populations now poor.

First, if the benefits of abatement were shared uniformly over the global population, about 90 percent would accrue to the countries now considered undeveloped. The well-to-do are now about a fifth of the world's population; in 2075 the populations in countries now undeveloped are expected to be somewhere between seven-eighths and eleven-twelfths of the global population. At that rate those populations will comprise most of the beneficiaries.

Second, material productivity in the developed countries currently appears to be substantially immune to weather and climate; production in less-developed countries depends much more on outdoor activities, especially agriculture, and is potentially much more susceptible to the adverse effects of climate change. Therefore, besides outnumbering the descendants of the currently developed countries, those in less-developed countries can suffer greater greenhouse gas damage per capita. (In absolute terms, the more developed countries could incur more lost GDP per capita, though the damage might not be noticeable.)

Finally, the currently developed countries enjoy GDP per capita ten times or more that of the undeveloped; during the second half of the coming century they will probably still be ahead by a factor of four or more. So the marginal utility of consumption of the poorer nine-tenths of the population will be several times that of the richer tenth, and the benefits in utility increments from material consumption will therefore be overwhelmingly inherited by the descendants of those who are currently poor. For example, if Chinese per capita income increased at 4 percent per year for the next fifty years and 2 percent for the following fifty years, and U.S. per capita income increased at 1 percent over the hundred years, Chinese per capita income would still be less than half the U.S. level at the end of the century. At those rates of improvement, the Chinese will be approaching the present U.S. level toward the end of the century; before then, interest will probably be lost in further increments.

Earlier it was stated that the implications are startling. One of them has already been mentioned: virtually all the benefits from enhanced consumption will accrue to countries that will not participate much in financing the abatement. The transfers will be from the currently rich to the descendants of the currently poor, who will—when the benefits begin to be felt—be much less poor than they are now but still poorer than the descendants of the currently rich and probably still significantly poorer than the abatement-financing countries are now.

Another is that the implicit "discount rate" based on marginal utility comparisons will be negative. The currently popular optimization models can't show this negative rate, because GDP per capita is assumed to rise everywhere. Even if it does, however, disaggregating shows that the beneficiaries will be both poorer and more numerous than those who finance the increments in consumption.

THE DEVELOPMENT CONTEXT

A third implication is that if GDP per capita continues to increase in most of the developing world, as can be expected and as the optimization models assume, over the next hundred years marginal utilities of the beneficiaries will be much higher during the first fifty years—before abatement benefits become significant—than in the second fifty years. This factor substantially tilts the priority toward whatever investments can raise living standards in the first and second generations. Those investments are likely to be direct investments in economic development, which should also reduce dependence on climate rather than investment in climate stabilization.

Even more drastic, if marginal utilities will be higher in the fifth decade than in the sixth, in the third than in the fourth, and in the first than in the second, today's undeveloped populations have stronger claims, on the basis of marginal utility, than the populations two or four generations in the future. Once the world's population is disaggregated by income level, it becomes logically absurd to ignore present needs and concentrate on the later decades of the coming century. An initial interest in climate and its impact on welfare should not insulate one from alternative means to the same end. That then means that no framework for considering the benefits and costs of greenhouse gas abatement should isolate itself from the opportunity cost: direct investment in the economic improvement of the undeveloped countries. Abatement expenditures should have to compete with alternative ways of raising consumption utility in the developing world.

Greenhouse gas abatement, which is largely identified with energy policy, is insulated in optimization models from economic development. An answer to how much (and when) to abate is given in optimization models independently of what else is going on. When greenhouse gas abatement is identified as a mechanism for making income transfers to future generations—especially to those whose consumption levels are still comparatively low—it should have to compete with transfers for investment in economic development.

Carbon dioxide abatement is probably "target efficient," helping mainly those society would prefer to help. Poorer countries are usually going to be more vulnerable to climate change than wealthier countries. But direct investments in public health, birth control, training and education, research, physical infrastructure, water resources, and so on can also be directed to target populations, so abatement does not necessarily have the advantage.

It is doubtful that developing countries would choose to defer consumption increments to later generations, whether what is deferred comes out of their own resources or out of resources made available by wealthier countries. If offered a choice of immediate development assistance or equivalent investments in carbon abatement, it is likely that potential aid recipients would elect the immediate. So if we, the developed, elect carbon abatement for their benefit, it is *we* who choose their descendants over themselves.

NOTES

1. William R. Cline, *The economics of global warming* (Washington, DC: Institute for International Economics, 1992); Samuel Fankhauser, *The*

social costs of greenhouse gas emissions: An expected value approach (University College and University of East Anglia, Centre for Social and Economic Research on the Global Environment, Norwich, U.K., 1993); Alan S. Manne, "The rate of time preference: Implications for the greenhouse debate," *Energy Policy, 23* (1995): 391–394; William D. Nordhaus, *Managing the global commons: The economics of climate change* (Cambridge, MA: MIT Press, 1994).

2. Fankhauser, *Social costs of greenhouse gas emissions.*

Commitment as Self-Command

5

Self-Command in Practice, in Policy, and in a Theory of Rational Choice

■ An increasingly familiar occurrence for obstetricians is being asked by patients to withhold anesthesia during delivery. The physician often proposes that a facemask be put beside the patient, who may inhale nitrous oxide as she needs it. But some determined patients ask that no such opportunity be provided: if gas is available they will use it, and they want not to be able to.

The request is interesting for decision theory, and raises questions of ethics, policy, and physician responsibility, even if the woman is merely making a mistake—if she simply does not know how painful labor will be and how glad she will be, even in retrospect, if the pain is relieved. But some women who make this request have had earlier deliveries during which they demanded anesthesia and received it. They are acquainted with the pain. They anticipate asking for relief. And they want it withheld when they do. They expect to regret afterward any recourse to anesthesia.

This particular instance of attempted self-denial has features that are special but many that are common. The woman is, so far as we know, in good health physically and mentally. She anticipates a transient period when her usual values and preferences will be suspended or inaccessible. She has reasons for wanting to frustrate her own wishes at the critical time. She needs cooperation. She may ratify her choice afterward by expressing herself grateful that no anesthesia was offered, even when requested. There are ethical dilemmas and legal issues,

63

and there is conflict, if, say, the husband disagrees with the physician in the delivery room about what his wife really wants.

I. ANTICIPATORY SELF-COMMAND

This obstetrical example, though special in certain respects, is not a bad paradigm for the general anomaly of anticipatory self-command. That is the phenomenon that I want to discuss—that a person in evident possession of her faculties and knowing what she is talking about will rationally seek to prevent, to compel, or to alter her own later behavior—to restrict her own options in violation of what she knows will be her preference at the time the behavior is to take place. It is not a phenomenon that fits easily into a discipline concerned with rational decision, revealed preference, and optimization over time.

Attempting to overrule one's own preferences is certainly exceptional, as consumer behavior goes, but not so exceptional that anyone who reads this is unfamiliar with it. Let me remind you of some of those behaviors that share with obstetrical anesthesia the characteristic that a person may request now that a later request be denied. Please do not give me a cigarette when I ask for it, or dessert, or a second drink. Do not give me my car keys. Do not lend me money. Do not lend me a gun.

Besides denial there are interventions. Do not let me go back to sleep. Interrupt me if I get in an argument. Push me out of the plane when it's my turn to parachute. Don't let me go home drunk unless you can remove my children to a safe place. Blow the fuse if you catch me watching television. Make me get up and do my back exercises every morning. Keep me moving if I am exhausted in the wilderness. Pump my stomach if you catch me overdosed with sleeping pills.

Then there is restructuring of incentives, often with somebody's help. Wagers serve this purpose, and are often used by people who share an interest in losing weight. Confessing something incriminating that can be revealed in the event of a lapse, or just making a ceremonial display of determination to exercise or to stay off cigarettes, can threaten oneself with shame.

Most of the tactics used to command one's own future performance probably do not depend on someone else's participation. I mentioned some that do, partly for comparison with the obstetrical example, partly because our experience with purely individual efforts is usually restricted to our own and we are unaware of the efforts of others unless a need for cooperation makes them visible. Further, the legal, ethical, and policy issues arise mainly when a second party is enlisted. And these are the cases that appear to call for a judgment about the ambivalent person's true interest—which set of preferences deserves our loyalty or sympathy.

The obstetrical case is rich in its ethics and legalities. To which patient is a physician obligated? The one asking for anesthesia or the one who asked that it be withheld? Can the physician enter a contract that will both protect against malpractice and compel compliance with the woman's earlier preferences? Do we like policies that make such contracts possible; do we like policies that make such contracts void?

Physicians, of course, are bound by a professional code as well as their personal ethics, and are subject to criminal and civil complaints. In the same way, our personal ethics are challenged when the drinking guest who entrusted us with his car keys wants them back, or snatches them and heads for his car. Our ethics are even challenged when he didn't ask but we know he intended not to drive himself home, he has a momentary alcoholic confidence in his driving ability, he will certainly thank us tomorrow if we disable his car, but he demands now that we let him alone.

Professional discussion of suicide indicates that anticipation of changing preferences is common. There are two symmetrical cases here. One is preventing suicide when a person has asked for protection against his own determination during periods when he unmistakably prefers to be dead. The other is the contrary, being begged to expedite someone's departure in the event of some ghastly condition, even if the condition is accompanied by such horror of dying that he will beg us to perpetuate that horror in violation of our earlier promise. There is also the person who elects death but cannot face the finality of bringing it about, and, like the parachutist who asks to be shoved out if he grips the door jam, implores our help in getting him over the brink.

Legal issues arise in some attempts to abdicate rights that are deemed to be inalienable. I cannot get a court injunction against my own smoking. I cannot contract with a skydiving pilot to push me out of the airplane. I cannot authorize my psychiatrist in advance to have me hospitalized against my wishes in circumstances that we have agreed on. I cannot contract with a fat farm to hold me against my will until I have lost some number of pounds; they have to let me out when I ask. (If we are clever we can arrange it; I go to a remote fat farm that requires a twenty-four-hour notice to order a car, a notice that I can rescind during a moment's resurgent resolve to lose weight. I have heard that what keeps cruise ships from offering this kind of service is the inability to keep the crew from smuggling extra calories on board for the black market.)

An interesting issue is the ethics of prohibition—against, say, the display and sale of rich desserts in the faculty dining room, or against cigarette smoking in the workplace—not to keep others from overeating or smoking, as is usually the motivation behind prohibitions, but to keep ourselves from succumbing and to reduce the pain of temptation. There is a legal test in Massachusetts now of whether nicotine addiction is a protected species of handicap and a person has a right to relief through smoking in the workplace.

The most serious cases are those that involve, one way or another, actively or passively, taking your own life—one of your selves taking the life that you share. The law takes sides with the self that will not die. Someone who lives in perpetual terror of his own suicidal tendencies can welcome the law's sanctions against people whom he might, during a passing depression, beg to help with suicide. People for whom life has become unbearable but who cannot summon the resolve to end it have the law against them in their efforts to recruit accomplices. In December a California judge ruled against a quadriplegic woman who wished to die and asked the hospital's help in starving herself to death. The judge ordered forcefeeding, with the comment that "our society values life."

Besides legal issues there are regulatory policies. Nicotine chewing gum has been introduced as a prescription drug. The National Academy of Sciences has proposed that cigarettes low in tar and high in nicotine be developed to see whether people can better regulate their intake of tars, carbon monoxide, and other gases if they can more readily satisfy their need for nicotine. And female hormones are being administered to violent male sex offenders who volunteer for treatment.

There are now remote monitors that can be attached to a parolee that will transmit encrypted messages at scheduled times through an attachment to the parolee's telephone to monitor whether he is abiding by a curfew. But he could voluntarily submit to surveillance by a friend, spouse, or other guardian; and I remind you of the electric-shock dog-training collars that can administer a deterrent to misbehavior. There is no technical difficulty in devising an unremovable blood-alcohol monitor that could activate a radio signal, or even administer a painful shock.

There are dangers. One can imagine a variety of self-restraining or self-compelling measures that could be used as conditions for employment, for election to office, for borrowing money, or for parole or probation, if it were known that one could incur an ostensibly voluntary enforceable commitment. The polygraph is a current example. Sterilization is another.

Many heroin addicts are alcoholics. Methadone is legally available for some heroin addicts; it replaces the need for heroin. Antabuse is legally available for alcoholics; it interacts with alcohol to produce extreme nausea, and precludes drinking. Methadone is attractive—at least in the absence of heroin—but antabuse is unattractive when alcohol is available. Some therapists provide the methadone only after the patient has taken the antabuse in the presence of the therapist.[1]

II. SELF-COMMAND AND THE RATIONAL CONSUMER

How can we accommodate this phenomenon of strategic self-frustration in our model of the rational consumer? We can begin by asking whether there is a single phenomenon here, one that can be epitomized by addiction, appetite, or pain.

Adam Smith, by the way, included a chapter on self-command in his *Theory of Moral Sentiments*. He meant something different—courage, generosity, and other manly virtues. In my usage, self-command is what you may not need to employ if you already have enough of what Adam Smith meant by it. You don't need the skillful exercise of self-command to cope with shifting preferences if you've already got your preferences under control. I cannot resist quoting a passage that I'm sure he'd like an opportunity to edit once more. "We esteem the man who supports pain and even torture with manhood and firmness; and we can have little regard for him who sinks under them, and abandons himself to useless outcries and womanish lamentations."

There is a quite heterogeneous array of types and circumstances and it will be useful to recall them. What they have in common is that they invite efforts at anticipatory self-command. Many of them are quite ordinary.

We can begin with behavior anticipated when one is fatigued, drowsy, drunk, or coming out of a sound sleep. Or for that matter asleep: people do misbehave in their sleep. They scratch; they remove dressings from wounds; they adopt postures not recommended by orthopedists. Wearing mittens to frustrate scratching or putting the alarm clock across the room are perfectly familiar techniques of self-command.

Quite different are acute thirst and hunger, panic, pain, and rage; some athletes drink water through straws to avoid gulping, and many people forgo the advantages of a gun in the house for fear they'll use it.

There is captivation—books, puzzles, television, argument, fantasy —that engages a person against his earlier determination not to be so engaged. Keeping your mind from misbehaving on its own is somewhat different from keeping it from making wrong decisions; still, the mind that sneaks off into reverie without permission, or that won't stop chewing on some logical paradox, can be thought of as actually consuming—against orders.

There are phobias—reactions of admittedly unreasoning fear to heights, enclosures, crowds, audiences, blood, needles, reptiles, leeches, filth, and the dark. These, too, look sometimes like the mind misbehaving; several of them can be brought under some control by shutting one's eyes. It is not only pediatricians who suggest looking away when the knee has to be drained through a four-inch needle. I've seen many references to a phenomenon I experienced as a child—the dark is not so frightening if you shut your eyes, especially under the bedclothes.

There are compulsive personal habits involving faces and fingernails that are difficult to frustrate because we cannot take a trip and leave our cuticles behind.

Certain illnesses entail such protracted depression that, just as a person may attempt to make decisions now that he cannot change when he becomes aged, a person may put certain decisions beyond reach during an anticipated postoperative depression. It is not for nothing that we have the phrase, "a jaundiced view"; hepatitis does change one's outlook profoundly. Medication can change a person's values; self-administration of drugs, stimulants, and tranquilizers is used deliberately to alter one's effective preferences, and can have similar effects inadvertently. Alcohol makes some people brave when they need to be brave and some fool-hardy when they can't afford to be. People for whom medicinally induced swings in mood are an unavoidable chronic way of life shouldn't be disqualified as the rational consumers that our theoretical assumptions are supposed to represent.

Some of those behaviors, like falling asleep, may not sound like consumer choices, possibly because we do not usually identify them with the marketplace, and some may not seem altogether voluntary. They do remind us that attempts to achieve self-command are familiar, not necessarily abnormal, and when abnormal not uncommon.

There are many such behaviors that we have to acknowledge do look like consumer choice: smoking, drinking, overeating, procrastination, exercise, gambling, licit and illicit drugs, and shopping binges. And remember, I am speaking only of people who want to deny themselves later access to the foods, drugs, gambling, sexual opportunities, criminal companionship, or shopping splurges that constitute their own acknowledged problems in self-command. Anyone who is happily addicted to nicotine, benzedrine, valium, chocolate, heroin, or horse racing, and anyone unhappily addicted who would not elect the pains and deprivations of withdrawal, are not my subject. I am not concerned with whether cigarettes or rich desserts are bad for you, only with the fact that there are people who wish so badly to avoid them that, if they could, they would put those commodities beyond their own reach.

It is not an invariable characteristic of these activities that there is a unanimously identified good or bad behavior. Some dieters try to stay below a healthy body weight. Some people are annoyed at teetotalers, successful dieters, compulsive joggers, or people who never lose their tempers. And somebody who pleads for help in taking his own life, and alternately pleads not to be heeded on the occasions when he does, offers no easy choice as to who it is we should prefer to win the contest. The same is true of people who take steps to prevent their own defection from some religious faith.

While all of the cases I mentioned, from scratching to religious conversion, are within the subject of self-command, not all of them need to be recognized in a theory of rational decision. The person who prefers not to get out of bed we can consider just not all there; there are chemical inhibitors of brain activity that play a role in sleep, and until they have been metabolized away his brain is not working. His case may typify important decisions, but not the ones our theory is about. You can't make rational decisions when you're not rational, and you should rationally keep yourself from trying. Noisy alarms out of reach represent a rational choice.

What we can do is to append to our consumer a list of disqualifying circumstances in which his decisions are likely to be mistaken ones, and we make it the ordinary consumer's business, if he can't keep out of those circumstances, to take steps in advance to keep himself from making any decisions, or to arrange in advance to have his decisions disregarded. An important part of the consumer's task is then not merely household management but self-management—treating himself as though he were occasionally a servant who might misbehave. That way we separate the anomalous behavior from the rational; we take sides with whichever consumer self appeals to us as the authentic representation of values; and we can study the ways that the straight self and the wayward self interact strategically. We can adopt policies that, if they don't cause troubles elsewhere like interfering with civil liberties, help the consumer in his rational moments to control that other self and to keep important decisions from falling into the wrong hands.

But what about the person who, having given up cigarettes six months ago, succumbs after dinner to an irresistible urge to light a cigarette, who does so in apparent possession of his faculties, who six months earlier, or six hours, would have paid a price to ensure that cigarettes would be unavailable at the moment he changed his mind? If he were crazed with thirst or acutely suffering opiate withdrawal we could disqualify the decision: the mind is partly disconnected, a level of mind has taken over that is incapable of handling more than a couple of primitive dimensions of desire. But the person lighting that cigarette doesn't look as though he's bereft of his higher faculties.

The conclusion I come to is that this phenomenon of rational strategic interaction among alternating preferences is a significant part of most people's decisions and welfare and cannot be left out of our account of the consumer. We ignore too many important purposive behaviors if we insist on treating the consumer as having only values and preferences that are uniform over time, even short periods of time.

Just to establish the magnitude of the problem, consider cigarette smoking. There are thirty-five million Americans who have quit smoking. Most of them had to make at least three serious tries in order to quit. Of those thirty-five million, about five million are in danger of relapse, and two million will resume smoking and regret it. Most of those will try again, and three-quarters will fail on the next try. There are fifty-five million cigarette smokers, among whom some forty or forty-five million have tried to quit; nearly half have already tried three times or more, and some twenty million of those cigarette smokers made a serious try, and failed, within the past year. More than half of all young smokers, of both sexes, tried to quit within the past year and failed. A third of all young smokers have unsuccessfully tried three times or more. They know that smoking is dangerous, and we know that it is worth some years of their life expectancy. Smoking behavior alone is a major determinant of consumer welfare, one that a theory based on stable preferences and rational choice cannot illuminate without some modification; and smoking is only one such behavior.

There has been interesting work on how time preferences, as among future points in time, can change as time goes by—how one's preferred allocation of resources between the decade of the 1990s and the next decade after that can change between 1980 and 1990. I have in mind ideas associated with Robert Strotz (1956), Edmund Phelps and Robert Pollak (1968), Pollak (1968), and Jon Elster (1977, 1979). And we know the anecdote of the politically radical twenty-year-old whose conservative father infuriates him by putting a sum of money in trust that the son may use for political contributions only when he reaches the conservative age of forty. I propose we admit not only unidirectional changes over time, but changes back and forth at intervals of years, months, weeks, days, hours, or even minutes, changes that can entail bilateral as well as unilateral strategy.[2]

There are different ways to say what I'm describing. Two or more sets of values alternately replace each other; or an unchanging array of values is differentially accessible at different times, like different softwares that have different rules of search and comparison, access to different parts of the memory, different proclivities to exaggerate or to distort or to suppress. We know that the sight of a glistening bowl of peanuts can trigger unintended search and retrieval from memory, some of it subliminal, and even changes in the chemical environment of the brain. In common language, a person is not always his usual self;

and without necessarily taking sides as between the self we consider more usual and the other one that occasionally gains command, we can say that it looks as if different selves took turns, each self wanting its own values to govern what the other self or selves will do by way of eating, drinking, getting tattooed, speaking its mind, or committing suicide.

III. STRATEGY AND TACTICS

From this point of view we can be quite straightforward in examining the strategies and tactics with which different selves compete for command. Here are some of the strategies I have in mind.[3]

Relinquish authority to somebody else: let him hold your car keys.

Commit or contract: order your lunch in advance.

Disable or remove yourself: throw your car keys into the darkness; make yourself sick.

Remove the mischievous resources: don't keep liquor, or sleeping pills, in the house; order a hotel room without television.

Submit to surveillance.

Incarcerate yourself. Have somebody drop you at a cheap motel without telephone or television and call for you after eight hours' work. (When George Steiner visited the home of Georg Lukacs he was astonished at how much work Lukacs, who was under political restraint, had recently published—shelves of work. Lukacs was amused and explained, "You want to know how one gets work done? House arrest, Steiner, house arrest!")

Arrange rewards and penalties. Charging yourself $100 payable to a political candidate you despise for any cigarette you smoke except on twenty-four hours' notice is a powerful deterrent to rationalizing that a single cigarette by itself can't do any harm.[4]

Reschedule your life: do your food shopping right after breakfast.

Watch out for precursors: if coffee, alcohol, or sweet desserts make a cigarette irresistible, maybe you can resist those complementary foods and drinks and avoid the cigarette.

Arrange delays: the crisis may pass before the time is up.

Use buddies and teams: exercise together, order each other's lunches.

Automate the behavior. The automation that I look forward to is a device implanted to monitor cerebral hemorrhage that, if the stroke is severe enough to indicate a hideous survival, kills the patient before anyone can intervene to remove it.

Finally, set yourself the kinds of rules that are enforceable. Use bright lines and clear definitions, qualitative rather than quantitative limits if possible. Arrange ceremonial beginnings. If procrastination is your problem, set piecemeal goals. Make very specific delay rules, requiring notice before relapse, with notice subject to withdrawal. Permit no exceptions.[5]

IV. IMPLICATIONS FOR WELFARE JUDGMENTS

An unusual characteristic of these two selves, if you will permit me to call them selves, is that it is hard to get them to sit down together. They do not exist simultaneously. Compromises are limited, if not precluded, by the absence of any internal mediator. I suppose they might get separate lawyers or agree on an arbitrator. If the obstetrician with whom I began this essay insists on taking the pain somewhat more seriously than his patient wanted him to, we would have an arbitrated compromise between the two selves.

For this reason we should expect outcomes that occasionally appear Pareto nonoptimal compared with the bargains they might like to strike:

Not keeping liquor or rich foods in the house, both selves suffering the detriment to their reputation as host;

Not keeping sleeping pills in the house, both selves suffering occasional insomnia;

Not keeping television in the house, both selves missing the morning news.

The simplicity with which we can analyze the strategy of self-command by recognizing the analogy with two selves comes at a price—a price in terms of what we value in our model of the consumer. When we identify a consumer attempting to exercise command over his own future behavior, to frustrate some of his own future preferences, we import into the individual a counterpart—I think an almost exact counterpart—to interpersonal utility comparisons. Each self is a set of values; and though the selves share most of those values, on the particular issues on which they differ fundamentally there doesn't seem to be any way to compare their utility increments and to determine which behavior maximizes their collective utility.

I should remark here that it is only in talking with economists that I feel at all secure in using the terminology of "selves." Philosophers and psychiatrists have their own definitions of the self, and legal scholars may resist the concept of the multiple self when it seems to raise questions about which "self" committed the crime or signed the contract, and whether the self on trial is the wrong one and we must wait for the "other" to materialize before trial, sentence, or incarceration. It is only in economics that the individual is modeled as a coherent set of preferences and certain cognitive facilities; and though economists are free to deny the phenomenon I'm discussing, if they recognize the phenomenon I think they have little difficulty with the language of alternative selves.

What about that woman who denies herself anesthesia, pleads for it during delivery, and denies it again at the next delivery? What about the person who drops by parachute with survival gear into the wilderness to go a month without smoking, drinking, overeating, or sleeping late as he beats his way back to civilization, cursing all the way the self that jumped, then pleased with himself when the ordeal is over? Is there a way to formulate the question, did the individual maximize utility? Or can we only argue that one of the selves enhanced its own utility at the expense of the other? When we ask the mother who an hour ago was frantic with pain whether she is glad the anesthesia was denied her, I expect her to answer yes. But I don't see what that proves. If we ask her while she is in pain, we'll get another answer.

As a boy I saw a movie about Admiral Byrd's first Antarctic expedition and was impressed that as a boy he had gone outdoors in shirtsleeves to toughen himself against the cold. I decided to toughen myself by removing one blanket from my bed. That decision to go to bed one blanket short was made by a warm boy; another boy awoke cold in the night, too cold to go look for a blanket, cursing the boy who removed the blanket and swearing to return it tomorrow. But the next bedtime it was the warm boy again, dreaming of Antarctica, who got to make the decision, and he always did it again. I still don't know whether, if those Antarctic dreams had come true, I'd have been better able to withstand the cold and both boys would have been glad that the command structure gave the decision to the boy who, feeling no pain himself, could inflict it on the other.

The person who can't get himself up in the morning I said was not quite all there. Why does that count against him? Apparently because he cannot fully appreciate what it will be like to be late to work. But does the self who sets the alarm, and arranges with a tennis partner to roll him out of bed, fully appreciate the discomfort of getting out of bed? My answer is yes. But notice: I am not in bed. I lecture only when I am awake, and the self that might prefer to stay in bed goes unrepresented.

In another respect I am not impartial. I have my own stakes in the way people behave. For my comfort and convenience I prefer that people act civilized, drive carefully, and not lose their tempers when I am around or beat their wives and children. I like them to get their work done. Now that I don't smoke, I prefer people near me not to. As long as we have laws against drug abuse it would be easier all around if people didn't get hooked on something that makes them break the law. In the language of economics, these behaviors generate externalities and make us interested parties. Even if I believe that some poor inhibited creature's true self emerges only when he is drunk enough to admit that he despises his wife and children and gets satisfaction out of scaring them to death, I have my own reasons for cooperating with that repressed and inhibited self that petitions me to keep him sober if I can, to restrain him if he's drunk, or to keep his wife and children safely away from him.

Consider the person who pleads in the night for the termination of an unbearable existence and expresses relief at midday that his gloomy night broodings were not taken seriously, who explains away the nighttime self in hopes of discrediting it, and pleads again for termination the next night. Should we look for the authentic self? Maybe the nighttime self is in physical or mental agony and the daytime self has a short memory. Maybe the daytime self lives in terror of death and is condemned to perpetuate its terror by frantically staying alive, suppressing both memory and anticipation of the more tangible horrors of the night. Or the nighttime self is perhaps overreacting to nocturnal gloom and depressed metabolism, trapped in a nightmare that it does not realize ends at dawn.

The question, which is the authentic one, may define the problem wrong. Both selves can be authentic. Like Siamese twins that live or die together but do not share pain, one pleads for life and the other for death—contradictory but inseparable pleas. If one of the twins sleeps when the other is awake, they are like the two selves that alternate between night and day. The problem seems to be distributive, not one of identification.

A few years ago I saw again the original *Moby Dick,* an early talkie in black and white. There was a scene—not in the book—of Ahab in the water losing his leg, and immediately afterward below deck under a blanket, eating an apple with three of the crew. The blacksmith enters with a hot iron to cauterize the stump. Ahab begs not to be burned. The crewmen hold him down as he spews out the apple in a scream, and steam rises where the iron is tormenting his leg. The movie resumes with Ahab out of pain and apparently glad to be alive. There is no sign that he took disciplinary action against the blacksmith or the men who held him while he was tortured.

When I first began contemplating this episode I thought it an incontestable case of the utility gain from denying freedom of choice and ignoring revealed preference. I wondered whether Ahab might have instructed the blacksmith that in the event of a ghastly wound to any member of the crew it was the blacksmith's responsibility to heat an iron and burn the wound, even if the wounded man were Captain Ahab. However much he implores us now not to burn his leg, Ahab will surely thank us afterward. But now I wonder what that proves.

If one of *you* were to be burned so that *I* might live I would probably thank the people who did it. If you burn *me* so that I may live I'll thank you, afterward, but that is because I'll be feeling no pain and not anticipating any when I thank you. Suppose I were to be burned and Ahab in the next room needed to be cauterized, too. Would you, while holding me down in disregard of my plea, ask my expert advice on whether to burn Ahab, and his advice on whether to burn me?

How do we know whether an hour of extreme pain is more than life is worth? Alternatively, how do we know whether an hour of extreme pain is more than death is worth?[6] The conclusion that I reach is that I do not know, not for you and not for me.

I do feel sure that if I wanted in such circumstances to endure the pain I would have to rely on people who were tough enough in spirit to hold me down, or at least to tie me down. And if any violation of the Captain's express orders constituted mutiny punishable by death, you would have to gag Ahab to keep him from screaming "don't" and thus condemning himself to a fatal infection. (Still, if the Captain himself presides over the trial of the mutineers who held him when he shouted "stop," they will be in no danger of his wrath; so, anticipating acquittal with thanks, they may as well hold him down.)

I have found, in conversations about Ahab's plight, that people like me approve of his being burned against his express wishes, not merely burned despite his involuntary screams and thrashings but against his horrified begging before he went out of his mind with pain. I interpret that to mean that people like me prefer a regime in which we ourselves would be held and burned even if we asked not to be. Yet our willingness to consider the need to be held against our will is an acknowledgment that, being certainly no braver than Ahab, we would in the event react as he did. That could mean that, at a position remote in time or in likelihood from the event we are better able to appreciate the relative merits of pain and death. But when I examine my own attitude, I usually find the contrary. If I try to imagine my way into Ahab's dilemma I find myself becoming so obsessed with immediate pain compared with immediate death that I begin agreeing with Ahab.[7]

If there is any wisdom in my current choice, which is to be held and burned if I am ever in Ahab's situation, it is the wisdom of choosing sides without fully acquainting myself with their merits. What I avoid is identifying myself with that person who may be burned, even though I know that it could be me. In the same way afterward, I shall thank you because I do not much identify with the historical I who was burned in the recent past. But I shall know then that if I had to do it again I would prefer death. It is hard for two selves that do not simultaneously exist to compare their pains, joys, and frustrations.

In exploring this problem of identity I have been tantalized by some imaginary experiments: imagine being offered a chance to earn a substantial sum, say an amount equal to a year's income, for undergoing an exceedingly painful episode that would have no physical aftereffects. Upon hearing what the pain is like, you refuse; maybe you'd undergo it for twice that sum. The experimenter is embarrassed; anticipating your favorable response, he has already initiated the experiment with you, perhaps through something you drank. You suffer the pain and are confirmed in your original judgment that you wouldn't do it for a year's income. When the pain is over and you've recovered from the shock, you receive the money. Question: when you see the experimenter on the sidewalk as you test-drive your new Porsche, are you glad he made that hideous mistake?

A second experiment: some anesthetics block transmission of the nervous impulses that constitute pain; others have the characteristic that the patient responds to the pain as if feeling it fully but has utterly no recollection afterwards. One of these is sodium pentothal. In my imaginary experiment we wish to distinguish the effects of the drug from the effects of the unremembered pain, and we want a healthy control subject in parallel with some painful operations that will be performed with the help of this drug. For a handsome fee you will be knocked out for an hour or two, allowed to sleep it off, then tested before you go home. You do this regularly, and one afternoon you walk into the lab a little early and find the experimenters viewing some videotape. On the screen is an experimental subject writhing, and though the audio is turned down the shrieks are unmistakably those of a person in pain. When the pain stops the victim pleads, "Don't ever do that again. Please."

The person is you.

Do you care?

Do you walk into your booth, lie on the couch, and hold out your arm for today's injection?

Should I let you?

NOTES

I am grateful to the Russell Sage Foundation and the Alfred P. Sloan Foundation for support and encouragement in this work.

1. There is an "interaction effect" that sometimes has to be taken into account in judging the merits of voluntarily incurred coercion, or even involuntarily. Physicians who advise their cardiac and pulmonary patients about smoking, and psychiatrists who deal with hospitalized (incarcerated) heroin addicts, report a common phenomenon. Addicts suffer noticeably less withdrawal discomfort when in an establishment that has a reputation for absolute incorruptibility, unbribable guards and staff, and no underground market anywhere, compared with a hospital in which it is expected,

rightly or wrongly, that appropriate effort and willingness to pay will produce relief. Cardiac and pulmonary patients who are told flatly that they must stop completely, at once, if they want to survive the year not only quit more frequently than patients merely advised to quit if they can, or, if they can't, to cut down or switch brands, but—this is the parallel to the heroin example—report surprisingly less withdrawal discomfort than those who succeed in quitting after getting the less absolute advice.

2. An imaginative and comprehensive treatment of this subject, including comparisons with animal behavior, is George Ainslie (1975). An intriguing philosophical approach is Elster (1977, 1979). In economics there are attempts to fit self-control within the economics tradition and some outside that tradition. The best-known effort to fit self-control within the economics tradition is George Stigler and Gary Becker (1977); their formulation denies the phenomenon I discuss. On the edge of traditional economics are C. C. von Weizsacker (1971) and Roger McCain (1979). Outside the tradition and viewing the consumer as complex rather than singular are Amartya Sen (1977), Gordon Winston (1980), Richard Thaler and H. M. Shefrin (1981), and Howard Margolis (1982). Winston, Thaler-Shefrin, and Margolis recognize a referee or superself, or planner-doer dichotomy, that I do not see; whether the difference is perception or methodology I am not sure. The most pertinent interdisciplinary work I know of by an economist is the brilliant small book by Tibor Scitovsky (1976). For related earlier work of mine, see my 1984 book.

3. These strategies exclude "seek professional help," even "get a good book." There are therapies: some are based on fairly unified theories and some are quite eclectic. Good examples of the more eclectic are K. Daniel O'Leary and G. Terrence Wilson (1975) and David Watson and Roland Tharp (1981), intended for use as college textbooks, and Ray Hodgson and Peter Miller (1982), a serious work designed for popular use. Many of the strategies I mention are represented in books like these. A more focused self-help book is Nathan Azrin and R. Gregory Nunn (1977), now unfortunately out of print; it deals mainly with "grooming" and other personal habits.

4. There is a cocaine addiction clinic in Denver that has used self-blackmail as part of its therapy. The patient may write a self-incriminating letter that is placed in a safe, to be delivered to the addressee if the patient, who is tested on a random schedule, is found to have used cocaine. An example would be a physician who writes to the State Board of Medical Examiners confessing that he has violated state law and professional ethics in the illicit use of cocaine and deserves to lose his license to practice

medicine. It is handled quite formally and contractually, and serves not only as a powerful deterrent but as a ceremonial expression of determination.

5. My back book prescribes exercises that are to be done faithfully every day. I am certain that some of them need to be done only two or three times a week. But the author knows that "two or three times a week" is not a schedule conducive to self-disciplines. My periodontist tells me that patients told to perform certain cleansing operations faithfully every day are pretty good at it, but told they can get along on two or three times a week relapse to two or three times every two or three weeks; he cannot then credibly insist they go back on the daily schedule.

6. Many discussions of ambivalence toward suicide, especially for the wretchedly or terminally ill, suggest a comparison with the case of Ahab. The ambivalence appears less an alternation between preferences for life and for death than a preference for death and a horror of dying. Death is the permanent state; dying is the act of getting there, and it can be awesome, terrifying, gruesome, and possibly painful. Ahab can enjoy life— minus a leg—only by undergoing a brief horrifying event, just as the permanent relief of death can be obtained only by undergoing what may be a brief and horrifying event, especially if the healing professions will not help or are not allowed to.

7. I find it difficult to predict my choice if I were in a situation comparable to Ahab's but with a choice whether to initiate my remaining life with the agonizing episode or to postpone the pain until later. It always seems to me that anyone able to elect the pain at all would be tempted to take it now. Pain in the future may be discounted, but pain past is discounted more. Faced with an episode of frightening pain, people often do try to get it over and done with.

REFERENCES

Ainslie, George, "Specious Reward: A Behavioral Theory of Impulsiveness and Impulse Control," *Psychological Bulletin,* July 1975, *82,* 463–96.

Azrin, Nathan H. and Nunn, R. Gregory, *Habit Control in a Day,* New York: Simon and Schuster, 1977.

Elster, Jon, "Ulysses and the Sirens: A Theory of Imperfect Rationality," *Social Science Information,* 1977, *41,* 469–526.

———, *Ulysses and the Sirens,* Cambridge: Cambridge University Press, 1979.

Hodgson, Ray, and Miller, Peter, *Self-Watching—Addictions, Habits, Compulsions: What to Do About Them*, New York: Facts on File, 1982.

McCain, Roger A., "Reflections on the Cultivation of Tastes," *Journal of Cultural Economics*, June 1979, *3*, 30–52.

Margolis, Howard, *Selfishness, Altruism, and Rationality*, Cambridge: Cambridge University Press, 1982.

O'Leary, K. Daniel and Wilson, G. Terrence, *Behavior Theory: Application and Outcome*, Englewood Cliffs: Prentice Hall, 1975.

Phelps, Edmund S. and Pollak, R. A., "On Second-Best National Saving and Game-Theoretic Equilibrium Growth," *Review of Economic Studies*, April 1968, *35*, 185–99.

Pollak, R. A., "Consistent Planning," *Review of Economic Studies*, April 1968, *35*, 201–208.

Schelling, Thomas C, "The Intimate Contest for Self-Command," in Schelling, *Choice and Consequence*, Cambridge: Harvard University Press, 1984, 57–82.

———, "Ethics, Law, and the Exercise of Self-Command," in *Choice and Consequence*, 83–112.

———, "The Mind as a Consuming Organ," in *Choice and Consequence*, 328–46.

Scitovsky, Tibor, *The Joyless Economy: An Inquiry into Human Satisfaction and Consumer Dissatisfaction*, New York: Oxford University Press, 1976.

Sen, Amartya K., "Rational Fools: A Critique of the Behavioral Foundations of Economic Theory," *Philosophy and Public Affairs*, Summer 1977, *6*, 317–45.

Smith, Adam, "Of Self-Command," in *The Theory of Moral Sentiments*, Section III, Part VI, 1759.

Stigler, George J. and Becker, Gary S., "De Gustibus Non Est Disputandum," *American Economic Review*, March 1977, *67*, 76–90.

Strotz, Robert H., "Myopia and Inconsistency in Dynamic Utility Maximization," *Review of Economic Studies*, no. 3, 1956, *23*, 165–80.

Thaler, Richard H. and Shefrin, H. M., "An Economic Theory of Self-Control," *Journal of Political Economy*, April 1981, *89*, 392–406.

von Weizsacker, C. C., "Notes on Endogenous Changes of Tastes," *Journal of Economic Theory*, December 1971, *3*, 345–72.

Watson, David L. and Tharp, Roland G., *Self-Directed Behavior: Self-Modification for Personal Adjustment*, Monterey: Brooks/Cole Publishing, 1981.

Winston, Gordon C., "Addiction and Backsliding," *Journal of Economic Behavior and Organization*, 1980, *1*, 295–324.

6

Coping Rationally with Lapses from Rationality

■ A man gave up smoking three months ago. For the first six or eight weeks he was regularly tormented by a desire to smoke, but the last three or four weeks have been less uncomfortable and he is becoming optimistic that he has left cigarettes behind for good. One afternoon a friend drops in for a business chat. The business done, our reformed smoker sees his friend to the door; returning to the living room he finds, on the coffee table, an opened pack of cigarettes. He snatches up the pack and hurries to the door, only to see his friend's car disappear around the corner. As he will see his friend in the morning and can return the cigarettes, he puts the pack in his jacket pocket and hangs the jacket in the closet. He settles in front of the television with a before-dinner drink to watch network news. Twenty minutes into the news he walks to the closet where his jacket hangs and takes the cigarettes out of the pocket, studies the pack for a minute, and walks into the bathroom, where he empties the cigarettes into the toilet and flushes it. He returns to his drink and his news.

What have we witnessed? I think we can confidently guess that our subject came to anticipate that in the presence of the cigarettes something might occur that he did not want to happen; by disposing of the cigarettes he has made it not happen. Wasting a few dollars' worth of his friend's cigarettes was an inexpensive safeguard. He has coped rationally with the risk that he would do something he did not—at the moment of flushing the cigarettes—want himself later to do.

I shall look in more detail at what may have been forestalled, but for the time being let us just interpret the man's act as a rational attempt to prevent some nonoptimal behavior that the presence of the cigarettes might motivate. Tentatively we might suppose that the man would explain his behavior as anticipating some "irrational act" that he strategically precluded by acting while still "rational."

My usual interest is in how people actually exercise strategy and tactics, successfully or unsuccessfully, in constraining their own future behavior. Often the ways people try to constrain their own future behavior are like the ways they would try to constrain someone else's behavior; they appear to be treating their "future self" as if it were another individual. If our man had never smoked but his wife had, and she had recently with great discomfort forsworn cigarettes and was not yet confidently weaned, and his business friend had left cigarettes behind, he would surely dispose of the cigarettes before his wife came home. So whether we want to say that he treats his ten o'clock self as if it were "another self," or only that he treats it as he would "another's" self, makes little difference.

Most literature on this subject in economics and philosophy concerns what is usually described as an apparent change in preferences. At five o'clock the man does not want to smoke; at five o'clock he does not want to smoke at ten o'clock; at ten o'clock he may want to smoke, remembering perfectly well that five hours ago he did not want himself to smoke at ten o'clock, remembering that three months ago he did not want himself to smoke at any time. Just describing what the man is doing if he lights the cigarette that even a few moments ago he may have hoped he wouldn't smoke is not easy. Whether it is "rational" that he satisfies an urge to smoke, exercising his unalienable sovereignty at ten o'clock, may not be answerable within the classical paradigm of rational choice; neurologically there may be a resolution of the question, but I prefer at this point to postpone examination of whether and how that succumbing at ten might be judged rational or irrational. I'll settle for calling it *nonoptimal as of five o'clock;* I'm willing to let the man refer to his anticipated lapse as "irrational" if he wants to call it that; at least, it so appears to him as of five o'clock.

These apparent changes in preference as time goes by, or as events trigger them, are important and interesting—maybe the most important and interesting of the "lapses from rationality." They can involve addiction to legal and illegal drugs—heroin, nicotine, Valium, caffeine; they include thirst, sex, and appetite; they include some hard-to-manage behaviors like gambling and video games.

Just to be clear: I do not consider the injection of heroin or the smoking of nicotine to raise any issue of rationality. It is only when the user of heroin or nicotine makes a serious attempt to stop and has difficulty doing so, suffering occasional relapse or suffering torment on the verge of relapse, perhaps attempting to restructure his or her environment or his or her incentives, that the issue arises whether some preferences are "true" and some are interlopers, whether fulfilling one preference is rational and fulfilling an opposing or alternating preference is not.

But, as I said, I shall defer treatment of those conflicting preferences. I want to introduce a number of conditions and behaviors for which a judgment about "irrationality" will be less problematic. Whether these conditions and behaviors appear less important or more important than drug addiction, binge eating, or nymphomania, they at least offer a spectrum into which the more notorious addictions and compulsive behaviors can be fitted. The latter may then be seen as members of a family not all of whose members are so difficult to understand.

OUTLINE OF WHAT'S TO COME

Asleep
Drowsy
Depressed
Euphoric
Drunk
Extremes of motivation
    Pain
    Fear
    Panic
    Rage
    Thirst
Phobias
Compulsions
Captivations

Nervous interaction
Giggling
Embarrassment
Misbehaving minds
Temptations

SLEEP

A good place to begin is sleep. Many people do things in their sleep that awake they want not to do. Children suck their thumbs and wet the bed; children and adults scratch lesions or tug at bandages; people lie on their bellies whose back doctors recommend against it, or lie on their backs and snore. (When I was young sleepwalking was ubiquitous; I don't know what became of it.) Probably we would not call it "irrational" to tug at our bandages, sleep being out of bounds to rationality. But a child can desperately want to stop sucking its thumb, and an adult male may badly want not to sleep on his back and snore. And the child can rationally put on thick mittens at bedtime; and the snoring adult can strap a lumpy object to his back. These coping behaviors surely do not raise any question of what the person "really" wants to do.

Nightmares and bad dreams can be a problem. Having an alert partner to wake one up is a help. Certain before-bedtime activities can be avoided, and certain foods; and one can experiment with tranquilizers.

And of course there is oversleeping. We set an alarm.

DROWSY

Even an alarm may not solve the problem. People put the clock across the room so they cannot turn it off without getting out of bed. When it is important they call a friend who will call, and call repeatedly, in the morning. (In a foreign city, without an alarm, I found a waking service in the yellow pages and left a call. I got the call on time; five minutes later I got another call, and another five minutes after that.) Is it "irrational" not to get out of bed when the alarm goes off? People have missed important engagements; others have had to skip shaving and breakfast. Rather than say a strong preference for an extra half hour's sleep exercised a legitimate claim, we'd probably prefer to say that the barely awakened drowsy person is not quite all there; his metabolism is depressed, his brain is awash with "sleep." By the standards of the night before when the alarm was set, and by the standards of the person cursing his lateness to work, staying in bed was "irrational."

Falling asleep is a problem. Actually it is two, but I defer insomnia for later. The soldier on guard may sit with his chin on his bayonet: when he droops, the pain awakens him. Truck drivers can purchase a noisemaker that is activated when a button is released; if they doze, they relax their grip and the noise startles them awake. Is it "irrational" to fall asleep when doing so will get one in trouble? Descriptively, this may depend on whether one chooses to say a person "succumbed" to a strong temptation—as surely sometimes one does—or instead the person's brain "turned off" on its own. I don't think it matters: what matters is that people need to cope, and often can rationally cope, with undesired dozing.

Drowsiness can be due to fatigue, lack of sleep, medicinal drugs, alcohol. Precautions can include coffee, a nap, and not drinking.

Besides falling asleep when drowsy, people can be inattentive or absentminded—failing to turn off the stove, missing telephone messages, not hearing the baby cry. Anticipating drowsiness, one can try to avoid drowsiness, can warn others that one may be too drowsy to be responsible, or otherwise avoid responsibility that one anticipates being unable to fulfill.

DEPRESSED

Depressed, people do things, decide things, and say things they deprecate in advance and regret after. Some depression is predictable: postoperative for surgery patients, postpartum for mothers. Some medicinal drugs induce depression, as do some illnesses, notably hepatitis (as preserved in the expression "a jaundiced view"). Some depression is treated with dietary supplements or medicines, some (seasonal affective disorder, SAD) with light.

Some of the behaviors associated with depression can be anticipated and guarded against. If a pregnant woman eschewed alcohol and tobacco during pregnancy, and hopes to remain nicotine-free now that she has several months invested in that condition, she can be advised that the onset of depression may lead to relapse and her husband would be wise not to leave cigarettes around the house. The husband's giving up smoking is especially valuable at this time, even if he can keep it up only for a few weeks. Postsurgical depression may need to be guarded against by cardiac patients who wish, on the adamant recommendation of their physicians, to give up smoking.

Depression is a condition in which it may be important to rid the house of means of suicide—a gun, sleeping tablets, even car keys—or to keep company on hand, a watchful friend or a telephone line.

EUPHORIC

There is a euphoric counterpart to depression, although it is comparatively rare. People become impetuously generous as a result of success or good luck; gamblers who win heavily are said to become instantly spendthrift. And Jeppo in *The Informer*, newly rich and surrounded by flatterers, squandered in one evening the entire twenty pounds reward that was to buy his steamer ticket out of Ireland.

DRUNK

Alcohol is one of the many temptations people try to avoid, but here I refer not to abstinence but to regrettable behavior, behavior that one hopes in advance to avoid and that one regrets after. The person who enjoys drinking and has no intention of giving it up may need safeguards against behaviors that, when he is under the influence, will seem perfectly rational but, when remembered the next day—if remembered—will seem foolish and unwise, or worse. The classic case is the person whom alcohol encourages to think he can actually drive a car safely; the solution is to leave the car at home and take a taxi, or to deliver the keys to the host with the request not to return them if the host thinks that best.

People who when drunk abuse their spouses or children, insult their friends or employers, fight, bet large amounts of money, or otherwise behave outrageously may have to remove their children in advance, leave their money at home, and do their drinking away from the people whose presence is conducive to bad behavior.

The same disregard of consequences that can get one into trouble after drinking can at times dispel inhibition and provide the "Dutch courage" to say what, sober, one hadn't the nerve to say, or to do what, sober, one hadn't the nerve to do, like proposing marriage, or proposing divorce, demanding a promotion, or quitting a job, making up to one's children, or disowning them. Just as people rationally drink to conquer stage fright or fear of flying—or are served drinks for that purpose—they can "rationally" drink to rise to the occasion. Whether we should say, then, that they rationally drink to achieve rationality—it being irrational not to say what the occasion calls for—or to achieve irrationality—it being irrational to be insensitive to the consequences, is a choice I leave to the reader.

EXTREMES OF MOTIVATION

Pain

American women about to give birth have been known to request that anesthesia be withheld; they want to be fully aware, they want the newborns not drugged, they want to display loving courage. An obstetrician may respond that nitrous oxide will be available for self-administration, otherwise anesthesia will be used only in an emergency. The woman asks that nothing be available on demand—if it is available she will demand it and get it, and she wants her demands unattended, she wants not to receive relief even if she asks for it. (There are evident legal and ethical issues, as well as medical; and if the husband is present in the delivery room there may be conflicts of interpretation.)

Advance self-denial may be formulated as not wanting to succumb "irrationally" to a level of pain that makes clear thinking and clear recall unavailable. The brain may have evolved when pain was something to be avoided, not welcomed; and a "primitive" response to pain may overwhelm any earlier resolution, taken perhaps in a more recently evolved part of the brain, to eschew relief—may even overwhelm the very recollection of that resolution or the reason for it.

Fear

Let me quote the first paragraph of the first chapter of my favorite book about baseball (Koppett 1967).

"Fear."

That's the paragraph. The second paragraph begins, "Fear is the fundamental factor in hitting, and hitting the ball with the bat is the fundamental act of baseball." If one has decided, fully aware of the risk, to lean into the plate, bat poised, awaiting a white object traveling ninety miles an hour toward one's face, ducking away at the last moment may be "irrational." Or maybe not doing so is irrational.

Rationality may be somewhat intertwined with voluntariness. If, during the third of the three-fifths of a second the ball is traveling, one changes one's mind and backs off, doing so may be irrational—it contradicts what one earlier decided in full knowledge of the danger. If one uncontrollably, involuntarily, perhaps by reflex, flinches and withdraws, maybe the act is something like "transrational," beyond considerations of rationality. Surely if one blinks the act does not qualify as irrational, any more than sneezing while hiding from an enemy is irrational.

A World War II movie showed an officer removing fuses from unexploded bombs in London. He wore a headset into which he described every move so that when he disappeared there would be a record. His was a calling that was very demanding: one's fingers mustn't tremble. In training, nobody trembled during practice; it was only confronting a live bomb that anyone learned whether or not he qualified. Tranquilizers were unavailable; they reduced the sensitivity of the fingers. Possibly a fully rational person could not control his own trembling; maybe there is something "wrong" with a person so nerveless. Again we confront the question of what "rationality" covers: if one knows rationally that it is safer not to tremble . . . ?

Suppose that trembling over the bomb's fuse made detonation extremely likely, while a calm hand could almost surely remove the fuse safely. Now should I be able rationally to persuade myself there is no danger—none unless I create it by needlessly trembling—and not tremble? I can either correctly believe the operation safe, because I am not trembling, and not tremble—a rational response—or I can correctly believe the operation extremely dangerous, because I am trembling, and tremble—two "equilibrium" pairs of belief and behavior.

When I was young I read that dogs could smell fear in me if I was afraid. (I believe it was adrenaline or some such hormone that affected the chemistry of my breath or my perspiration.) And the smell was said to infuriate dogs and make them (irrationally?) aggressive. Decades later I remembered, as I jogged occasionally pursued by dogs. I was not particularly afraid of dogs, never had been; but remembering, I realized I might well be *afraid of being afraid* of dogs. I tried to be "rational," to be unafraid because there was nothing to be afraid of. But I was subject to a sneaking "rational" recognition that if I *were* afraid there was plenty to be afraid of! Again two "rational"(?) equilibria.

I'll come to phobias shortly. Here the issue is whether justifiable fear may overcome one's resolve to face it, and one needs to cope in advance in order not to give way. Alcohol on the battlefield may be administered by one's superiors, or self-administered in the interest of not acting the coward. (Maybe my drinking alcohol could keep those dogs tranquil.) A sufficient level of terror may induce paralysis when action is needed; a sufficient level of terror may lead to flight, when fleeing courts disaster. That leads to our next topic.

Panic

Many people know that when the car skids in snow the worst thing is to slam on the brakes, and they slam on the brakes. Technology has come to the rescue; before that, practice—skidding practice—helped overcome the impulse. Novice skiers can knowingly do the wrong thing when they slip; some of us can even watch ourselves helplessly doing the wrong thing.

Mountain lions have returned to Colorado and have been seen near some of the hiking trails, even near towns; signs have appeared advising appropriate behavior in the event one confronts a mountain lion. Some of the advice sounds sensible: make continuous noise, for example, carry a little bell that is always dingling; the lions will hear and you'll never see them. The advice that scares me is: never turn your back and run!

Rage and Temper

Rage is sometimes a wonderful substitute for courage and often a source of energy. But rage usually distorts judgment and triggers impulsive actions that are futile, destructive, or embarrassing. Losing one's temper is a mild sort of rage. I don't know of any programs of training for rage control, but there is the traditional prophylactic, count to ten before speaking. If I am too enraged to mind my behavior, how can I make myself count to ten? Actually people do, and it helps. How

COMMITMENT AS SELF-COMMAND

can I simultaneously be rational enough to count to ten and at the same time not rational enough to contain my rage? Maybe the mind is not altogether singular; watching myself uncontrollably losing my temper I count to a controlled ten and watch myself regain control.

When rage or loss of temper is predictable one can often avoid the stimulus or the occasion. There was a member of my department who was incapable of speaking, on any subject, without provoking me into bad humor and a futile argument. I eventually learned that whenever he began to speak I should simply go to the bathroom. I'd miss my chance to lose my temper and never regret the lost opportunity.

Thirst

If a person suffers a stomach wound and must not drink for forty-eight hours, and no intravenous technology is available, it is important not to leave a glass of water nearby. Eventually, we are told, the person will drink and die. People at sea will drink salt water and die; in the desert, poisonous water and die. I think we should not conclude that the person prefers instant relief to long life, but we should infer that his central nervous system was programmed, through millions of years of biological evolution, to relieve extreme thirst at any cost. As the hours go by the stomach-wounded person's thirst increases, his mind's capacity to think about the consequences of drinking the water steadily diminishes while his mind's preoccupation with the need to quench his thirst increases. He didn't "decide" he would rather drink than live: he was under the control of a brain that knew that dehydration could kill and didn't know that drinking could.

Is it irrational to drink? I propose that it is neither rational to drink nor irrational. It is rational to drink only if one is capable of rational action and drinking is the right thing to do; it is irrational to drink only if one is capable of rational action and drinking is the wrong thing to do. The dehydrated nervous system is not capable of rational choice: there is no choice, there is an absolute demand for rehydration. Maybe we could identify *a primitive rationality* that takes charge. By evolutionary experience, drinking the water is the right thing to do; drinking is the wrong thing to do only at a level of mental activity that has been shut down in the interest of survival.

Most of us do not get lost in the desert or at sea, or suffer stomach wounds where intravenous liquid is unavailable. But thirst may be a useful model for the nature of choice *in extremis,* when the conscious mind cannot get our attention, when the more primitive brain kicks in and takes charge. I think this idea applies to extreme pain, discussed earlier.

PHOBIAS

Dictionaries make phobias irrational, or at least behaving under their influence irrational. They are defined as fears not based on reasoning or evidence, or fears greatly exaggerated. "Fear" may be too restrictive: some appear to be revulsion, and some induce nausea, fainting, or paralysis. Alfred Hitchcock's *Vertigo* revolved around Jimmy Stewart's reaction to heights; Howard Hughes's antiseptic withdrawal late in life was reportedly phobic.

There are many phobias; a score have their own Greek or Latin names: acrophobia, claustrophobia, agoraphobia, and in a 1990 movie, *Arachnophobia.* In addition to heights, enclosures, open spaces, and things that crawl, there are needles, blood, reptiles, filth, feces, viscera, leeches, and the dark. For some people it is submersion in water, for some it is the furry animals that other people love. Stage fright can reach phobic proportions. Some phobias appear to be induced by traumatic experience, some are thought to be partly genetic in origin. Acrophobes get a physical sensation that sometimes attracts and repels, and bears little relation to "fear." Some monkeys react to reptiles with panic; removing one of the frontal lobes of the brain, it is reported, and putting a patch over one of the monkey's eyes, sends the monkey to the ceiling in panic if there is a snake in the cage, or alternatively lets the monkey calmly pass the snake in pursuit of a banana, according to whether the unpatched eye corresponds to the intact hemisphere or the one lacking the frontal lobe.

Most phobias can be seen as abnormal or unhealthy; some agoraphobes' lives are shaped by an incapacity to leave home, and Hughes's life was reportedly devastated by his compulsive antisepsis. But acrophobes are typically normal except for their phobia. A hospitalized soldier in *M*A*S*H** who sexually harassed a nurse was punished by her dropping his blood sample and telling him that he'd have to give blood again tomorrow; the soldier was ordinarily brave enough, but he spent the night in horror of tomorrow's needle.

Heights, needles, and even fear of the dark often yield, at least somewhat, to closing one's eyes, although if one needs to navigate a precipice closing the eyes is not an available option. Fear of flying appears phobic in some people who acknowledge that their fear is not rational; perhaps they just cannot control their imaginations, or cannot keep their nervous systems from interpreting every slight jolt of the plane as a warning signal. Airsickness and seasickness seem to be aggravated by, if not generated by, an inability to distinguish the signals from the noise.

Some phobias have a potential to be therapeutic. "Aversive conditioning" has been occasionally successful against nicotine addiction: people are instructed to oversmoke to induce headache, to keep wet cigarette butts in open containers to emit disgusting odors, and so on. Evidently if phobias could successfully be induced, they would have great potential.

Not altogether unlike phobias are some more apparently "natural" or normal aversions. Some people cannot kill spiders, some cannot drown kittens, some cannot kill the horse that broke its leg. The inability to inflict suffering may be a welcome, recent cultural evolution.

COMPULSIVE BEHAVIORS

One class of compulsive behaviors has been named "grooming behaviors." These are biting fingernails, picking scabs, plucking hairs and whiskers, squeezing earlobes, chewing on lips and cheeks, and doing other things with face, head, and hands that are unsightly or painful. (The name implies efforts to remove surface imperfections.) Where one can avoid driving home drunk by leaving the car at home, and avoid a spending binge by leaving money and credit cards at home, one cannot leave cuticles, eyebrows, and cheeks at home. The number of Americans who suffer significantly from these grooming behaviors has been estimated in excess of twenty million. These behaviors are usually partly conscious, partly unconscious, and when conscious may be quite irresistible.

An interesting method of coping—interesting partly because it has application to other deprecated behaviors—is identifying precursors, behaviors that tend to precede, as preliminaries, the unwanted actions. (Alcohol is often a precursor to smoking relapse; if one has trouble giving up cigarettes but not alcohol, giving up the latter for a period can help to prevent smoking relapse.) Azrin and Nunn (1977) explain that many of the offending facial features that invite compulsive "grooming"—a whisker the razor missed, an errant eyebrow, a small scab—are "discovered" while a hand is idly exploring the face. Once discovered, the item's demand for attention becomes irresistible; but if one never discovers it by hand it doesn't offend and won't be noticed. The manual exploration is a habit that is nowhere near as compulsive as the irresistible sequel. If one can learn to keep hands away from the face—eliminate the precursor activity—one may escape the irresistible invitation to groom. Keeping hands off the face requires only breaking a habit, not resisting a compulsion.

For cuticles and fingernails the authors recommend professional manicures until the compulsive habit has subsided.

CAPTIVATION

Many of us waste time we cannot afford to waste by watching an old mystery or western, often something we had no intention of watching, something we got caught in the middle of while idly scanning the channels. For most of us there is a precursor that is not too hard to cope with: turning the set on in the first place. Like not eating the first peanut or potato chip, not getting a glimpse of the police chase can be crucial to not staying to the end. But it is not always easy to resist looking for the late news, or something "really" worth watching; the set does get turned on, with the risk of a lost hour. I often wish the hotel would disconnect the television in my room; I'd happily pay extra for a TV-less room.

For some of us reading can be as bad as television, and a cheap mystery isn't over in one hour or two. Puzzles can be captivating, and people who can't afford the time to solve them have learned they cannot easily be laid down unfinished, or put out of mind.

NERVOUS INTERACTION

Interacting with dogs was mentioned earlier, an interaction that could generate "irrational" fear in me and possibly irrational aggressiveness in dogs. More widespread is interaction among people leading to undesired feelings and behaviors. Yawning and coughing are examples; so are giggling and embarrassment.

Giggling

Giggling is never solitary. Two youngsters, even teenagers, can be seized with uncontrollable giggling; scolded, they may stop, but just looking at each other starts it again. To control it they must avoid catching each other's eyes—sit facing away from each other, or in separate rooms. Some years ago, with a group studying the role of television in American culture, I watched an episode of the *Mary Tyler Moore Show* "The Death of Chuckles the Clown." A beloved clown had died when the episode opened; everybody felt the need to grieve but nobody could help laughing whenever Chuckles was mentioned. The climax was a funeral at which the entire congregation giggled uncontrollably; the minister finally assured them that Chuckles could only have been delighted at their inability to control their laughter. Fifteen minutes into the program the group I was with was laughing uncontrollably. It was nervous laughter, self-conscious laughter, participatory laughter; whenever we managed to stop, someone among us would try to stifle a giggle and at the sound we were rocking back and forth again, choking with uncontrollable laughter. I am sure if I had seen the show alone in my room I would have kept my poise; and I would have missed a convincing demonstration of the show's authenticity.

Embarrassment

Embarrassment is an interactive phenomenon: it takes two to make somebody embarrassed, and usually both are. A lone astronaut stranded on the moon can do nothing to embarrass himself.

("Consider the following problem. Suppose you were to find yourself on a lifeless moon with no possibility of returning to, or communicating with, the earth. Suppose also that you were in a frame of mind to do something bad. What would you do?" [Braybrooke 1965, 73].)

A poignant experience was driving to a friend's home with another friend who began to complain about the treatment he had received from an anonymous referee. As he enumerated the errors and fallacies of the referee's report I recognized the manuscript: I was the referee. The author's name had been removed and it had not occurred to me that my friend might be the author. He assumed my complete sympathy because this manuscript was in the style and methodology of an earlier manuscript that I had told him I admired.

I had a choice. I could confess at once, guaranteeing mutual embarrassment, or I could feign sympathy and risk a worse embarrassment if he discovered that I not only was the referee but had deceived him during his diatribe. I took the chance; he never knew; we were not embarrassed.

Suppose he had caught on. He might, for example, have been quoting something from the referee's report that he had not thought to associate with me, but with me beside him the attribution to me had become inescapable. He might have turned to me in shock as he discovered my dirty secret; my treachery would have been the greater because of my claim to have admired the earlier manuscript. As we looked in each other's faces, and he knew that I knew that he knew that I knew that he knew I was the referee, our "common knowledge" of my role would have allowed no escape from an embarrassment that might have afflicted us both forever.

Suppose instead—and conceivably this is what happened—that he had caught on, just while complaining to me, to who the referee was and appreciated the mutual embarrassment that would ensue if he let on; he might have kept secret that he knew my secret and spared us both. If it had become apparent to me that he had caught on and was not letting on that he had caught on, I should have cooperated in disguising my awareness of his awareness. The important thing was to avoid "ratification," mutual acknowledgment of the mortifying fact that I was the referee. "Ratification" is Goffman's term (Goffman 1955). "Poise" is Goffman's term for skill in disguising or hiding one's own embarrassment to cut the positive feedback between one's own and the other's embarrassment, or the talent to be casual in dismissing the occasion for embarrassment.

So there are rational ways to reduce the likelihood or the intensity of embarrassment, but whether embarrassment itself is rational or irrational, or neither of the two, is not easy to assess. Usually embarrassment is a mutual awareness of something that causes an unpleasantness that is due entirely to the awareness. If we could agree that there is nothing unpleasant except the mutual awareness, we might rationally agree to ignore whatever it is that is making us uncomfortable. Knowing that if I do not become embarrassed the mutual embarrassment will be aborted, should I rationally be able to make myself unembarrassed? Just as there were two equilibria in the fear-of-dogs cycle—rationally fearing them and providing grounds for fear, or rationally not fearing them and giving no grounds—there appear to be two possible equilibria for mutual embarrassment, being embarrassed and providing each other grounds for embarrassment, or not being embarrassed and providing no grounds. Whether this makes embarrassment "irrational" I do not know.

MISBEHAVING MINDS

It is an interesting question whether rationality should be construed as including command over one's mind, or how much command might be demanded. Guilt and regret, bad memories, apprehension of painful experiences to come, even a tune playing over and over in the mind, are hard to expunge by a rational act. One can sometimes "forget" by becoming absorbed—the student worried about tomorrow's exam can go to an exciting movie to displace the anxiety—but it is hard to teach one's mind the principle of sunk costs.

Being able to fall asleep at appropriate times is a help and a comfort that many of us miss, regularly or occasionally. Insomnia is a perverse phenomenon: awareness of it, remembering that one is insomniac, aggravates the insomnia. Some people report that they become so sensitive to their own sleeplessness that, as they finally begin to drift off, they notice it and jolt themselves awake. The best antidote to insomnia is to forget that one is afflicted.

I love sashimi. I read some years ago that there is a rare occurrence of a live worm in raw fish, a worm that is not destroyed by either the chewing or the digesting of the fish. There are two such worms, one of which is serious because it can do harm to the intestine; the other is less serious but uglier: it can be regurgitated and come out of one's mouth. I know the odds on this happening, and there is no reason to think that suffering such trauma is more likely than dying in an automobile crash on the way to a Japanese restaurant. But I could not, for a long time, keep myself from thinking about that dreadful worm, the one that might come out of my mouth, and wondered whether I could ever eat sashimi again.

Daydreaming, a.k.a. fantasy, is ambivalently irrational. Imagine an adult playing out a scenario in his or her mind, finding large amounts of money, heroically saving a child, making passionate love, delivering a lecture to an enraptured audience: what is the person *doing?* There are two interesting possibilities: the person is wasting good time unawares, idly letting his or her mind play at his or her expense; or the person is enjoying a good enough facsimile of the real thing to be getting genuine pleasure at little material cost. Either way there is some form of self-deception; both the wayward enjoyment of the autonomous fantasy and the counterfeit pleasure of the "authored" fantasy depend on a somewhat convincing pretense that what is being imagined is real. If I don't say this right, I'd like to know how to say it with higher fidelity to what is actually going on.

What could be more irrational than caring what happens in the final chapter of a book that someone has written? You tell me that someone is finishing a poignant novel and hasn't decided whether the heroine's kidnapped daughter will survive the final chapter; you ask me whether I care how it turns out. The final chapter is merely binary digits on a diskette that will become letters on a page; change the letters and the daughter is murdered, change them again and the daughter is rescued—letters on a page: no such daughter exists! But if I read the book, I care; I may weep if the daughter doesn't survive. Weeping is part of my enjoyment of the book, my utterly irrational participation. It is fantasy, but fantasy that I do not control; the author does. And here's what is so wonderful: if I could discipline myself to think rationally, and reduce the daughter to digits on a diskette, I would lose some of the best of life in a world of art and civilization. My ungovernable and irrational mind gives me nightmares, worms in the sashimi, embarrassment at things past and fears of things to come; but it lets me identify with characters in a play or novel and lets me experience, at least momentarily, feelings that money cannot buy.

And then there is absentmindedness—forgetfulness—and we learn tricks to cope. Forgetting, or having faulty memory, may be thought of as a sort of intellectual irrationality, a little like computing wrong or reasoning faultily. If one knows that one forgets, or knows that one remembers certain things wrong, one can try to cope—for example, don't call people by name if you know you are likely to get the name wrong, and write down where you parked the car.

The reader will probably acknowledge that most, or at least some, of the conditions I have described can reasonably be called "lapses from rationality," perhaps "normal, justifiable lapses from rationality." Turning around and running from the mountain lion, or yanking back the hand that needs its wound cauterized with a hot iron, is an act that I know is wrong, that somehow I cannot help at the time, an act for which I may seek some coping strategy or device, and an act for which I need not apologize.

By "temptations" I mean the kind of circumstance or phenomenon that I illustrated at the beginning of this essay with the cigarettes flushed down the toilet. I have in mind the temptations that people wish to resist and find hard to resist, often resolve to resist and fail to resist, sometimes with serious consequences. The distinguishing characteristic is that, notwithstanding the cliché of the "drug-crazed" addict, the person succumbing to what I call temptation is usually quite aware, while succumbing, that he or she is violating an earlier resolve to abstain and will eventually regret the momentary lapse and any ensuing longer-lasting relapse. (Remember, I am interested only in the "temptations" that people wish to resist; the contented overeater, addict, or nymphomaniac is outside my subject.)

I have been particularly interested in the ways that people try to govern their behavior in relation to temptations by avoiding the opportunities or the stimuli, by manipulating their own incentives or capabilities, or by affecting the functioning of their nervous systems. (The cigarette example represented one or more of these; we'll explore it further.) Some of these strategies may require an understanding of the nature of the lapse; some just require understanding how to prevent it. I can know that if there are peanuts on the coffee table I'll eventually start eating them and that I can avoid eating them by having them removed; that doesn't mean I can describe how my mind will be working when I reach the point of putting a peanut in my mouth fully aware that I didn't want to and didn't intend to and will shortly wish (or am already wishing) that I hadn't done it.

There are many behaviors that display the paradox that a person, quite uncrazed, fully conscious, apparently "voluntarily" does what the person is simultaneously fully aware one shouldn't do. Scratching hives, poison ivy, or chicken pox almost always aggravates the burning and itching, the person scratching knows that it does, and as he or she scratches can be amazed at what he or she is doing. The boy who believes masturbation is evil, harmful, or contrary to God's command, continues to believe it as he watches himself masturbate. The man or woman who is persuaded that sexual infidelity is fraught not just with risk but with the near certainty of awful consequences continues with the persuasion while engaging in the act. This phenomenon, altogether different from that of the thirst-crazed water drinker, the pain-crazed evader of the cauterizing iron, or the panicked confronter of the mountain lion, is utterly tantalizing. One sees oneself doing what one knows one should not be doing; there is no loss of awareness of consequences, only (this is one way to say it) loss of command from one part of the brain to another.

ADDICTION

A central role in what I call "temptations" is played by addictive substances. I appreciate the different needs of different groups—psychiatrists, lawyers, pharmacologists, legislators, psychologists, neurologists—for their own specialized definitions of addiction; but I believe understanding the nature of the lapse from rationality that occurs when someone succumbs to temptation can be advanced by comparing a wide range of behaviors: gambling, eating, drinking, smoking, sniffing, inhaling, injecting, masturbating, or watching television. What is happening when the reformed alcoholic accepts the drink, the reformed smoker rushes to the store before it closes to buy cigarettes, the conferee reaches for the Danish on the table, or the boy convinced that masturbation is evil masturbates, is not yet susceptible, as far as I can tell, to scientific description. (In my opinion, too little attention is paid to introspective reports.)

To illustrate what I have in mind I return now to our friend who flushed his friend's cigarettes away at the beginning of this essay. I averred, and expected no dispute, that the man's action was interpretable as a rational act, probably taken in anticipation of some lapse in his later rationality. This anticipatory preemption is easy to describe. Harder to describe is what that later action, the one he wanted to avert, would represent, what the state of his "rationality" would have been, at the later time, had he later engaged in smoking, or perhaps what the state of his rationality is still going to be at that later time when he might have engaged in smoking but does not. (Actually, maybe he will; his preclusive act may not have been decisive.)

An interesting question is whether he, at the time he disposed of the remaining cigarettes, had a good understanding of what his later state of mind was going to be. Might he, if we could ask him, be able to tell us just what the mental or emotional circumstances were going to be that he wanted to guard against?

There are a number of possibilities.

ALTERNATIVE SCENARIOS

One possibility is that he anticipates drinking alcohol and knows by experience that drinking interferes with his reasoning so that he succumbs to the temptation of cigarettes if cigarettes are readily available. If the individual believes that what alcohol does is to distort or to anesthetize some of the functions or characteristics that go under the name of rationality, we can call this situation "anticipated irrationality." We discussed it earlier.

This drinking contingency can be divided in two. The simpler case is that he enjoys relaxing in the evening with a few drinks even though it impairs somewhat his "rationality," because nothing he plans for the evening places demands on that part of his rationality that is subverted by alcohol. He could keep his smoking under control by going without alcohol, but for the price of a pack of cigarettes he can eliminate the danger and have his drink, and that is what he has chosen.

The second is that he wishes not only not to smoke but also not to drink, but he has a drinking problem that he knows he may not be able to control this evening: to be on the safe side—with respect to smoking, not to drinking—he destroys the cigarettes. We need here some reason why he doesn't pour the liquor down the toilet, too. Maybe he is going out for the evening where he will be confronted by an opportunity to drink, expects to succumb against his (currently) better judgment or expects to feel obliged to drink among his friends, and fears coming home with impaired rationality to find cigarettes on the coffee table. (Our story might have been more tantalizing if, upon discovering the cigarettes his friend left behind, he had studied the pack momentarily, had then put it back on the coffee table and gone to the pantry and poured his whiskey down the sink!)

Counting the alcohol contingencies as the first two, a third possibility is that cigarettes by their physical presence—the sight of them, perhaps the smell of them, or the mere unforgettable knowledge of their presence—stimulate a craving, a craving that is a serious discomfort and distraction unless satisfied by the smoking of a cigarette. This contingency in turn breaks down into three.

One is that the craving is such a discomfort and distraction that it will produce an unproductive and disagreeable evening; at the risk of complete relapse it would be rational to avoid such a dismal and unproductive evening by going ahead and smoking. The presence of the cigarettes is an irritant that if not removed will make it rational to smoke. (An alcoholic might be considered rational to drink before undergoing some exceedingly painful procedure, the risk of relapse being a lesser evil than the pain.)

A fourth possibility, the second of these craving contingencies, is that he knows he will *not* succumb—will not suffer a lapse from rationality—but will be sufficiently distracted by the presence of cigarettes to make it worthwhile to dispose of them. In the same way he may, when it is time to get to work, turn off the television, not because he expects to succumb to it but just because the flickering screen continually disturbs his concentration.

The third craving contingency—the one I find hardest to understand, though not to recognize—is that he expects to succumb "irrationally," not merely to be distracted, and not to be so distracted that it would be better to go ahead and smoke, but simply to be unable to maintain his resolve not to smoke. He wants now not to smoke later no matter how strong the craving, and he cannot trust his brain to function "rationally" under the stimulus of cigarettes present. (The case of extreme thirst mentioned earlier may be an exemplar.) He would rather handcuff himself to the radiator across the room than be free to succumb. He doesn't need to; it is the presence of the cigarettes, or the knowledge of their presence, that will influence his brain chemistry, and *that* he can take care of in the toilet. Less poignantly, people often remove the peanuts, or the Danish, from the conference table or the nearby buffet, either in fear of succumbing or just to remove the distraction. (Clinicians have told me that recovering heroin addicts suffer much less craving when in a "clean" place where they know there is no chance to obtain heroin than when they believe, rightly or wrongly, that there is some possibility of obtaining the stuff.)

A sixth possibility is that the craving is independent of the presence of cigarettes. He knows that late-night fatigue (or late-night awakening) or some circadian change in brain chemistry—he needn't know what—will produce an irresistible craving for tobacco. It is the same whether the cigarettes are in open view, stowed in a cupboard, or five miles away in a vending machine. Destroying the cigarettes has no effect on his choice to smoke, only on his ability.

Here, too, we can distinguish two cases. One is that there will be no other cigarettes available at reasonable cost. No stores will be open, no one will be on the street from whom to bum a cigarette, or perhaps the man lives out of town without a car and no buses will be running. Tossing the cigarettes effectively denies the wayward choice.

The other—the seventh case—is that the craving is the same whether or not cigarettes are present, but their absence affects his ability to avoid surrender. I can think of two reasons. One is that an impetuous urge might control his behavior for a minute or two, but not for an hour, and if he grabbed his car keys and drove away his better judgment would overtake him within the time it would take to get to the store and park the car, and he'd be safe. (Maybe knowing that he'd return without cigarettes suffices to keep him from getting the car.) Alternatively, in self-discipline some lines are harder to cross than others: he might allow himself "just one cigarette" if this act of God offers the opportunity, whereas getting the car and driving in search of cigarettes would be a flagrant violation of the regime he has imposed on himself, and the prospective loss of self-respect would suffice to deter.

An eighth case is that the individual simply believes that if the cigarettes are there he will smoke. It may not matter where his belief came from. If instead his problem were alcohol, it is easy to believe he may have been authoritatively told that if there is liquor in the house he will drink it, or is likely to. Therapies to cope with cigarette addiction have not institutionalized any such lore about the inexorable consequences of spending an evening in the company of cigarettes, but our man could have received strong advice to that effect and takes it seriously even without a theory of his own of how the breakdown occurs in the presence of cigarettes. If his belief is based on his own experience with earlier attempts to quit, it may be a belief in behavioral phenomena that he can analyze in retrospect.

His belief could be true, and it serves his purpose that he destroyed the cigarettes. His belief could be false, and he has wasted a few dollars for his friend. And there is a third possibility.

The proposition that if cigarettes are available he will ineluctably smoke before the evening is over may be the kind that is true of anyone who believes it and false of people who do not. Anyone who "knows" that with cigarettes around he will smoke before midnight knows that as midnight approaches he will have an irrefutable argument for going ahead and not waiting for midnight.

Somewhat akin to belief is suspense. Suspense produces discomfort, anxiety. If one spends an evening watching oneself, wondering whether one is going to succumb to temptation, two things can happen. One is that the evening can be exceedingly disagreeable; the second is that the suspense goes away once a cigarette is smoked. Until the cigarette is lit one is uncomfortably apprehensive that he may light a cigarette; lighting the cigarette is an escape. Is there something irrational here? There is a painful uncertainty whether I shall survive the night without smoking, an uncertainty that is dispelled upon smoking. Can the certainty that failure has occurred bring relief from uncertainty whether it will occur? (Again if it were alcohol, the anesthesia might enhance the relief.)

We have so far, I believe, somewhere from nine to eleven distinct scenarios, depending on how we count subcases. But they are all scenarios of what the person might have in mind when he "rationally" disposes of the cigarettes. That is an important part of our subject, and in several of the cases may be an adequate diagnosis of just what later would happen if the cigarettes were not made to disappear.

RECAPITULATION

Drinking contingencies
1. Wants *to drink,* knows he may smoke.
2. Wants *not to drink;* knows he may drink, may smoke.
    Pour away the whiskey

Craving *induced by presence* of cigarettes
   3. Discomfort so great it would be *rational to smoke.*
   4. Discomfort enough to be *worth the dollars.*
   5. Craving so great he will *lose control* and smoke.
      Analogy to thirst

Craving *independent of presence* of cigarettes
   6. If available will smoke, if not, can't.
   7. Local absence affects *ability to resist.*
      7a. Lose control only *briefly,* not long enough to acquire
          cigarettes.
      7b. Act of God vs. flagrant violation.

Belief in *inevitability*
   8. Belief is *true;* good to dispose of the cigarettes.
   9. Belief is *false;* he wasted the cigarettes.
   10. Belief is true *if (and only if)* he believes it.

Suspense
   11. Not craving, not belief, but *suspense* so disagreeable he will
       succumb to the need to dispel it.

POSTSCRIPT

But the tantalizing case, in terms of sheer description, is the third
"craving" contingency: no alcohol or other exogenous chemical influence, no brainwashing about inevitability, just the anticipation that, either gradually or impetuously, the resolve not to smoke will be, or may
be, replaced or overwhelmed by the desire to smoke, and in full consciousness that he badly wanted (wants?) not to, he will voluntarily
smoke. This is often a correct anticipation; it is the anticipation of
something that actually occurs. But what "it" is that occurs continues
to defy description.

REFERENCES

Azrin, N. H. and Nunn, R. G. *Habit Control in a Day.* New York: Simon
   and Schuster, 1977.

Braybrooke, D. *Philosophical Problems of the Social Sciences*. Macmillan, 1965, 73.

Goffman, E. On Face-Work. *Psychiatry: Journal for the Study of Interpersonal Processes*, 1955.

Koppett, L. *A Thinking Man's Guide to Baseball*. New York: E. P. Dutton, 1967.

7

Against Backsliding

■ Albert Hirschman observed some years ago that countries that are technically backward are far better at maintaining airlines than maintaining roadbeds. The point had to do with incentives: you can patch the road surface cheaply and over the years let the roadbed invisibly go to ruin, but airplanes don't go to ruin invisibly. Had he been an observer of urban economies in advanced countries he might have made the same point about fire engines and sewers in New York. Individuals display similar behavior: in a hurry, a man will shave rather than brush his teeth.

This is an essay on the theory and practice of backsliding. As a phenomenon and as a problem, backsliding concerns individuals, groups, and even governments. Not only is backsliding in general characteristic of both families and governments, but some specific kinds have counterparts at both those levels of aggregation. The federal government's statutory debt ceiling, so regularly and so easily elevated, and the often proposed balanced-budget amendment to the Constitution must be among the most widely understood self-denying legislative acts and proposals because so many families poignantly share the problem. Cruel and unusual punishment has tempted most parents at one time or another. White lies and small secrets can accumulate like some environmental poison, for husbands and presidents. And gamblers who know and even repeat the maxim "Don't throw good money after bad" are notoriously unable to heed it in the casino, in repairing an automobile, or in Vietnam. "Lest we forget," we build monuments to men and women, dead and alive, who risked and sometimes gave their lives. Still we forget, as a nation, or as close buddies who shared an "unforgettable" experience and want to celebrate an anniversary a decade from now. Building a preference for veterans in a state or federal civil service system is something of a safeguard against the inevitable decline in how much we care, saving for them a modest privilege that, thirty years later, they probably could not successfully claim.

Collective self-binding is richer in its dimensionality than individual attempts to resolve now for the future and to bind oneself. Collectively there are more kinds of mistrust.

Each of us—to identify one way—may doubt the steadfastness of his own resolve, be concerned only with his own resolve, and join in collectively requiring daily exercise or banishing dessert. This would be *using* some collective authority—typically not the kind of authority we think of as "government"—to make ourselves behave as we now resolve to behave, converting what is sometimes called "self-paternalism" into genuine paternalism, the authority making each of us do what it (we) thinks is good for us. That is not the situation that Hirschman had in mind, but once we are on the subject we may as well sort out the different motives and situations.

A second motivation for collectively binding ourselves, one that is especially pertinent to government, is the incentive structure that in the last couple of decades has become widely known as the many-person Prisoners' Dilemma. These are the situations in which each individual wants all the others to perform or abstain, but everybody would prefer to be a free rider and knows that everybody else would. All will be better off with an enforceable contract, and the authority of government can be invoked in lieu of contract. This is the commonest motive for collectively binding ourselves through statute and ordinance, but it is so common and so well understood that it altogether lacks the paradoxical quality of antibacksliding measures. It could, though, be pertinent to Hirschman's airlines and roads, if the roads are mainly worn out by people who use and depend on them but who drive overweight vehicles or park on the shoulders or otherwise do what is cheap or convenient, aware that others do too and that this is what is ruining the roads, sorry that the rules can't be enforced. But this is not backsliding, and I mention it only to lay it aside.

There is the important possibility that we do not doubt the durability of our own conscientiousness and concern but are not altogether sure of each other. We have identified some temptations that we have resolved to resist, having just hanged an innocent man or been almost defeated by a surprise attack, and I know that I'll never forget this stunning lesson and never again get carried away but some of you look to me like the kind of people who could do it again. (University departments often find themselves to have succumbed to a temptation to lower their standards—examinations, admissions, appointments, discipline—and everybody agrees that "they" will go and do it again sometime in the future unless "we" find some preclusive measure to forbid it.)

A less symmetrical motivation is that we are a system of individuals who interact together. I can trust myself as long as those about me are not losing their heads or their tempers or their resistance to temptation; I can drive slowly or keep my temper or do without dessert or maintain grading standards or leave promptly when the fire alarm rings as long as the rest of you do. But my resolve, like yours, gets demoralized when the whole system relaxes. The backsliding of each of us affects the backsliding of others, and we need protection against our common tendency to undermine each other's morale as we lose our own.

The interest in this case can be joint or several. It can be attendance, say, at a department meeting or a legislative session, each of us acknowledging a share in that weakness that would ultimately lead to empty chambers, to the detriment of our collective interest. Or it could be an attempt to quit smoking, each of us solely concerned with his own success but each being part of the other's environment where smoking is concerned, supportive or erosive according to how well we abstain, our several personal interests coming together in a no-smoking rule while we work together.

Sometimes when this interactive feedback has the right bias, just forming a collectivity reinforces everyone's resolve: four people who jog together three times a week at lunch hour may go on for years as a team; jogging separately on different days they all might have been early dropouts. S. L. A. Marshall in *Men against Fire* (Magnolia, Mass.: Peter Smith, rpt. 1985) discussed the phenomenon that in all armies in World War II most individual soldiers never fired their rifles—no matter how long a battle lasted, how brave they were, or what targets presented themselves—while weapons that required joint action by two or three soldiers, like feeding a belt of ammunition into a machine gun or loading and aiming an artillery piece, were regularly fired as intended.

Often the collective self-binding appears oriented not so much toward the loss of resolve or control that can occur when the members of the collectivity pass through a disturbing episode or grow older and change their values with age, as toward successor members of the collectivity. We want to bind later generations to our current values. These can be generations in the literal demographic sense, or the people who replace us when we retire or are voted out of office. The First Amendment was undoubtedly less intended by those in the Congress to keep themselves as individuals from turning around, contrary to their own sentiments at the time the amendment was passed, and establishing a religion or abridging speech, than to guard against unconsidered actions of later generations who would not have fresh in mind the experience of colonial subordination or the intense exposure to constitutional debate.

Again there is a comparison with individuals, couples, or extended families. In the days when life insurance and retirement annuities were more sexually asymmetrical it used to be proposed that husbands might wish to structure benefits so that a surviving wife could not spend her resources impetuously or invest them unwisely. But sometimes even the husband, contemplating retirement, was advised to guard against his own spendthriftiness by tying up his resources in a life annuity, even setting something aside for burial expenses or modest bequests for his grandchildren. An occasional feature of primogeniture was that an inheriting scion could legally allow *his* successor to dispose of the land and property but could not convert it to cash himself, the expectation being that each would preserve the restriction on his successor. It sounds a little like the principle, sometimes expressed in legislation, that a pay increase for the members of a legislature shall take effect only after the next election.

Among techniques, one is simply delay. Delay can be imposed by rules that specify delay, if the rules themselves are subject to the same delay or have a constitutional status that requires a greater majority to change them than is required for ordinary legislation. Some parliaments have a constitutional rule that a bill must have a second or even a third "reading" before enactment. Certain proscriptions, like the delay rules, can themselves have constitutional status, requiring greater majorities or some further ratification, such as by three-quarters of the states in the United States. The balanced-budget amendment, in contrast to the merely statutory debt ceiling, is an effort to take advantage of the extreme difficulty of repealing an amendment, and the failure to date of that amendment reflects the success of the Founding Fathers in making such amendments rare and difficult. Faculties often impose "constitutional" restraints, including delay, to guard against their own impetuosity or the decay of their standards, or to be more immune to coercion. Individuals even use mandatory delay, successfully at least sometimes, to guard against backsliding where cigarettes, food, or alcohol may momentarily become so tempting that one forgets what is so wrong with just one cigarette after dinner. The rule that you may change your mind any time you want to and go ahead and smoke a cigarette but not until twenty-four hours have elapsed, with the change of mind subject to rescission during the interim, has, when it works, some of the qualities of an unwritten constitution—the reason why "just one cigarette after dinner" is so damaging now is that it violates and threatens the former smoker's own constitution.

Precautions against backsliding are typically nondiscriminatory or undiscriminating. A constitutional provision that states may not deny due process applies to all the states, without regard to whether some of them may need the restraint more than others. Bicameral legislatures often have, by design or by tradition and evolution, somewhat different safeguards against backsliding in the two houses. The Senate's six-year overlapping terms can make that body more immune to momentary popular passions than the two-year coincident terms in the House, and where backsliding takes the form of action rather than inaction there needs to be only one steadfast chamber.

But when we use some governing body for self-paternal reasons, to guard ourselves as individuals against our own backsliding, the motive is potentially discriminating. I may be desperately willing to subscribe to rules that will keep me from gambling or squandering my inheritance, driving too fast after drinking, smoking or neglecting to exercise, or even talking too much in a heated meeting, but not care whether you smoke or squander your money, or, if you don't attend the same meetings I attend, waste other people's time. Furthermore, some of these constraints may be feasible while discriminating and others capable only of uniform enforcement. I may want to ban high-calorie desserts in my faculty dining room because just knowing they are available, especially seeing them, destroys my resolve, but if we can have two dining rooms and my resolve against dessert is all right at the time that I choose between rooms and only dissolves as dessert time approaches, we can let the ban on dessert apply only to volunteers. I might have license plates that waived my right to refuse a Breathalyzer test or subjected me to lower speed limits than other drivers. There are some modern technologies that might permit some of us to submit to curfews or that could put drinking places off limits, by monitoring the signaling devices that had been irremovably implanted in or attached to us. We have to be careful: it is constitutional for my state to forbid the sale or serving of alcoholic drinks, but not to keep me home on weekends or out of bars that are open to the public, even if I have volunteered the authority to them, because some of my rights are not alienable, even by myself.

I have spoken about legislative safeguards against backsliding. Executives and departments of government, military services, schools, the courts, and even such estates as the media and the churches need ways to police themselves against backsliding. For some governments a most demanding issue is how to keep from being taken militarily by surprise again, as the United States was at Pearl Harbor or the Israeli government was on Yom Kippur. Apparently what does not work is *routines* designed to avoid surprise. In the school where I teach we have had uncommonly numerous false fire alarms in the past five years; most of us are remarkably good at stopping in midsentence and insisting that we all head instantly for the exits. Possibly it's because we have had enough false alarms to keep the question of appropriate behavior on our minds, but not so many as to make us disregardful. I also notice, in the same school, that the signs saying "no food or beverages in the classroom" are regularly disregarded although the faculty supported that prohibition when it went into effect.

What Irving Janis called "groupthink" is a malady for which it is hard to find an antidote even among people who acknowledge together that they are collectively susceptible to it (*Groupthink*, Boston: Houghton Mifflin, 1983). Members of an athletic team have trouble effectively reminding themselves not to become overconfident. I have attended many senior department meetings that spent an hour and forty-five minutes clearing away the trivia in order to get down to some serious business, like a new tenured appointment, only to discover that there was no time left even to get started, remembering that that was exactly what happened at the preceding meeting, and the one before that, trying to resolve next time to leave the trivia for the end of the meeting, recognizing with some sense of futility that it is characteristic of trivia that it always looks like something that can be disposed of promptly.

Agencies, like people, worry about growing old and conservative, losing the capacity for adventure, initiative, innovation. Agencies, like people, worry about becoming too large, about becoming too susceptible to habit. And agencies, like people, should worry, if they do not, about how to make a graceful exit when life's work is done and it is time to expire.

## 8

Addictive Drugs:
The Cigarette Experience

■ Half the men who ever smoked in this country have quit, and nearly half the women. At the end of World War II, three-quarters of young men smoked; the fraction is now less than a third and going down. Fifty million people have quit smoking, and another fifty million who would have become smokers since 1945 did not.

This dramatic abandonment of a life-threatening behavior was entirely voluntary. Until recently there was virtually no regulation of smoking by any level of government. The situation changed sharply in the late 1980s after dramatic changes in smoking behavior were well under way.

Surveys documented that the public was aware of the risks.[1] Ninety percent or more answered yes to whether smoking caused cancer and heart disease. The facts were impressive. In 1982 the surgeon general estimated 130,000 premature cancer deaths, in 1983 170,000 deaths from heart disease, and in 1984 50,000 deaths from lung disease.[2] The total was later increased to more than 400,000.

Where do people learn about these dangers? Newspapers reported the annual reports of the surgeons general, but smoking was rarely news and inherently a dull subject. Only recently have city ordinances, airline restrictions, liability suits, advertising bans, and excise taxes made cigarettes occasional front-page news. Magazines rarely mention smoking; some of the most popular magazines report more than 25 percent of their advertising revenues from cigarettes.

The only emphatic repetitive communications about the hazards of smoking are the advertisements on billboards, and in magazines and newspapers. For two decades the central theme has been tar and nicotine. The message sent is that lighter cigarettes are safer but the message received must also be that smoking is dangerous. It is anybody's guess whether the cumulative impact is to entice people into smoking and to keep them smoking, or to drill home the deadly message about tar and nicotine.

No surgeon general has ever publicized the benefits of lower tar and nicotine, but the tar and nicotine have fallen by half. Smokers can infer that the government would not require labeling unless tar and nicotine made a difference.

Thirty years ago smoking was not much associated with social class. It is now. In 1980, a quarter of professional men smoked, a third of white collar men, and almost half of blue collar men (40 percent overall); for women the figures were similar (30 percent overall).[3] Among high school seniors in the 1980s, more than 20 percent of the non-college bound smoked half a pack or more daily, but less than 10 percent of the college bound.[4]

Which is more astounding, that some 50 million people have quit smoking or that nearly 50 million still smoke, most of them knowing that it is potentially fatal? Why don't they try to quit?

The answer is that they do. In 1980, two-fifths of all current smokers said they had made three or more serious attempts to quit. Among the youngest age group, more than half said they had made an attempt within the preceding twelve months. In fact, a third of the men of all ages and two-fifths of the women who smoked in 1980 said that they had attempted to quit within the preceding twelve months.[5]

Quitting is evidently attractive and, even more evidently, hard. Is it that some can quit and already did and others cannot and never will? Probably not. In 1970, 1975, and 1980, former smokers, both women and men, had smoked as many cigarettes per day as current smokers.[6] And while two-fifths of the men and women still smoking in 1980 had made three or more attempts to quit unsuccessfully, in 1975—the question was not asked in 1980—more than half the former smokers, men and women, claimed to have made three or more attempts before they succeeded.[7]

Quitting was hard for those who succeeded and hard for those still trying. Why so hard? I shall turn to that shortly but first will review some history. For those who hope to quit and desire reinforcement through restrictions on their smoking, the situation changed dramatically in the second half of the 1980s. The military services not only took cigarettes out of the field rations but banned smoking in most buildings and vehicles. The General Services Administration imposed controls on smoking in all federal buildings under its jurisdiction. Major cities were imposing tight restrictions on smoking in public places and the workplace. Smoking was eliminated on all domestic airline flights. Only 10 or 12 percent of the nation's largest corporations had restrictions on smoking in the early 1980s, mostly to avoid the risk of fire and contamination; more than half had restrictions by the late 1980s, and the increase was due to the publicized hazards to health as well as to complaints about the disagreeableness of environmental smoke.[8]

The trend toward restriction was given a push by the Surgeon General's Report of 1986, which concluded that secondhand smoke could cause respiratory cancer and could aggravate respiratory difficulties in children. (That the estimate of deaths due to environmental smoke was two orders of magnitude smaller than deaths due to smoking did not weaken the impact of this new report.) Two committees of the National Academy of Sciences expressed concern about the effects on health of environmental tobacco smoke, and especially the contamination of air in passenger airlines.

It remains your choice whether to be more impressed, and heartened, by the massive change in smoking behavior in the United States over the past two or three decades or to be more impressed, and disheartened, by the massive recalcitrance of smoking among forty-five million continuing smokers, most of whom have tried unsuccessfully to quit. Both phenomena are impressive. Can we expect the growing unpopularity of smoking to continue, and, if so, can we foresee the end in this country of a dangerous and somewhat offensive behavior?

It is too soon to declare victory. Still, fewer are smoking in all occupations and social classes. It is not surprising that those with more favorable life prospects, like those who go to college, should be the most sensitive to information about behaviors that affect mortality late in life, whereas people lower in socioeconomic status with lower life expectancies follow a decade or two behind.

Why is it so hard to quit? How does nicotine compare with other drugs?

Cigarettes in this country have been cheap; until very recently a pack a day cost less than half an hour's work at the federal minimum wage. Cigarettes are quickly available; smokers are rarely more than a few minutes from the nearest cigarette. Smoking requires no equipment other than a match. Cigarettes are portable and storable; a pack fits in a shirt pocket and requires no refrigeration. Being commercially available and brand named, cigarettes pose no problem of quality control. There is no fear of overdose; nicotine is a poison in large quantities, but a smoker feels the effects before any dangerous quantity can be inhaled.

Until the last few years, when regulations began to restrict smoking, the habit had an almost universal compatibility. People smoked anywhere, indoors and out, at work and at play, alone and with others, on the telephone, on horseback, with coffee or soft drinks or alcohol, at any time of day or night. There is almost no moment in a former smoker's life when a cigarette might not have been appropriate, and the former smoker's day is full of occasions and activities that would once have prompted a cigarette and still may prompt the thought of one.

Cigarettes produce no impairment of any faculty. There is no intoxication, no slurring of speech or loss of balance, no loss of visual acuity. Smoking is the only drug, with the possible exception of caffeine, that my airline pilot may indulge in without my being the least concerned.

Until smoking began to fall into disrepute in the last few years, there were hardly any social norms governing where or when or with whom it was appropriate to smoke. A person would not think of attending an afternoon conference with a bowl of hot soup or a pitcher of martinis— usually not even a sandwich or a candy bar—but smoking was never impolite. Perhaps the most powerful norm governing smoking behavior was that one offered a cigarette to a companion before lighting one's own.

Smoking is a socially facilitating activity. People who want to appear poised get support from the motions of extracting a cigarette, lighting it, exhaling the smoke, and holding the cigarette. This benefit is probably independent of the nicotine. Smoking is something that every smoker is good at.

The damage is slow in arriving. The people who suffer cancer and lung and heart disease from smoking have typically smoked for three decades or more before symptoms appear.

ADDICTION TO NICOTINE

Cigarettes are extremely addictive. Most users are addicted; few who have smoked regularly for a year or more find it easy to quit. Relapse rates may not measure the "strength" of an addiction, in the sense of pain, discomfort, and obsession upon withdrawal, but in the balance between desire to quit and desire to stay free, cigarettes are among the hardest to stay away from. Most studies indicate a success rate—at least two years' abstinence—at about one in five per attempt. (That half of all smokers in this country eventually made it is due to repeated attempts.) The surgeon general devoted his entire annual report for 1988 to the behavioral and chemical criteria according to which nicotine is a highly addictive substance.

Inhaled nicotine in cigarette smoke provides an instant response— ten seconds or less to reach the brain—and a short high. Unlike any other addictive or psychoactive substance, cigarettes have a pleasurable effect that lasts no longer than the lighted cigarette. The recycle time is short, less than an hour on average. With the possible exception of benzedrine inhalers when they were still on the market, there is no drug that has been taken with comparable frequency or in which the user is so practiced; a pack a day is 7,500 cigarettes per year, 75,000 inhaled puffs.

It is generally thought that nicotine is the main chemically addictive substance in cigarette smoke. The Surgeon General's Report treated nicotine exclusively as the addictive agent. There are two additional possible contributors to addiction. One is the taste of tobacco smoke. Without the nicotine one probably would not become addicted, but after smoking tens of thousands of cigarettes the association of nicotine with the flavor may give the flavor itself addictive qualities. The taste of cigarettes gives the addict something tangible to crave; if there were no tobacco it is not clear what a nicotine addict would crave other than relief from withdrawal symptoms.

The other possible dimension of addiction may be in mood control. A person may smoke at one time to calm down and at another time to perk up. (This homeostasis is almost unique to cigarettes; most drugs are stimulants or depressants but not both.) Once a person has smoked several thousand times to reduce tension or to stimulate alertness, lighting a cigarette may be an acquired habit that makes a person keep lighting up after saturation, when all the effect is gone. Many smokers smoke so much that they report getting little pleasure except on those occasions when, unable to smoke for an hour or two, they have gotten rid of the overdose.

From all I have read, users of most drugs, including prescription and over-the-counter drugs, have a good idea of the effect they are seeking, especially of drugs that produce a high or a rush or a "euphoria" of some kind. Most tobacco smokers cannot describe any attractive effect except what they might describe as the "taste" of tobacco smoke in their mouth and lungs and nasal passages. Being addicted to cigarettes is more like being addicted to chocolate than to hard drugs, more like the flavor of a dinner wine than the perceived alcohol content. True, as mentioned, some rely on a cigarette to calm down; but what a deprived smoker is conscious of wanting is usually not the calming but the taste of the cigarette. I belabor this point because it is an important contrast between nicotine, which is always administered through tobacco smoke that is the object of craving, and drugs that need no such medium. (Possibly people who chew coca and betel leaves have a sense of appetite for the leaves, not just a desire for the medicinal effects.)

Some addictive substances require increasing doses to get a given effect as one cumulatively experiences the drug; most smokers within the first few years stabilize on a steady diet. A narrow range of daily dosage covers most smokers; the preponderance of smokers smoke between one dozen and four dozen cigarettes per day. There appears to be greater variance among users of coffee, alcohol, marijuana, hard drugs, and medicinal drugs.

There is, in contrast, great variability in the time it takes to get over withdrawal symptoms and especially the craving for cigarettes. For some the worst is over in three days, for others three weeks, for others three months, and for some three years. How much of that variability is physiological and how much due to environmental stimuli is hard to guess.

Few smokers attempt to reduce the amount they smoke. The two responses to the publicized hazards are trying to quit and switching to lower tar and nicotine.

There is experimental evidence that people who switch to low nicotine compensate by inhaling more deeply, holding the smoke longer in the lungs, smoking more cigarettes or more of each cigarette, and even holding the cigarette in a way that lets less ventilation into the cigarette (reducing the dilution of nicotine). They probably end up with less tar and nicotine than they used to get but nothing like proportionately less unless they smoke extremely low nicotine cigarettes. (They may get more carbon monoxide.)

In the drug literature there is evidence that many people mature out of their habits. Other interests take over, use of the drug ceases to match a more mature lifestyle; marriage, job, or parenthood becomes incompatible with continued use. Hardly anybody "matures out" of cigarettes. Smokers quit, but not through loss of interest; quitting requires determination.

A few medicinal substances have shown an apparent ability to suppress a craving for cigarettes for people undergoing withdrawal. But the interesting drug is nicotine itself. For some years a chewing gum with the trade name Nicorette has been available by prescription. Nicotine is released through controlled chewing and absorbed through the mouth to maintain a steady level of nicotine in the blood. The instructions are to use it with a dosage that tapers off over ninety days. It is reported to reduce the withdrawal discomfort but to provide no pleasure; it reduces the craving for cigarettes but is not itself desired. The principle is like that of methadone, which reduces withdrawal discomfort for heroin addicts but provides little of the pleasure that heroin can provide. There are also other less troublesome methods of self-administering nicotine during withdrawal. (Nicorette requires a lot of chewing, enough to fatigue the jaws.)

There have been a few reports on the efficacy of Nicorette: the permanent success rate may be as high as one-third or better; that would be about double the usual estimate of successful quitting. If the reports are true, the self-administration of pure nicotine on a tapering-off schedule is the first major advance in quitting technology to be successfully marketed.

Nicotine may not deserve all the credit. Nicorette is available only by prescription; every user is under the supervision of a physician, who may be an important support. And just having something to do at regular intervals through the day, every day, may keep the patient engaged in a constructive quitting regime. We should keep in mind that the users of Nicorette are self-selected, and limited to people who see a physician, either to seek help in quitting or in circumstances that make the subject of smoking pertinent to the visit.

An altogether different approach would be to deliver the nicotine in the quantity a smoker wants and in a form that offers the usual satisfaction but causes less damage. One proposal has been to develop tobacco that is high in nicotine but low in tar. This is not easy to do naturally; nicotine and tar are highly correlated in the tobacco leaf. One method would be to add nicotine to a low tar, low nicotine cigarette. As far as anybody outside the cigarette companies seems to know, that has not been done.

An extreme version has been tried. R. J. Reynolds (RJR) spent nearly $1 billion developing, and tested in three cities, an almost pure nicotine delivery device, a glass tube the size of a cigarette with ignited charcoal that heated the air drawn through it and vaporized nicotine in a controlled way. Some glycerine was added solely to produce "smoke," and a bit of tobacco was included. (Whether the tobacco was for flavor or to permit classifying the device as a "cigarette," and not as a nicotine delivery system, we do not know.) There was an effort to get the Federal Trade Commission to declare jurisdiction over this "nontobacco" device. Organizations concerned about smoking were unanimously opposed to its introduction. The device was withdrawn after a few months of testing; newspapers reported that it had not caught on with smokers. Maybe RJR will tinker with the flavor and try again. Presumably there would be little or no danger of respiratory or oral cancer, and most lung disease might be eliminated. Such a device might be a replacement for regular cigarettes or perhaps only a replacement where cigarette smoking is not allowed. (The Department of Transportation would have had to decide whether the use of that device in an airplane was "smoking.")

Whether the device should be welcomed or deplored is not obvious. It has been almost unanimously deplored, just as cigarettes low in tar and nicotine have been almost invariably disparaged by organizations concerned about smoking and health. If there are smokers who would like to quit but cannot, denying the pure nicotine condemns them to getting what they need only with carcinogenic tar and poison gases. The alleged objection is that the device gives smokers who might otherwise quit an excuse for inhaling pure nicotine instead.

LESSONS AND OBSERVATIONS

One heartening observation is simply that there can be massive changes of behavior in the direction of abstinence with a highly addictive substance. And they occurred in the absence, until recently, of any even mildly coercive efforts by government or any other institutions in our society. Eventually changes in behavior on this scale are associated with changes in attitudes, expectations, and norms. When the efforts at abstinence are numerous enough to be unmistakably noticeable, they generate a social environment that is supportive of efforts to abstain. But the change was very, very slow.

A related observation is less heartening. A habit that was widespread among all socioeconomic groups, with only a gender differential that was on the way to disappearing, has become markedly identified with lower education and employment status. The motivation for quitting is probably strongest among people who are in a condition to appreciate longevity and are best positioned to receive and understand health messages from credible sources. Cigarettes are distinctive among addictive drugs in the extreme delay from use to symptoms. This convergence of use, over several decades of intense efforts to publicize the harm, on the least advantaged and least influential social classes may be proving typical of other drugs. The effects on the politics of prohibition could be substantial.

The information about the health effects of smoking came from a source that never lost its credibility. The surgeon general's reports patiently brought together, year after year, biomedical and other evidence and presented conclusions that were never really challenged from any reputable quarter. And the one surgeon general whose face became familiar had a style that inspired trust. In contrast, children had little reason to trust the information they used to be given about marijuana and other drugs. Of course, the surgeon general had a message that did not need exaggeration.

A possible inference from the cigarette experience is that "society" can tolerate addiction to a chemical substance if the behavioral consequences hurt only the addicted consumers. The drugs policy literature reveals a widespread belief that addiction to any drug is morally offensive and socially degrading. Until recently few Americans were morally offended by the widespread smoking of cigarettes or thought it an index of social depravity. The only behavior that smokers engaged in that nonsmokers did not was smoking. The increasingly explicit mention of nicotine as an addictive substance, the increasing objection of nonsmokers to smoking in their presence, and the increasing identification of smoking with lower classes may succeed in making nicotine addiction per se objectionable.

Even among the youngest adults who smoke, both men and women have been persuaded to try to stop. Except for those lowest in socioeconomic status, motivating people to quit is no longer the problem. The problem is relapse. And there are two parts to coping with relapse.

One is to avoid relapse. Few people who quit just come to decide that quitting is not worth the hardship and resume smoking. Most people who relapse had no intention, the day before relapse, of resuming smoking.

The second aspect of coping is recovering from the relapse. When somebody does break down and have a cigarette or two, it is usually not a brief interlude in a quitting program but a crash finish.

One reason why relapse is so common is the shortness of time between loss of resolve and having a cigarette in one's lips. Most smokers who have quit are rarely more than five minutes from the nearest cigarette, and it takes only the briefest loss of control to consummate the urge to smoke. If one had to wait until the next day to acquire cigarettes there might be plenty of intervening changes in the stimuli, and plenty of opportunity to get one's self under control; one could wake up the next morning relieved at having been rescued by the unavailability of cigarettes the night before.

Furthermore, as mentioned earlier, there is almost no moment in a former smoker's life when a cigarette might not have been appropriate, and the former smoker's day is full of occasions and activities that once would have prompted a cigarette and still may prompt the thought of one.[9]

NOTES

1. A 1985 Gallup poll, "Survey of Attitudes toward Smoking" reported that 94 percent of Americans believed smoking was hazardous to health (American Lung Association, *News*, 5 December 1985).

2. *The Health Consequences of Smoking: Cancer*, a report of the Surgeon General (U.S. Government Printing Office [GPO], Washington, DC, 1982); *The Health Consequences of Smoking: Cardiovascular Disease*, a report of the Surgeon General (GPO, Washington, DC, 1983); *The Health Consequences of Smoking: Chronic Obstructive Lung Disease*, a report of the Surgeon General (GPO, Washington, DC, 1984).

3. *The Health Consequences of Smoking: Cancer and Chronic Lung Disease in the Workplace*, a report of the Surgeon General (GPO, Washington, DC, 1985), p. 25, table 2.

4. L. D. Johnston *et al.*, *Drugs and American High School Students, 1975* (GPO, Washington, DC, 1984), p. 12.

5. *The Health Consequences of Smoking: Cancer*, a report of the Surgeon General (GPO, Washington, DC, 1982), pp. 372–373, tables 5 and 6.

6. Ibid., p. 369, table 2.

7. Ibid., p. 372, table 5.

8. For a review of private and public regulations on smoking, see *Reducing the Health Consequences of Smoking: 25 Years of Progress*, a report of the Surgeon General (GPO, Washington, DC, 1989), chap. 7, pp. 465–644.

9. Condensed from a study for the RAND Drug Policy Research Center with a grant from the Alfred P. Sloan Foundation.

Society and Life

9

Life, Liberty,
or the Pursuit of Happiness

■ The history of individual liberty in the United States is a history of triumphant, if uneven, progress. Whether measured by individual dignity, access to the marketplace, or access to the political system, the signs of that progress are everywhere.

Furthermore, the practical results of most of these advances in individual liberty are as welcome as the improvements in human rights. Most of us not only believe in the principle that ethnic minorities should not be discriminated against in the workplace, but also would like to see them earn more, participate more, and raise healthier families. Most of us probably want contraceptive information available not only because suppressing it is intolerant but because we believe that people should be able to plan and limit their pregnancies.

But social objectives and civil liberties are not always in tune. Preventive detention can reduce crime but reduces freedom; wire tapping can identify terrorists but invades privacy; control of handguns may reduce accidental deaths and homicides but only by denying a right that some people believe is guaranteed by the Constitution. These are straightforward conflicts; a person calculates a trade-off and picks a side or selects a compromise.

Not all the conflicts are straightforward. Individual rights clash not only with social goals but, increasingly, with one another. The constitutional protection of pornography has been alleged to violate the rights of women. The rights of parents to decide on medical treatment for se-

127

riously defective newborns conflict with the rights of newborns to be protected from their parents' decisions, and even with the rights of physicians and nurses to practice medicine in accordance with their consciences. The right of a person to decide in advance, while mentally competent, what treatment may or may not be administered when the person has later become incompetent conflicts intertemporally with the person's subsequent right to choose, however incompetently, the person's own treatment. Abortion confronts a fetus's right to be born with a woman's right to control the functioning of her body and the size of her family (and even, in some interpretations, the same fetus's right *not* to be born).

Moral and religious values collide with civil rights in the issues of abortion, euthanasia, nonviable births, and the new technologies for conceiving and bearing a child. In 1983 a California judge ruled against a quadriplegic woman who wished to die and had asked a hospital's help in starving herself to death. The judge ordered force-feeding, with the comment, "Our society values life." Any right to die apparently conflicts with, and even was overruled by, a value attributed by the judge to our society; it conflicts with deeply held religious values, and these in turn conflict with such social objectives as reducing, for terminally ill people, and for some who can only wish their illness were terminal, the pain, the horror, the loss of dignity, and even the medical expense.

Social objectives, individual rights, and moral and religious values are all involved in the question of whether contraceptive education should be provided in junior high school. The right of children to have knowledge conflicts with the right of parents to deny knowledge or to provide the knowledge in their own fashion; the moral issues in abetting premature sex conflict, for many Americans, with the social objectives of reducing schoolgirl pregnancies, controlling venereal disease, and protecting individual children against acquired immune deficiency syndrome (AIDS) and the entire population against an epidemic. And, as is often the case, people disagree about the social objectives themselves or about the efficacy of the proposed program: some believe, or claim to believe, that safer sex—safer against pregnancy, against traditional venereal disease, and against AIDS—may so increase sexual activity as to aggravate, on balance, what the sex education was supposed to ameliorate.

To explore some of the ways that rights, values, and social objectives conflict with one another, this chapter has to be arbitrarily selective. Potential candidates for examination are as diverse as genetic engineering, markets for human organs, surrogate motherhood, the terminally ill, homosexual marriage, capital punishment, animal experimentation, and the burning of cigarettes in public. Each raises a different cluster of issues, problems, and values.

This chapter concentrates on one topic, the right to die. The right to die is one of the many conflictual issues brought into prominence and near-universal interest as a side effect of spectacular advances in medical technology, and by the consequent drastically changing demographic profile of our population. Pneumonia and other violent infections used to perform an often welcome euthanasia that ran afoul of nobody's values or the laws of any state; now the paralyzed victim of stroke can stare vacantly at the ceiling indefinitely with antibiotics and nasal and intravenous tubing to keep that fatal infection at bay. This issue, like syphilis until the *Reader's Digest* lifted the rug off it fifty years ago, is ineluctably going to preoccupy more and more Americans not only as a political, social, and moral issue but as a matter of intimate personal involvement.

The astonishing advances in medical technology that have, in the past few decades, made it increasingly easy (and costly) to keep people alive in discomfort, indignity, and despair have been paralleled by increasing attention—in the courts, the legislatures, and the press; among professional ethicists; and among patients and their families—to the questions whether, in what circumstances, and by whose decision these life-extending medical procedures might be eschewed. The questions arise similarly but not identically for patients at the beginning of life and for patients who are, or who hope they are, near the end of life.

Everyone who reads this book recognizes the names Karen Ann Quinlan and, after 2005, Terri Schiavo and most will have read about more than one judicial decision on the subject within the year. Many older readers have already signed, before witnesses, a "living will." In the late 1970s no state had passed any form of living-will legislation; now nearly all the states and the District of Columbia have provided some statutory recognition of this modest instrument, endorsing some limited and qualified "right to die."

In order to draw the line, or even to identify the line, that circumscribes this limited right not to be kept alive against one's wishes, it is useful to identify the spectrum of circumstances in which the issue arises and the kinds of acts and omissions that may fall within or beyond the lines. I shall try to list them in increasing order of moral complexity or ambiguity.

THE DEAD, THE UNCONSCIOUS, AND THE INCOMPETENT

The most primitive case involves the question of what constitutes death. Whether a *body* can survive after the *patient* has died is a metaphysical question as well as a scientific one. The patient at that stage is no longer concerned, but the patient's "interests" may still be a legitimate consideration—publicity, organ donation, and especially the stress on family members for whom no funeral ceremony can yet help them begin to get over their grief, to say nothing of the expense if the costs are not fully covered. By moving the definition from one of heartbeat and respiration to one of brain activity, some of the patients who might have preferred to claim a right to die in these circumstances can simply be declared already dead.

The next situation worth distinguishing is that of a patient permanently in coma. By no reasonable definition is the patient dead, although many of us in that condition might be happy to be treated as though dead—not fed, not respirated, not administered antibiotics. This is one of the borderline areas that the courts have been struggling with; two crucial aspects have been who has the right or obligation to decide, and how one establishes the wishes of the patient who cannot communicate.

The third stage has been the most difficult of all in this country: that of the patient who is alive but incompetent, neurologically unable to speak or, if able to speak, unable to comprehend, or physically unable to see or to hear or to speak or to write. Unlike comatose patients, these people suffer and their suffering can be terminated only by death. (If they do not manifestly suffer pain and frustration, the question of letting them die does not arise.)

Unlike the comatose, these people can be presumed to have preferences in the matter, although it may be hard to define what "preferences" mean for a person who has thoughts and feelings but perhaps no comprehension of any alternatives. But getting at what the patient would answer if the patient could give an answer; what the patient would decide if he or she could understand the choice; whose testimony counts in that inquiry; and whether the patient's prior testimony as expressed to family, physician, attorney, or pastor, possibly in a signed statement with witnesses, should be determining—these are the questions that have occupied the courts and the professional witnesses who appear in court and those who write on the subject in journals devoted to medicine and ethics.

A question that cannot be pursued here, but one that has been raised by legal and ethical scholars, is whether a formal and unambiguous instruction signed before witnesses and issued to all who may be eventually concerned should be binding. That is, should a competent person have the right to decide in advance for when he or she will be incompetent? Or instead is the right to decide for oneself a right that can never be relinquished? Do prior instructions have only the status of evidence for deciding what the patient in his or her present state would choose if the patient could choose?

THE COMPETENT PATIENT WHO CANNOT DIE

The fourth stage worth distinguishing is that of the competent patient who would rather die than go on living but cannot die without the passive or active help of people who have been keeping him or her alive. Courts have been of several minds about this, some ruling that patients have a right not to be "artificially" kept alive by extraordinary and heroic means but that they must be provided nourishment, respiration, and drugs, at least the drugs that do no great violence.

Complications arise, of course, in determining just how competent a patient is; some participants in debate on this subject go so far as to assert that a desire to terminate one's own life is itself evidence of incompetence. The hardest cases are probably those patients who continually express preferences but whose preferences change. Sometimes they plead to be disconnected from life support, other times they appear to welcome it. Sometimes they attempt, when one preference governs, to discredit the contrary expressions that issue from time to time. And even if the patient is unwavering in requesting to be allowed to die, the people who are reluctant to permit it can always propose that if the ultimate decision is postponed the patient may yet undergo a change of mind.

Court decisions in recent years have been more sympathetic to these patients' wishes, allowing patients the right to be unfed and unrespirated while being treated for terminal pain and discomfort.

To this point the patients discussed are those incapable of taking their own lives. Some of them can try, by yanking tubes from veins and nasal passages, but they are usually at the mercy of people who can immediately replace them. What the patients can request, or what can be requested on their behalf—the removal of some essential part of a life support system—is at the borderline between what is sometimes called "passive euthanasia" and "active euthanasia." The former is usually taken to mean the omission of some life-extending act, the latter the commission of some life-shortening act. The removal or withdrawal of life support is sometimes construed as the commission of a life-shortening act, sometimes as merely a reversion to the nonadministration of life support and identified with omission rather than commission. (It is letting the patient die "naturally," not accelerating death.)

UNREQUESTED EUTHANASIA

Euthanasia ("the action of inducing the painless death of a person for reasons assumed to be merciful") that is neither requested by the patient nor otherwise known to be desired is not considered here. Whatever the merits and moral values of painlessly killing someone who wants to stay alive, even if the person clings to life only out of sheer horror of dying itself, there are legal and other practical reasons for leaving this case outside the realm considered here. It deserves and receives attention (and an actual case of a man who shot and killed his hopelessly ailing wife was featured on network television), but euthanasia at the initiative of the killer is better treated here as extenuated homicide and left at that.

ASSISTED SUICIDE AND EUTHANASIA

Finally we come to two actions or circumstances that have to be discussed together. One is euthanasia of the active kind, provided on request; the other is assisted suicide. They have to be discussed together because they are sometimes indistinguishable. (Unassisted suicide in this country is no longer subject to any legal sanction, the "right" being freely exercisable, except in a few important special cases that will be treated later.)

When the hindquarters of my fourteen-year-old dog could no longer support his body, I took him to a veterinarian who injected a couple of cc's of something into his foreleg. Nothing happened for about five seconds and the doctor explained that circulation is slow in the elderly. The dog then shuddered, relaxed, and was dead. I suffered no trauma, only envy.

Active euthanasia is exemplified by what my dog experienced. In this country when such an injection is administered to human beings it is murder. It is murder whether or not the patient requests it. Laws could be changed to specify conditions and procedures that would make such euthanasia the legal practice of medicine.

The only country in the world in which a terminally ill competent patient can request and receive a physician's assistance in dying is the Netherlands. In that country there are formal procedures intended to ensure that the decision is the patient's and that the patient is adequately informed of the nature and prognosis of his illness. The procedure can be done in hospital or at home. And the death-inducing medical procedure can be almost as simple as what my dog received.[1]

Hopelessly ill patients are often incapable of performing their own intravenous injections, but in principle a physician could hand the syringe to the patient who would administer it to himself; or the physician could write a prescription that the spouse could have filled; or the physician could simply advise on a combination of drugs and the best procedures for administration; or the physician could write a column in the health section of a newspaper providing the pertinent information. There is thus a progression from active euthanasia through "assisted suicide" to medically informed but unassisted suicide.

So far only the physical or technological dimension of euthanasia and suicide has been considered. Equally important, though less susceptible to legal restraint and specification, are the several kinds of moral and psychological assistance that patients may need to reach a responsible and informed decision with which they are comfortable, to arrange their affairs with decency and dignity, to reduce the psychological trauma to family and friends, to minimize feelings of guilt among those who participate in the decision, and to protect them from suspicion or accusation of duress or precipitate action.

Because of the criminal sanctions and possible malpractice suits, physicians are exceedingly uneasy about, and usually reluctant to be accomplices in, mercy-suicides, and they are almost always unwilling to acknowledge publicly that they play a role or how they do it. Courts in most jurisdictions have not explored the line that may separate medical advice from complicity in suicide. It is generally assumed that many physicians do try to be of help but discreetly, indirectly, noncommittally.

In the United States, recipes for painless suicide can be published and distributed through the mail. This has been done by the National Hemlock Society. In Britain a similar book by a similar society was not allowed to be commercially sold but could legally be distributed to members of the society upon payment of the society's initiation fee. In France, bootleg copies of such a book have circulated illegally, publication not being allowed.

What has been published in this country makes clear that the direct services of a physician can be important in selecting the drugs to be used. The patient's medical history, including drug history, is pertinent to the selection of appropriate drugs—often a combination of drugs for prompt unconsciousness and drugs for timely death.

What the public thinks about it is interesting. A Roper Poll taken in 1986 inquired whether or not doctors should be allowed by law to end the life of a suffering, terminally ill patient if the patient requests it. The results are surprising! Ten percent of the Americans polled did not know or gave no answer; among the 90 percent who stated that such help should be or should not be allowed, favorable answers outnumbered unfavorable answers by more than two to one, 62 percent answering yes, 27 percent answering no. When the answers were categorized by the religion of the respondent—Protestant, Catholic, Jewish, other, none—the responses in every category were preponderantly favorable, even Catholics favoring such assistance by 59 to 31 percent, 10 percent not answering or not knowing.

Education made little difference: the range of answers from college graduates to respondents who had not finished high school was narrow and more than two to one in favor for each category. Democrats, Republcans, and Independents differed by minuscule amounts, as did "conservatives," "moderates," and "liberals." Responses in the four major geographic areas of the country differed hardly at all. Male and female answers were virtually identical. Least in favor were blacks with 46 percent in favor to 39 percent against and 15 percent expressing no preference. Age made no difference. Income made some difference, respondents with high incomes being more than three to one in favor and those with the lowest incomes not quite two to one in favor. The occupational category in which the responses were least favorable was blue-collar, but even people in that category were more than two to one in favor.[2]

This was a stunning finding.

As mentioned earlier, most states have adopted varying forms of living-will legislation. Standard forms for living wills have been available for many years; they have been freely available from Concern for Dying. Living wills and the surrounding issues have been discussed frequently in *The Hastings Center Report*. The typical key statement in such a document is something like the following:

> If the time comes when I can no longer take part in decisions for my own future, let this statement stand as an expression of my wishes and directions, while I am still of sound mind. If at such a time the situation should arise in which there is no reasonable expectation of my recovery from extreme physical or mental disability, I direct that I be allowed to die and not be kept alive by medications, artificial means, or "heroic measures." I do, however, ask that medication be mercifully administered to me to alleviate suffering even though this may shorten my remaining life.

The statement is signed, dated, and witnessed by two persons not of the immediate family. The document may append a list of treatments to be specifically excluded, and may appoint someone to make decisions—a kind of executor.

In most jurisdictions, courts have been responsive to living wills or equivalent prior expressions on the subject by people who are no longer competent. What, then, does the legislation add? Clearly, the legislation gives moral support to those who will be responsible for not administering the proscribed procedures. Legislation can reassure attending physicians and nurses and hospital authorities fearful of damage suits. And a few technical issues, like the applicability of suicide clauses in life insurance policies, can be taken care of by statute. The most important effect, however, is to build an impressive nationwide legislative record in favor of a right to die, a record that will probably encourage efforts to liberalize rights to more active assistance on the part of physicians under appropriate safeguards.

Except for institutionalized persons, the right to unassisted suicide is freely exercised. But as in the case of physician assistance, ambiguity—partly legal, partly moral—surrounds what constitutes illegitimate complicity in suicide. Providing ten grams of Barbital with a chaser of alcohol and Valium to a person who is awake and knows exactly what he or she is drinking and for what purpose may feel to the provider like a merciful assistance to suicide; injecting an equivalent substance intravenously, especially while the patient sleeps, after full and conclusive discussion by the patient with all appropriately interested parties, may feel more like killing. The difference in feeling may be even more stark when the alternatives are between procuring a handgun and ammunition that the patient can fire into his or her own head, after the helping person has left the room, and firing the shot when the patient lacks the physical strength or dexterity to handle the weapon or, more tantalizingly, lacks the nerve.

THE INSTITUTIONALIZED

When people are arrested and jailed, they typically surrender anything with which they could hang or cut themselves, even their eyeglass lenses. The law does not recognize the prisoners' right to die by suicide. The justification is unclear, aside from the avoidance of embarrassment to the custodians (or accusations of murder). But nationwide the incidence of suicide in jail is high, and for many people the psychological trauma of sudden incarceration might be feared to produce a transient despondency that could lead to an act of suicide that, were it prevented, the prisoner would ultimately be glad to have been spared.

A final important category of patients whose "right to die" is typically not acknowledged is one so complex that it can be only mentioned briefly here. I once asked the dean of a school of public health which classes of medical patients—emphysema, bone cancer, phantom limb syndrome, stroke-induced paralysis—he thought the most wretched and the best candidates for assisted easy termination of life. His answer was prompt and unequivocal—people who remain in state mental institutions. Some of these people are "incompetent" in the full sense, unable to hang or cut themselves or even to appreciate that a suicide option might be available. Others are sufficiently competent to cut, strangle, or bash themselves to death without assistance, as long as they are not restrained or denied the simple instruments for taking their lives. To prevent exactly that they are denied cords or belts or pointed or sharp-edged instruments of any kind; sometimes they are physically restrained and sometimes they are kept in padded rooms. In a legal sense it has been determined that they are incompetent to make the decisions for themselves, even if they are competent to carry out those decisions.

And what most starkly distinguishes these patients from the ones to whom living wills are typically applicable, or from those whose expressed preferences for death may be acknowledged, is that they are *not* terminally ill. Wretched, hopeless, they can be kept alive for decades by the most ordinary means. These institutions may ultimately be the ugliest and most difficult arena in which to attempt to define an appropriate right to die.

GUNS AND DOCTORS

A poignant statistic relates the right to die to the right to bear arms. A study of 743 deaths from gunshot in the Seattle area of Kings County, Washington, from 1978 to 1983, found that 333 of these deaths were suicides.[3] In the nation as a whole, according to Joseph Fletcher, 57 percent of suicides are accomplished by gunshot. According to Fletcher,

> The plain fact is that those who plan self-deliverance, usually for reasons of broken health, find that it is often extremely difficult to get drugs in lethal forms or quantities, and that suffocation may be awkward and too open to interference (for example, monoxide in closed garages). Gunshot, on the other hand, is quick, solitary, simple. Booklets advising people of ways and means to self-deliverance by methods

other than gunshot have been published . . . but the average run of people, at least to date, have found their recommendations sophisticated and difficult to carry out. Guns, especially pistols, are much more familiar and available.[4]

Dr. Pieter V. Admiraal, who has participated in patient-requested euthanasia in the Netherlands, once closed an address with the words:

Let me then end here, by submitting to you my sincere hope that already the next generation will be profoundly puzzled by the length of time our generation has taken to come to the unconditional acceptance of euthanasia as a recognized, natural human right.[5]

The argument is powerful but not absolutely compelling. The Netherlands is not the United States. There are strategic considerations that need to be carefully examined.

Some rights bring responsibilities and verge on obligations. The "right" of seventeen-year-olds to volunteer in wartime can subject them to a sense of obligation. The right to early retirement can be construed as an obligation of older workers to get out and clear the way for younger people. The right to depart this world at least raises the question for dying persons whether the decent thing to do might be to discontinue being a burden, an annoyance, an expense, and a source of anxiety to the people caring for the dying person. One's terminal disability is a burden shared with one's spouse as long as no alternative is available; it is a burden of which the spouse can be relieved if the option of dying is known to be available. And it is an option that can preoccupy both of them, whether or not there is any immediate intention of taking advantage of it.

If a man could die and relieve his wife of the burden and the expense, how could the wife persuade him she truly wanted him to live? Saying so, repeatedly, may only demonstrate awareness of the option and remind him of it. If the man's survival gains him a few years of life of exceedingly low quality and condemns his wife to the same when she could have been free had he exercised his right to go, and a friend feels this keenly, how does the friend perceive the obligation to the wife, including the obligation to respect what the wife believes to be her own obligations? How does the man manage his guilt upon awakening every morning, knowing he is spoiling another day of her life? And how does he evaluate the guilt she will feel if he takes his life for her sake?

These are real, not just rhetorical questions. Procedures and safeguards will have to be devised, and the medical conditions in which assisted dying is a legitimate option appropriately circumscribed, so that these nagging questions can be dealt with.

The issues are not only legal and strategic, they are psychological and political. Legislative efforts to replace a fuzzy area in which some right to die is ambiguously perceived by a clear line that deliberately enlarges the area may only push that fuzzy borderline farther outward. Thoughts and feelings on the subject may be pushed various distances in different directions in ways that are hard to foretell.

The line between abortion and infanticide may exist primarily in people's minds and feelings, not just in the science of neurology or in court-interpreted statutes. The same may be true of the line between freely undertaken, mercifully assisted suicide and something that invites an uglier name.

NOTES

1. Dr. Pieter V. Admiraal, "Active Voluntary Euthanasia," *Hemlock Quarterly,* no. 21 (October 1985):3–6.

2. *Hemlock Quarterly,* no. 24 (July 1986):2–3. Louis Harris, *Inside America* (New York: Vintage Books, 1987), 154–58, reports similar responses to similar questions going back to 1973. On whether it was right "to give a patient who is terminally ill, with no cure in sight, the right to tell the patient's doctor to put the patient out of his or her misery," the percentage answering yes was only 37 in 1973 and was 61 by 1985. Those opposed declined from 53 to 36 percent over the twelve-year period.

3. Arthur L. Kellerman, M.D., and Donald T. Reay, M.D., "Protection or Peril," *New England Journal of Medicine* 314, no. 24 (June 12, 1986):1557–60.

4. Joseph Fletcher, "Guns and Suicide: A Personal Opinion," *Hemlock Quarterly,* no. 24 (July 1986):8.

5. Admiraal, "Active Voluntary Euthanasia," 6.

## 10

Should Numbers Determine Whom to Save?

■ The problem: there are two (or several) groups of people who are si-multaneously and equally mortally endangered; rescue is available but can serve only one group, but a group of any size. Someone must de-cide which group to save, letting the rest perish. Should the sizes of the groups be decisive in who gets saved? Specifically, should the larger group be the one saved?

We suppose that there is no individual whose "value" to society dominates, for example, no one who can save, if saved himself or her-self, some large number of lives that must be attributed to the rescue.

The question has been posed ex post. That is, there they are—two groups on an island subject to some catastrophe, one but only one of which can be lifted safely, or two railroad cars out of control, one but only one of which can be successfully diverted, the other doomed to crash fatally. The Coast Guard captain, the air traffic controller, the railroad switchman, or the dogsled driver who can take the antibiotics to only one infected village faces an immediate decision.

I propose that there is a more useful way to formulate the issue. Namely, ex ante. We ask, not whom should we save when the emer-gency is on us, but what rule should we adopt in anticipation of such emergencies? This would be a general rule, not specific to airplanes or railroad cars or tourist groups stranded on a volcanic island, but a rule applicable to any emergency decision about whom to save when not all can be saved. It would be a rule that disregarded not only the nature of the emergency but any quality of the people that might be at risk.

The latter notion is important. If the smaller of two endangered groups will usually be the young, or the old, or the women, or the men, or the Christians or the Jews or the Muslims, the sick or the well, the rich or the poor, the veterans or the draft-evaders, the felons or the law-abiding, there can be serious differences among us about who is most worth saving. So I postulate that nothing is known at the time the rule is adopted about who will compose the larger or the smaller groups in any unforeseen emergencies that may eventuate.

My proposal is that it should be easy to adopt a rule. And the rule that would be adopted is to save the more, not the fewer. And I propose that this rule can be expected to be universally desired, unanimously adopted.

There are at least two motivations for adopting the rule. One is simple self-interest. If I don't know in advance which among those at risk I—or my wife, or my child, or my friend or colleague—shall be, it is simply a matter of probability that I or my wife or my child or my friend is more likely to be in the larger group than in the smaller group. This is just a matter of numbers. If there are a 150 potential but unidentified individuals to be at risk, 50 in one group and 100 in a second group, and nobody knows or can know who is in which groups, anyone I want saved is twice as likely to be in the larger group as in the smaller. The reason we can't know who is in which group is that we are choosing a rule for future unidentified contingencies. If asked to accept or reject the rule of saving the group with more members, whomever I am trying to favor, myself or anyone else, I'll elect to save the larger group.

This reasoning may not entail moral value, except perhaps the value of democracy. People who are mainly concerned with being rescued in various contingencies may welcome a contract according to which they share with everybody else the maximum likelihood of being saved. If all wish to be saved—or their families to be saved, or their neighbors to be saved—all may be attracted to the rule that not only accomplishes what they wish but that does the same for everybody else in the society.

A second motivation is less selfish: I wish to save those who most deserve to be saved, whoever they may be. Again, it is a simple numerical judgment. Whoever it is who should be saved—if there is anyone who deserves more than somebody else to be saved—is more likely to be saved if we save the larger of the two—or largest of the several—groups at risk.

So whether I am selfishly motivated, voting along with other selfishly motivated members of society on a rule for whom to save, or I am selflessly motivated to wish salvation for those most deserving, or those most valuable to society, I achieve my goal in a probabilistic sense if I vote for the rule to save the greater number.

I conclude that intelligent voters who wish (a) to maximize the likelihood that they themselves, or whomever they most cherish, will survive contingencies in which the larger or the smaller group might be saved, or (b) to maximize the likelihood that those who most deserve to survive or who contribute most to society will survive such contingencies, will unanimously choose to save the larger number.

Again: this assumes the absence of any a priori expectation of correlation between sizes of groups and any individual or group characteristics that one would wish to enjoy a survival advantage. Since the rule is to cover all kinds of contingencies, mostly unforeseen, that may not be an implausible condition.

This schema is the kind that John Rawls used, incorporating a "veil of ignorance," but it does not use anything else of his.

Finding this argument compelling as to what the rule should be—that is, what rule should we expect people to adopt unanimously—I next ask myself how to solve the ex post kind of question. There they are, in mortal danger, and we are without a rule. What to do?

I personally find this one easy to answer in principle. It is to address the question, *if* we had had a rule, what would the rule have been?

I believe that often when we need to face a dilemma, this formulation yields an answer. Not always: sometimes there are alternative rules that claim some validity. But in this case of numerical determination of whom to save, I think there is a unique answer that is compelling, namely, the answer I gave above.

So the ex post resolution follows readily once we have resolved the ex ante questions.

The "rule" formulation leads directly into a second dimension, or second criterion for decision. It is a criterion that rarely gets raised with the ex post kind of formulation but arises naturally when one asks what might be the most efficacious rule. That is, what is the rule—or what are the rules—the anticipation of which leads to the most appropriate behavior?

Usually when one considers rules, the first issue, or at least an immediate issue, to consider is what behavior the rule leads to. Many rules, probably most, are rules to govern behavior. A rule that determines decisions is somewhat different from a rule that directly addresses behavior, but a rule that determines a court's decision is essentially a rule about the consequences of certain behaviors. A rule that says you must stay close to where you could be rescued in an emergency is much like a rule that says you will not be rescued unless you stay close. The former may be enforced differently, but both intend the same kind of behavior and intend to induce that behavior.

So we can properly ask, what rule about who should be saved, the larger or the smaller group, will lead to the appropriate behavior? And clearly the answer is that, in the interest of behavior, the larger is the one that should be saved.

If people can know which group is the safer group, they can make personal judgments about which group to adhere to. If you go off with a minority group, you are on notice that in an emergency you cannot be saved. You can decide the risks and choose accordingly. If you are especially worried about risk, stay where help is available, namely, with the larger group. If you are more concerned to go off in the smaller group for whatever the advantages are of separating from the larger group, you are forewarned. If the risk is significant, we prefer that people stay together, not split into smaller groups that are beyond rescue. If the risks are very great, perhaps all should stay together. If the value of separate exploration is compelling, some should go in the smaller group, but preferably not many. In Antarctica they know that going off separately has risks and advantages, and those who go along for the ride do so at their own acknowledged risk.

This is a case in which both criteria—(1) which decision rule would be adopted unanimously in order to maximize the likelihood of survival of whomever people most want to survive, and (2) which decision rule would induce behavior that optimizes the choices between staying together and splitting off into smaller groups—favor the same solution.

Economics and Social Policy

What Do
Economists Know?

■ The title of this chapter, originally delivered as a commencement address, was stimulated by a conversation I had fifty years ago with Peter Bauer, the distinguished Cambridge University economist. I arrived early at a dinner for him, and before other guests arrived he proclaimed, provocatively, that the number of things that economists knew that were true, important, and not obvious, was no more than the fingers on one hand. I waited to hear what the four or five things were that were true, important, and not obvious, but other guests arrived, the conversation was interrupted, and I was left forever in suspense.

I reflected on the question from time to time. I couldn't be sure whether he meant there were only five things altogether that together we know, or there are many important things known but no *one* among us knows more than five of them. So my program was just to take inventory of how many things I knew in economics that were true, important, and not obvious, and to see whether they added up to five.

Of course, to say that I know five things is to imply that they must be true: I can't be said to know them if they are false. But I could believe them wrongly to be true. Peter Bauer may have meant that there are many more things that economists think they know—they just aren't true. Believing something makes it true to me but not to somebody of a more skeptical persuasion.

This excursion on truth is not just a play on words: some important things are true in a different way from the way some other important

147

things are true. Similarly some things are obvious in a different way from other things; in fact some things are believed true precisely because they become obvious. I say "become obvious," because my candidates for Peter Bauer's collection all have the characteristic that, while at first glance they are paradoxical, once understood they are seen as incapable of being false.

These are what are sometimes called accounting identities. When I was an undergraduate they were often disparaged as "mere identities." They were unfalsifiable statements and did not count as scientific truths. They were said to be true by definition.

Actually the truth of all scientific propositions depends on careful definition; but the truth of the so-called identities depends *only* on careful definition. They are not merely definitions; if they were, they would be obvious. But they can be derived from definitions if the definitions are carefully made consistent.

The simplest possible identity—it sounds obvious when I say it—is that in any sales transaction the value of the item sold equals the value of the item purchased. The need for careful definition arises even here: if there is a sales tax we have to treat it as either received by the seller or as a side payment to the tax authorities. That even this simple identity is not always obvious was apparent, for example, in 1994 when values on the stock exchanges dropped almost 10 percent. At that time I heard several intelligent-sounding conversations on national public radio about where all the money was going. People obviously were anxiously liquidating their portfolios and it seemed important to know what they were doing with the proceeds.

What apparently wasn't quite obvious was that no money was leaving the stock market. No money could leave the stock market. No one can sell a share of stock without a buyer: taxes and brokers' fees aside, for every dollar liquidated there has to be a dollar invested. Individuals, yes, were taking money out of stocks; but all investors together could not. Where the liquidated money was going might be interesting; but then equally interesting was a question not asked: where is all the money coming from? Together they had to cancel out. We can't all get rid of our Canadian quarters by passing them along at the first opportunity.

The national-income accounts contain a number of important identities. What they are is quadruple-entry consolidated income statements. Double-entry bookkeeping is for a single individual: but with every sale of goods or services there are two entries for the seller, two for the buyer. These accounts help us to understand the futility of efforts to get consumers to save more by spending less. The United States has a private savings rate lower than it used to be, lower than other industrial states. We citizens don't accomplish enough saving to promote faster improvements in productivity. It is seriously proposed that if we didn't use our credit cards to buy so many needless consumer goods we could have a more respectable rate of saving.

What apparently is not obvious is that the only way private citizens can accumulate savings is to consume less than their incomes, that is, to earn more than they spend on consumption. But there is no way they can all earn more than they consume except by producing equivalent goods that are not consumed. Somebody has to buy those goods. They can be domestic investment, exports, or government purchases; if those do not increase, it is impossible for private saving to increase. I can save another $10 by going without a haircut; but my barber's income goes down by $10, and his savings too, unless he cuts his own spending, in which case he passes along the loss in a chain reaction that offsets my $10 saving.

If those of you who read this book have learned this truth, it may seem obvious; but it wasn't obvious to you until you learned it, it isn't obvious to most people out there, and it wasn't obvious to economists when I entered Berkeley in the early 1940s.

There are other important accounting truths. Most bankers understand their own balance sheets well; what most bankers don't know is that whenever they make a loan they increase the money supply. They don't know it because, as they see it, they only lend money that already exists, money in the bank's reserves. What they don't see is that the reserves still exist—they have simply migrated to other banks—while the customer's money also still exists; it, too, has migrated.

Most of the nonobvious accounting propositions are true only in the aggregate, not true for the individual. They do not correspond to the experience of the banker who lends only money that he has in reserve, or the consumer who forgoes the haircut. But they hold in the same way that the laws of conservation do—conservation of energy, mass, or momentum. If we launch a squash court into orbit, the momentum of its center of gravity will be undisturbed by the game being played inside.

In the physical sciences many of these accounting identities are digni-fied with the title "law"; and like the identities in economics they were not obvious without an intellectual struggle. The conservation of mo-mentum—that a moving object will continue moving at the same speed and in the same direction forever until resisted, pushed, deflected, or subjected to friction—has become obvious, but because it couldn't be observed anywhere in the universe until space flight became possible, its becoming obvious required laboratory experiment and intellectual struggle.

It is sometimes said, in textbooks and in learned volumes, that these accounting statements, being unfalsifiable, do not count as science. I don't care. The question is whether they tell you something important you didn't know. The history of our discipline demonstrates that they are not obvious. Disparaging them as "mere identities" at least testifies to their truth. They are the foundation of any macroeconomics. They have their counterparts in physics, chemistry, biology, genetics, and our sister discipline, demography. They are sometimes known as "bud-gets"; there is the earth's energy budget, its carbon budget, its water budget, even budgets for nondegradable substances like DDT.

There are many more than five important accounting identities in economics that are not obvious; I could have mentioned the balance of payments, or the input-output matrix. As to their importance, where I would draw the line—at five or ten—I don't know. Some of them were surely unknown to Peter Bauer; the carbon budget was unrecognized when I had dinner with him.

So if I am allowed five candidates, they are all accounting identities. I cannot hope to have persuaded you in twenty minutes, but I hope I have sensitized you to be on watch for them, to respect and appreciate them, and not to be afraid of counting them among the things you know that are true and important and were not obvious before you studied them, even though they do not count as empirically grounded, poten-tially falsifiable, scientific hypotheses.

I am tempted to close these remarks with a small investigation into what it is that economists know that are important, not obvious, and *not* true. Actually, what I have in mind is propositions or principles that are true but that unintentionally, the way they are formulated, appear to deny something that is also true, raising the question: which deserves the more emphasis, the truth contained in the proposition, or the truth the proposition appears to deny?

I have a candidate. It has become fashionable, not only among economists but among those who like to quote economists, to advert to an incontestable, absolute truth colloquially expressed as: there is no free lunch.

The truth that I think this assertion is intended to communicate is that resources are always scarce, there are competing ends and competing beneficiaries, redistributing in someone's favor is at someone's expense and there is no alchemy in economics: you can recycle, but it is hard to find the equivalent of a nuclear breeder reactor that produces, in burning fuel, more fuel than it burns.

Maybe it's because of where I've been in economics, but I prefer the alternative truth, that there are free lunches all over just waiting to be discovered or created. What I have in mind is what we technically call Pareto improvements, or the gains from trade. There are non–zero-sum games that permeate the economy that have settled into, or have been forced into, inefficient equilibria.

There are not just free lunches but banquets awaiting the former socialist countries that can institute enforceable contract, copyrights, and patents, or eliminate rent-free housing and energy subsidies. How the lunches get distributed matters; but the lunches are there.

Those of you who move into the economics profession, in government, academia, or in business, will spend much of your time exploring for opportunities to eliminate constraints on mutually beneficial trading, to overcome market failures and to create markets where they are needed, to identify removable deadweight losses, and to promote integrative bargaining.

This is what we do in economics. Technological innovation can push out the production frontier; it is economists who help to find where we are deep inside that frontier, diagnose what keeps us from the frontier, and propose institutional changes to bring us closer to the frontier. To those of you who become professional economists I urge you: get out there and help find those free lunches.

## 12

Why Does Economics Only Help with Easy Problems?

■ My title is only partly facetious, and is not intended to denigrate the science—or art?—of economics itself, but rather to observe how little difference economic analysis appears to make in most important policies. My observations are all from the United States, and in a few instances I am sure are unique to the United States. And I shall use "economic analysis" to imply policy analysis, including the decision sciences, systems analysis, operations research, statistics and econometrics, and "implementation analysis." I begin with a litany of issues on which policy analysis in the United States appears to have had little or no impact.

SOME SERIOUS EXAMPLES

Abortion

Abortion was a quiescent issue politically until about thirty-five years ago. For reasons I do not think anyone has yet adequately explained, abortion suddenly leaped into public consciousness, a few states drastically changed their antiabortion laws, and the courts quite suddenly reversed nearly a century of tradition. What would have happened had only the legal status of abortion been reversed, I find hard to predict retrospectively, but what did happen was that the issue of public financing of abortion arose in the context of publicly financed medical care; and on that issue the traditional opposition to abortion, which had been caught unorganized and surprised by the court decisions, rallied to counterattack. Where this will eventually all come out, it is still too early to tell. There are a few studies that empirically demonstrate what is already plausible to an economist, namely, that the public financing of abortion had comparatively little to do with the ease and frequency with which abortions would be obtained. One study I have seen indicates that for the United States neither the price of abortion nor Medicaid financing of abortion has a substantial impact on the number of abortions. Public funding, even funding in foreign-aid programs, is a favorite issue on both sides of the abortion debate, possibly for reasons independent of the economic analysis; but in any case nobody is listening to the analysis.

Race Relations

At least since the election of John F. Kennedy, no policy issues in the United States have been more divisive, more loaded with hope and tragedy, than relations between the races, especially between "whites" and "blacks." The defining moment was probably the Supreme Court decision in 1954 requiring the desegregation of public schools. What some call "affirmative action" and others call "reverse discrimination," pervasive in federal contracting, college education, and labor relations, has more recently come under severe attack. Issues of race overlap the issues of poverty, crime, and fatherless households. There was one moment of triumph for policy analysis when a study group produced a report that was used successfully before the Supreme Court in arguing that segregation by race, independently of the correlation between the race of the students and the quality of the schools, could impair educational outcomes. Since that time it is hard to find policy choices at any level of government that were substantially driven by analysis of the alternative outcomes that could be expected from alternative policies. The furor over the book by Herrnstein and Murray (1994), *The Bell Curve*, cast doubt not only on whether their results could stand up to criticism but on whether certain policy issues can ever be treated analytically without generating as much hysteria as analytical interpretation.

Illegal Drugs

Policy toward illegal drugs is another area apparently immune to analysis. On the issue of somewhat relaxing the penalties for possession of marijuana there is now the experience of a dozen states that drastically relaxed their laws on that subject two or more decades ago. There have been some studies, somewhat equivocal in their results, on whether the relaxation spurred consumption. They are never cited in debate. There are studies of the effect of clean-needle programs on the spreading of AIDS, but clean needles earlier became a litmus test of whether one was serious about the drug problem. The issue of what is usually called drug "legalization," which is not literally what most of its proponents have in mind, cannot even be raised in public by a senior government official without a resulting clamor for resignation. This policy area is substantially impervious to analysis.

Crime and Punishment

Crime and its punishment, of which drugs are a large part, are susceptible to analysis. A popular proposal has been the one referred to as "three strikes and you're out." Three felony convictions are to be followed by life imprisonment without benefit of parole. There have been studies of the cost, including medical care, of keeping a forty-five-year-old prisoner locked up for another thirty-five or forty years, compared with the likely committing of violent crimes by the middle-aged and the elderly, but in the policy debate there is so little interest that even newspapers don't bother reporting the analytical results. Some ingenious polls have demonstrated that people who like capital punishment believe in its efficacy as a deterrent and people who dislike capital punishment dispute its value as a deterrent, and both sides formulate their positions with great attention to the deterrent effect or its absence, but neither side appears interested in the evidence. A related issue, gun control, appears unrelated to any analysis of what kind of gun control might lead to what kind of result. Interestingly, people who tend to believe in gun control are often against legal controls on marijuana, because the marijuana laws cannot possibly be enforced; people who favor heavy penalties on the use of marijuana usually object to gun control on grounds that laws against possession of guns could not be enforced.

Health Care

Policy toward health care looks like a promising field for the application of economic analysis. It involves market incentives, demography, public support for medical schools, regulation of prescription drugs, income taxation of employer-provided health insurance, mandatory insurance in the workplace, and so on. The former president of the American Economic Association, Victor Fuchs, said in his 1996 presidential address that there has been a thirteen-fold increase in the number of PhDs in health economics in the last thirty years; nevertheless, he concluded, the health care debate of 1993–94 in the United States, a debate that led nowhere, reflected little influence of the health economists. I will have more to say later about his explanation for why that was so.

Budgetary Policy

Balancing the budget has consumed much time and energy on the part of presidents, senators, congressmen, high-level budget officials, and presidential candidates. The subject might have led to the first constitutional amendment in decades; and no candidate for congressional office, let alone for the presidency, could dare to question the wisdom of balancing the federal budget. Why an exactly zero deficit should be so compellingly attractive surely has nothing to do with economic analysis. Probably, like clean needles in the war on drugs, a "little deficit" in the war on the deficit is interpreted as a lack of seriousness, or as the equivalent of one little drink to a reformed alcoholic. Economists even outside the federal government were remarkably silent on this during the early 1990s when the issue arose, I suppose because they perceived that a full-page ad in the *New York Times* would not receive attention worth the cost of the ad. And in the 1996 presidential campaign the flat tax, the centerpiece of Steve Forbes's platform, for a while won a popularity contest with neither help nor hindrance from most of the economics profession, largely, I suppose, because they were caught by surprise.

Finally, the "new revolution" in American politics of the 1990s, reversal of the growth of federal responsibility and devolution of responsibility and authority to the states—"back to the states" as it was erroneously referred to—appeared to be popular not only because the federal government has become a popular scapegoat but because of the "self-evident" principle that state governments, closer to the people, can do a better job, and do it with a less expensive superstructure than the federal government. The truth of this hypothesis, considering how much hinges on it, would have deserved careful historical, empirical, and theoretical study. But that would have taken time, and politics often can't wait. Furthermore, it isn't at all clear that anybody would care whether that particular argument for devolution to the states had any validity. An indication of the lack of depth in this reasoning is that the argument almost always ran in terms of what governors wanted and what governors could do, rather than state legislatures.

■

There is one area of policy in the United States that has been exceptionally responsive to analysis. That is defense policy, which I will come to shortly. First let me draw on Fuchs's assessment of why economics has had so little impact on the health-care debate, and generalize what he has to say to the numerous policy arenas that I have mentioned.

HEALTH POLICY

Fuchs administered a questionnaire to the health economists "whom I considered to be the leading people in the field, plus some of the more promising recent PhDs. There were 46 respondents (response rate 88 percent)" (Fuchs, 1996, pp. 6–7). He asked twenty questions, and asked three experts from three different universities to identify which of the twenty questions were relatively "value-free" ("positive" questions), and which had substantial value aspects ("policy-value" questions). Their independent replies, he reports, were almost unanimous in identifying seven as "positive" and thirteen as "policy-value." Each question was in the form of a statement with which the respondent could agree or disagree.

Positive questions included "The primary reason for the increase in the health sectors share of GDP over the past thirty years is technological change in medicine," or "third-party payment results in patients using services whose costs exceed their benefits, and this excess of costs over benefits amounts to at least 5 percent of total health care expenditures." Policy-value statements included "The U.S. should seek universal coverage through a broad-based tax with implicit subsidies for the poor and the sick," and "Insurance companies should be required to cover all applicants regardless of health condition and not allowed to charge sicker individuals higher premiums."

What Fuchs found, so plausible in retrospect but what I might not have guessed, is that leading health-care economists in the United States, though not quite unanimous, produced a strong consensus on the positive questions. The answers to the two that I mentioned were agreed to by 81 and 84 percent, respectively. The policy-value questions found no such consensus. Only one of the thirteen questions had substantially more than two-thirds of the health-care economists agreed on the answer; on virtually all of the answers they divided close to 50–50 or within the range of two to one.

Fuchs's interpretation is that policy judgments are heavily dependent on values, and even people as similar in professional training and background as health-care economists, who can agree 80 or 90 percent on the positive questions, are split on the policy (value) questions. The value questions were almost entirely normative in expression: of the thirteen policy-value questions, nine contained the word "should" and the other four contained "inequitable," "is desirable," "inefficient," or "greater than is socially optimal."

There is a widespread judgment in the United States that economists, especially "mainstream" economists, are remarkably alike in their values, in what they take for granted, in their attitude toward markets, efficiency, and the use of incentives. And I do not dissent from that judgment. Furthermore, the health-care economists that I know, and I know a great many, do not seem to me to be heterodox in their methodology or dissident from the mainstream. It is remarkable to me that they could show such a powerful consensus on the positive statements—statements on which the economic theorists, who were also offered the same questions, differed drastically in at least two cases, suggesting that the "correct" responses were not self-evident—yet differ so widely on the policy prescriptions.

Before I heard Victor Fuchs's address I was going to conclude that the reason why economic analysis appears so impotent on so many big issues was that on those big issues it is values that predominate, not analysis. But I was also going to say that even on policy issues in which values predominate, economic analysis should be of help. My undergraduate students often choose policies according to the values they attach to the *outcomes* they anticipate, and they often anticipate outcomes wrong. I try to persuade them that they should keep their values on hold while they work through the analysis; then, when they have thought their way through to a correct anticipation of outcomes, it is time to apply their values. Students initially have strong reactions to issues like rent control, gasoline rationing, cash versus in-kind assistance, minimum-wage laws, electric-utility regulation, farm price supports, and tariffs; they often—American students, at any rate—favor or oppose a policy because it helps or hurts "the poor." If I can get them to withhold judgment until we have worked out the theoretical ramifications, and discovered who gains, who loses, and maybe how much, they can then bring their values out of storage and use them more wisely.

But Fuchs provides powerful evidence that the problem is not that economists cannot get heard on the policy issues on which they have expert judgment; it is that they differ among themselves on the value-laden policy judgments.

I have been asked to discuss the role of policy analysis in environmental policy. I shall in a moment, and I shall report that policy analysis has not only contributed little, but has often been overtly excluded. But first, a policy area where analysis has had an impact.

DEFENSE POLICY

I was once asked to lecture on the influence of academia on U.S. national security policy. In preparing the lecture I convinced myself that, in a manner probably unique to the United States, academic research had been not only more influential in defense policy than in any other policy area, but strikingly so. I shall describe that influence and make a few guesses about why that has been so.

Until the Second World War, military policy in my country, and especially the military services themselves, were virtually insulated from academia or anything intellectual. The subject of military strategy barely existed on any university campus before the Second World War. This situation changed immediately after the war. The air force established the forerunner of the RAND Corporation in 1946; it was incorporated as a not-for-profit research organization in California in 1948, had substantially independent command over a large research budget, and was deliberately kept out of the Washington area so that it could work on the long-range issues of its own choice rather than be available for quick answers to immediate questions. When Sputnik flew, in 1957, the RAND Corporation was the only source of information about possible earth-satellite orbits.

By the late 1950s strategic studies, mainly concerned with nuclear weapons policy and European alliance policy, had bloomed at many universities and think tanks, and through the 1960s the ideas generated in academia became powerfully influential in U.S. policy. I want briefly to survey the various channels and media through which ideas originating in academia found their way into policy. Mainly, but not entirely, the ideas penetrated the executive branch rather than the Congress, and in most policy areas it is not sufficient for ideas to be adopted in the executive branch. If the Department of Health and Human Services, or the Department of Housing and Urban Development, or the Department of Transportation, succumbs to policy ideas that originate in academia, the Congress is demonstrably capable of ignoring those ideas. The Congress is always much less likely to ignore policy ideas put forward by the Department of Defense, especially when there is no split between the civilian leadership and the senior officers of the uniformed services.

People

Beginning with the Kennedy administration in 1961, an obviously potent medium through which academic influence could penetrate into the American defense establishment was the appointment of academic people to senior positions. President John F. Kennedy's national security adviser was McGeorge Bundy, dean of Arts and Sciences at Harvard, and Bundy's deputy was another Harvard professor. Robert McNamara, Kennedy's secretary of defense, had an MBA from Harvard and appointed four academics as assistant secretaries. An MIT professor became director of the State Department Policy Planning Staff; a Harvard Law School professor became general counsel of the State Department.

These people brought not only the concrete ideas they had developed or learned in academia but an academic bent for analysis, a culture they shared with other academics, and personal acquaintances back in academia. They all became channels for ideas from academia and they drew on former colleagues to serve on advisory boards and committees.

Eight years after Kennedy's election President Richard Nixon introduced Henry Kissinger to his television audience as his new national security adviser. Kissinger's entire career, except for a stint in the army, had been academic. Generally Republican administrations have not used academics on the scale of the Democrats, but Kissinger's deputy (later President George H. W. Bush's national security adviser), Brent Scowcroft, was a military officer with a PhD in international relations.

President Jimmy Carter's national security adviser was an academic, as was his secretary of defense. And in the first Clinton administration a congressman with a PhD became secretary of defense and immediately nominated at least five academics to the rank of assistant secretary or higher. One of them later directed the Central Intelligence Agency.

People—academic individuals—appointed to senior policy positions give the American defense-policy establishment a porosity, a permeability, a penetrability to academic ideas that is surely unique among the governments of the world.

Institutions

But that is not all. The military services themselves operate four major "war colleges," nine-month academies for the advanced education of people on the verge of becoming admirals and generals. The senior one is the National War College in Washington, D.C. It takes each year roughly fifty from the army, fifty from the navy, fifty from the air force, and fifty from civilian agencies together with a few from Canada and other NATO countries. Most of the curriculum is government and politics, diplomacy, international economics, and military strategy. The faculty is half to two-thirds civilian, some permanent and some invited in for a year or two; the rest of the faculty is recruited from among the more outstanding students. Lectures are mainly by government officials and invited academics. Additionally the army, navy, and air force have their own war colleges of comparable size.

These war colleges have a serious academic atmosphere. My first experience was in 1959, when I lectured at the Air War College. At that time the colonels in the audience were people who had either gone into the Army Air Corps in World War II straight out of high school or had interrupted their college and never returned. Few in the class of 1959 had a bachelor's degree. The student body was not entirely receptive toward civilians from college campuses who wanted to talk to them about war, mobilization, military economics, or alliance politics. A dozen years later demography had run its course, the entire student body had the equivalent of a bachelor's degree, at least a third had higher degrees in management, economics, international relations, or engineering, and some had PhDs.

There were two other academic programs for military officers. One was to send officers at the rank of colonel or navy captain to centers for advanced study like the International Institute for Strategic Studies in London, the Council on Foreign Relations in New York, the Harvard Center for International Affairs, or the MIT Center for International Studies. These people spent an academic year in an academic environment. The other was a vigorous PhD program, more active in the army and the air force than in the navy. In my thirty years at Harvard I had at least thirty young officers getting PhDs in political economy, government and politics, or economics.

One consequence of this development over the past forty years or so is that the sharp distinction that once existed between the uniformed and nonuniformed policy people in the Pentagon has been substantially smoothed over. There was a time, early in the Kennedy administration and continuing for a while into the Johnson administration, when there were reported cultural incompatibilities between senior military officers and younger civilian "whiz kids" in the Department of Defense. But, healthily, the main reaction of the military services was to see that their own people got the kind of training that would allow them to hold their own with their civilian counterparts.

■

The question arises, why should "values" obstruct consensus on health economics but not on nuclear strategy? I can only conjecture. Perhaps it was the sheer novelty and unfamiliarity of the nuclear challenge. A little history may help. Three books appeared in 1961 that epitomized an emerging consensus on what arms control should be about. Each was a group effort, and each stimulated discussion while being written. During the summer of 1960 Hedley Bull's manuscript, *The Control of the Arms Race* (Bull 1961), was circulated by the Institute for Strategic Studies in preparation for that institute's second annual conference. That same summer a study group met on the outskirts of Boston, and Morton Halperin and I produced a little book (Schelling and Halperin 1961), discussed at numerous meetings of the Harvard-MIT Seminar on Arms Control during the fall of 1960, reflecting what we took to be an emerging consensus, one that was wholly consistent with the ideas that developed around Bull's manuscript circulated for discussion by the Institute for Strategic Studies, London. And that same year Donald Brennan organized a conference that generated *Arms Control, Disarmament, and National Security* (Brennan 1961). Participants in this activity were the White House national security adviser of the new Kennedy administration, the White House science adviser, the assistant secretary of defense for international security affairs, the assistant secretary for policy planning in the State Department, and many others. Unquestionably the ABM Treaty, which was ratified in 1972, was a direct outgrowth of those studies.

If military policy is the area that has been most receptive to policy analysis in general, and economic analysis in particular, my assigned topic—environmental policy—may be at the opposite extreme.

ENVIRONMENTAL POLICY

In environmental regulation, the need for economizing ought to be beyond dispute. Together the costs incurred in the federal government's budget and the costs imposed by regulation on farm, industry, and local government are estimated in the neighborhood of a quarter of a trillion dollars annually, without counting prospective huge costs of cleaning up after fifty years of nuclear materials production. Just getting the priorities straightened out could be enormously valuable, yet for cleaning up toxic waste the Department of Defense, the Department of Energy, and the Environmental Protection Agency recently had, and probably still have, altogether different philosophies of priority.

The two main contributions of economic analysis should be, I expect, the design of procedures for comparing benefits with costs, especially at the margin, and the design of incentives to substitute for direct regulation of technology. Why have economists been so unsuccessful for a quarter century in getting acceptance of these ideas at least in principle? I can see at least two reasons.

One is that much environmental regulation, as well as regulation of safety in the workplace, is, or is perceived to be, about saving lives, that is, about preventing deaths. Life and death are a subject that many people, including legislators and administrators, believe should not be contaminated by cost considerations.

The second reason is that, at least until recently, most environmentalists in the United States, including those on the staffs of congressmen, chose to treat pollution as a criminal activity, not an activity to be governed through the marketplace. Effluent charges were despised as "licenses to pollute."

■

The American Congress has passed a number of laws that overtly prohibit regulators from achieving a reasonable relationship between the costs of their actions and the benefits. The most publicized example is something called the Delaney Amendment, enacted under the Federal Food, Drug and Cosmetic Act, which bans any substance (except tobacco) that has been proven carcinogenic at any dosage in any animal test. This provision has survived even the great hullabaloo that occurred when the Food and Drug Administration declared that Diet Coke could not contain saccharine. In many cases brought by environmentalist organizations the courts have ruled that regulatory decisions had wrongly allowed costs to be taken into account.

In cleaning toxic waste sites any explicit criteria relating to risk tend to be extremely conservative. A commonly proposed standard is that the "most exposed person" should incur no more than one-in-a-million lifetime risk of death. And this without regard to cost.

On the matter of incentives, I received an inquiry from a former student who was in the Environmental Protection Agency's Office of External Research, in the late 1970s. He wanted to know why it was that nearly all economists believed that environmental regulation could be most efficiently handled through market incentives, and hardly anybody but professional economists did—not legislators, not administrators, not environmental lobbyists. I took his money and financed four studies, one of which was an opinion survey. The researcher interviewed congressional staff, workers in both business and environmental lobbying organizations, and administrators in several Washington agencies. He found that business lobbies liked market incentives more than environmental lobbies, and Republicans liked them more than Democrats. He found that neither paid attention to efficiency considerations: those opposed to market incentives primarily wanted to avoid anything that legitimized any level of pollution, and those who favored market incentives simply preferred the impersonal market to human regulators.

WINDING UP

I was once at a conference in Norway on the global environment and was interviewed for radio by a woman who asked me what Americans thought of "green taxes." I told her that I thought most Americans had never heard the term, but if they knew what it meant most environmentalists would be against green taxes. My response was mainly based on that survey of ten years earlier, and I believe now I was wrong in the answer I gave. For reasons I do not quite understand, the tide had turned in America and environmentalists were beginning to believe, as European environmentalists had already come to believe, that market incentives were often the superior mechanism.

In the same way, the notion that life is too precious to calculate its value is beginning to give way to the notion that resources devoted to human health and safety in the environment are limited, and should be focused on where they do the most good. But in many cases there will have to be changes in legislation to make it legitimate to prefer programs that can save many lives per million dollars spent to those that spend many million dollars to save a single life.

Economics is gradually penetrating the environmental community, but two decades was a long time to wait. Maybe during the interval economists spent too much time talking to each other and too little speaking clearly and simply in public.

REFERENCES

Brennan, Donald G., ed. *Arms Control, Disarmament, and National Security*. New York: Braziller, 1961.
Bull, Hedley. *The Control of the Arms Race*. New York: Praeger, 1961.

Fuchs, Victor. "Economics, Values, and Health Care Reform." *American Economic Review* 86, no. 1 (March 1996): 1–24.

Herrnstein, Richard, and Charles Murray. *The Bell Curve.* New York: Free Press, 1994.

Schelling, Thomas, and Halperin, Morton. *Strategy and Arms Control.* New York: Twentieth Century Fund, 1961.

13

Prices as Regulatory Instruments

■ Someone who spoils his own land without affecting drainage on other property, runs noisy equipment that no one else can hear, or contaminates his own water supply is not said to create an environmental problem. The problem is said to be environmental when lead and sulfur drift downwind to make somebody sick, an oil spill washes onto a public beach, acid drainage from an abandoned mine destroys marine life, or the burning of fuels changes the regional or global climate. Environmental effects are the consequences that are outside the purview, the cost accounting, the concern, or the responsibility of identifiable producers and consumers. They are outside the pricing system (except when damage suits can make the activities costly).

The activities that have environmental impacts are of many kinds. There are beneficial activities that go unrewarded and harmful ones for which neither price nor penalty is paid. There are some so natural, like the happy voices of children a little too early in the morning, that we hesitate to complain. However, the roar of a motorcycle gets little sympathy. There are individuals who pour crankcase oil down the storm sewer or throw cigarette butts out the car window, and there are businesses, large and small, that dump their waste on land and sea and in the air. There are activities, such as driving and parking, that are unobjectionable on a modest scale but on a larger scale cause obstructions. There is illicit disposal of hazardous waste, disposal that is legal but dangerous, and unwitting disposal of things that prove harmful. There are activities, such as burning fuel to make electricity, that are bound to continue, the issue being only the scale of the activity. Other activities, such as the use of certain herbicides or pesticides, need not and ought not to continue at all. There are damaging activities that are so beneficial that the harm is incidental and no "problem" is perceived, activities that pose difficult choices because of disagreement or uncertainty whether the benefits or the damages are greater, and activities that almost without question deserve to be discouraged or stopped. And when all those with any conceivable stake in the matter or any right to participate get together and determine that some investment in the environment is not worth the cost or that some depletion is more than compensated by the benefits, they may count the quorum unmindful of all the interested parties who have not been born yet.

Most of us play many roles on the environmental stage. We are assaulted by construction and aircraft noise, offended by roadside advertisements, endangered by lead and mercury, and delayed by double-parked vehicles. Our children are threatened by broken glass when they go barefoot. But somebody else is offended by our children's bare feet, and if that broken bottle wasn't ours we may have seen it and neglected to remove it before it got broken. We ourselves contribute to the Christmas-shopping congestion. Our chamber music annoys the teenager as much as her rap music bothers us. We rarely ask our neighbors what color they would like us to paint our houses. Some of us smoke and used to inflict disagreeable or toxic substances on others in elevators; some of us quit and chew gum, which may smell as bad as cigarette smoke. And if our automobile is fully insured against theft we may carelessly let it be stolen and abandoned or burned in a vacant lot. We complain about the high price of electricity while the utility companies try to keep costs down by avoiding expensive smoke abatement. We patronize an economical laundry that pours chemicals down the sewer. We pay higher prices for oysters without knowing that, whether or not the oystermen are suffering from pollution, the oysters are and it makes them expensive.

It takes some analysis to identify victims and beneficiaries. When electric utility companies are required for the sake of health, comfort, and agriculture downwind to clean up the hot gas that comes out of the smokestacks, it is not easy to figure out who is going to pay for those downwind benefits. A good guess is that, taking all the coal-burning electric utilities together, it will not be their stockholders. Electric rates are set by public boards and commissions that determine what costs are deductible and what rate of return is appropriate, and most of the cost is passed along to customers. Some of the customers will be industries; they, too, will pass most of the rate increases along to their customers. If the industries use much electricity, business may suffer some and wage increases will be less forthcoming or property-tax assessments less aggressive; and all the results are as complex as locating the ultimate incidence of a tax on electricity or on the coal used in utilities' boilers.

These complications remind us that efforts to preserve or improve the environment, protect against hazards, and abate the degradation of soil and forests and other resources entail a mix of gains and losses and of gainers and losers. And neither the aggregate size of gains and losses nor their distribution among gainers and losers is transparent. The distributional issues—who gains and who loses, by income size or region or occupation—are not easy to discern and are sometimes contrary to intuition. Even the relative magnitudes of gains and losses (those that accrue to individuals and those that are thought of as social values) are not easy to estimate. Not only is the analyst or observer hard put to be sure who is affected by how much in which direction, but even the victim of environmental damage (and the beneficiary of protective measures), like the beneficiary of environmental permissiveness, can be unaware of the magnitude of his gain or loss—even unaware of any concern in the matter. And those on whom the costs of environmental protection initially fall can have an exaggerated sense of being the ultimate victim of environmental policy, not recognizing how many of the costs get passed along to customers or suppliers.

Although this kind of analysis is difficult in practice, the theory with which to think about externalities is well developed. And in theoretical terms it matters little whether the externality in question is one that we would call environmental. Nevertheless, in assessing those impingements of people's activities on the welfare of others that are mediated by the physical environment, there are some elements that the theory of externalities cannot handle. The reason is that the theory is neutral toward the moral significance of activities and events, and excludes values that cannot ultimately be assessed in individual welfare.

Specifically, economic theory evaluates actions by their consequences and by the way the consequences are valued by the people who benefit or suffer, not by whether they are inherently good or evil or according to the spirit in which they are done. However, for many people concerned about the environment, activities are not adequately measured by a summation of individual gains and losses. That there is no one to speak for a particular endangered species or for the Earth itself does not, for some people, imply that, because nobody has a stake in the matter, there is no matter. And certain actions that can do grievous injury to innocent people or other living things are not always assessed (and possibly dismissed) according to the amounts of harm that accrue to individuals. An offense may be unpardonable independent of its consequences.

Environmental concerns are loaded with additional weight because they occasionally, as with climate, pose the possible risk of irreversible damage of an immensity difficult to agree on. And they entail chemical and biological hazards capable of causing, on a large or a small scale, those most awesome human tragedies, death and fetal abnormality.

EXTERNALITIES AND SOCIAL CONTROLS

So it is that people and businesses engage in activities that use up something scarce that doesn't belong to them, spoil something in which others have a legitimate interest, or harm other people directly. Or they do these things immoderately when on a modest scale they might be excused. And they can do it because they do not know they are doing it, or they know but do not care, or they know and care but have a conflicting interest of their own, or they do not know how to moderate their activities or redirect them in less harmful ways. They may enjoy the anonymity that allows them to get away with it, or they may regret their inability to identify their victims and make amends. And activities beneficial to the environment may go unrewarded for similar reasons.

Thus arises the need for some social control, some inducement to curtail or moderate the harmful activities or to enhance the beneficial ones. The generic term *environmental protection* implies that it is the harmful activities that deserve most urgent attention.

Self-Controls

For want of a better term we refer to the various ways environmental policy is implemented as *social controls*. The term has to include what might better be called *self-controls,* which are much relied on in social policy. It must include education that generates awareness and knowledge of the consequences of actions or the availability of alternatives. It includes prohibitions, regulations, fees, charges, tax incentives, and methods of enforcement. And it includes what may be done through private negotiation, civil law, and informal cooperative arrangements.

Unquestionably a large part of environmental protection depends on decency, considerateness, and self-control. Some of the most powerful social controls work through habit and etiquette. Four generations ago spitting was common, even indoors, and sanitary protection took the form of strategically placed containers; more recently, many elevator entrances were guarded by containers of white sand for the receipt of burning cigarettes. Three generations ago the spittoon had disappeared, but "No spitting" signs were everywhere, even on streetcars, and violations of the no-spitting ordinance were threatened by fines the way littering from a car window is today. One generation ago spitting had ceased to be a menace, probably because the technology of nicotine ingestion had shifted from plug to cigarette. Then butts became the problem and ashtrays the solution. Today the emphasis has shifted from the debris of smoking to the smoke itself. We have gone from "No spitting" to "No smoking" in half a century. The same was true of spitting seventy-five years ago, though, and today it is not the fear of that $50 fine that keeps people from throwing litter out the car window.

Considerateness and self-control deserve emphasis. A propensity for civilized behavior is a precious resource for protecting our environment, and the more overt social controls should be compatible with preserving that widespread sense of personal responsibility on which, especially in densely populated areas, we all depend so much.

Overt Controls

The more overt controls take a variety of forms. There are prohibitions on the transport of dangerous chemicals and regulations on where campfires may be lit, when noise may be made, how wastes may be disposed of, how much gas may be emitted, how many deer may be killed, what ingredients may be used in a pesticide, how fast a car may travel, how loud a noise may be, and what unsightly or dangerous objects may not be left in a public place. These can be enforced by fines, imprisonment, tax penalties, or loss of licenses and privileges.

Then there are the fees and charges collected at parking meters, toll booths, and entrances to national parks. There are tax credits for saving energy, weight-related license fees on heavy trucks, federal subsidies for municipal waste disposal, and even bounties for vermin and old containers picked up and delivered. (In some places there are finders' fees for leftover explosives from earlier wars.) And there is the civil justice system that allows private citizens to bring suit against those whose environmentally offending activities, licit or illicit, violate their rights and inflict harm. And the ballot box is a medium of social control when government is the offending party.

There are many ways to classify these media of control. They can be formal and legal or informal and voluntary, rigid or flexible, enforced or merely promoted, based on negative or positive sanctions, aimed at activities or substances or damages, universal or specialized, and with different degrees of reliance on citizen enforcement or enforcement by police power.

This chapter is about a particular set of measures of social control— measures of a kind familiar in some contexts and unfamiliar, even alien, in others. They are sometimes described as economic incentives, sometimes as measures that work through the price system. A list of measures of this kind would include fees and charges, subsidies, rewards, indemnities, auctions, the assignment of property rights, and the creation of markets. Familiar examples are parking meters and bottle deposits, income-tax credits for home insulation, stimulated markets in recycled paper, and low-interest loans on solar home-heating systems. Less familiar and more controversial are fees, fines, or taxes on the sulfur emissions of electric utilities, on airport noise, and on the venting of noxious fumes. Attempts to generate markets in which new firms that cannot operate without emitting into the atmosphere some quantities of regulated substances can buy the rights of existing and former firms, which in turn discontinue equivalent emissions, are a more recent innovation, as is the proposed "carcass deposit" on new automobiles, which would be refunded at the end of a car's life to whoever disposed of the remains at an approved site.

Pricing Systems

The distinguishing characteristic of these measures is not just the payment of money in consideration of damage done, resources depleted, or environmental benefits conferred. I exclude from this study the widely advertised fines for mutilating subway seats, throwing trash out a car window, or letting one's pet do what is known in London as "fouling the footpath." Fines levied on or damage payments collected from companies that carelessly or surreptitiously dump hazardous substances illicitly in rivers and ponds and vacant lots are not what I mean by prices, even though the anticipation of a fine may add an economic incentive for staying within the law. And rewards paid for information leading to the arrest and conviction of whoever set the woods on fire, defaced public property, or dumped toxic waste by the roadside at night, however much economic incentive is intended in getting people to do their clear public duty, are not what I would call price mechanisms.

The distinction is illustrated by the difference between a *fee* and a *fine*, or between a *charge* and a *penalty*. It is typical of fees and charges (whether a fee is collected on an activity or paid for its performance) that no moral or legal prejudice attaches to the fee itself or the action on which or for which it is paid. The behavior is discretionary. The fee offers an option: Pay it and deposit your rubbish here or take your rubbish elsewhere; pay it and park here or drive someplace else; pay it and swim at the public beach or don't swim. Whether used to cover the cost of cleaning up afterward, to maintain a public facility, to keep the facility from being overcrowded, or to indemnify those who may be discomfited or whose productivity is adversely affected, a fee entitles one to what one has paid for. It is not levied in anger, it does not tarnish one's record, and even if paid to cover damages it is not expected to be paid grudgingly and received resentfully. But a fine that is paid upon conviction for an offense does not erase the offense. "Paying one's debt to society" is not an apt metaphor. There is no thought that society breaks even when someone serves a prison term or pays a fine. The conviction stays on the books; the law has been violated and the behavior is reprehended.

The distinction is clear in principle, even though fines for traffic violations are modest in amount, excused or reduced for the first few offenses, and not counted as a police record. There may be cases in which willingness to pay a fine is a test of personal urgency, and the violation is publicly condoned or legally excused. But even then the action usually has to be excusable on its merits; the paying of the fine is only an earnest of seriousness and not a license for misbehavior.

Decentralized Decisions

The essence of a pricing system is that it leaves the decision to pay or not to pay to whoever confronts the price. The price is there to be paid—not to stand as a warning, an act of redemption, or an admission of liability. A pricing mechanism decentralizes the decisions. A central authority may determine the price, but paying or not paying is a decentralized choice. In contrast, a central authority determines that you may not park in front a hydrant—not you, not anybody, not for an hour, not for five minutes, not to make a phone call, not to go to the bathroom. The fine is an enforcement device. It may be calculated to deter; it may be thought commensurate with the offense; but there is no intention that, with the fine for an offense set, it is now freely up to you whether or not to park there.

In a similar way, some taxes on damaging behaviors are excluded from the category of price mechanisms. A tax intended to reduce some consumption or activity may embody disapproval and be equivalent to an imperfectly enforced prohibition. A tax is described as punitive when its political motivation makes it akin to a fine. (Taxes on liquor and tobacco reflect disapproval.) There are other taxes that are reminiscent of fees and charges because they are related to wear and tear or damage generated by the taxed activity, or to the cost of providing facilities for the activity. Gasoline taxes earmarked for public roads are like indirect fees to maintain highways.

What is crucial about a price is not merely that it is devoid of ethical significance or that it allows freedom of choice. A price is a *measure*. In the marketplace a price on a voluntary transaction must cover the cost of performance or provision, or represent adequate compensation. The transaction is voluntary. The price paid for a bottle of cola must cover the cost of labor, materials, energy, and anything else that went into producing it, delivering it, and handling it up to the time of sale. If people will not pay enough to cover those costs, we conclude that the drink is not worth what it costs; the labor, materials, and energy will be used elsewhere to produce things that consumers do consider worth the cost. And if the cost of cola delivered to the neighborhood store is well within the prices that consumers will pay, and if no single firm has a monopoly, we expect competition to produce all the cola that people want at a price that covers its cost. Thus, the amount of cola produced and sold will be the amount that consumers find worth the cost, where the cost reflects the alternative uses of the resources that go into making and bottling and distributing cola. The price serves simultaneously as a measure of the worth of the resources that go into the cola and the worth of the cola to consumers (more accurately, the worth when *that* amount of cola is being consumed—smaller quantities are valued more highly, whereas additional quantities would be worth less than the cost; otherwise people would be buying more).

Sometimes prices reflect a scarcity value. Most cities regulate the number of taxicabs. Under the medallion system there is some fixed number of licenses. Medallions are salable, like seats on the stock exchange, and the question of who drives the taxis is thus decentralized to the marketplace. There is a going price in each city. A medallion must be worth at least that price to its owner (because he has the option of selling), and must be worth less than that to anyone else (because otherwise somebody would bid the price up until the number of people to whom medallions were worth that much was the same as the number of medallions).

Thus, what is decentralized when goods and services and privileges are "priced" is decisions about who consumes or produces a service, which services are produced and consumed, where or when, and how much. Actually, nobody ever decides how much cola should be produced or consumed; each individual decides only how much he or she will produce or consume. For taxi medallions there is a centralized decision on how many, but the market determines who.

To translate the examples of cola and medallions into the environmental area, we can think of "bottle bills" requiring a deposit to be paid on returnable containers for beer and soda. Two generations ago beer and soda were sold in returnable containers. Most of us gave little thought to whether, having paid the deposit, we owned the bottles or had merely rented them and pledged with a small deposit to return

174   ECONOMICS AND SOCIAL POLICY

them. No matter. We paid enough deposit to cover a replacement if we lost or broke or kept the bottle. There were children who would collect bottles for profit if we thought them not worth transporting back to the store. And if we lost or broke one we never had to say we were sorry; the price covered the cost. Neither the store nor the manufacturer cared what we did with the bottle.

But somebody did care, or does now. Broken, the bottle was a nuisance, and intact it was unsightly. If I left a broken bottle on your sidewalk, I had paid for the bottle, but not for cleaning your sidewalk, or repairing your bicycle tire, or treating your dog's paw. But because the bottles cost money I was careful, and if I left behind an unbroken bottle some youngster might retrieve it and redeem it at the store for two cents before it got broken. Now that our standard of living is so high and the technology of disposable containers so cheap that most of us prefer throwaways, the failure of the price of the bottle to reflect the costs of cleaning up or the compensation for damage done is a greater discrepancy than it used to be. The deposit on a returnable container has been reinvented for regulatory use.

Actually the deposit, as a control mechanism, need not be associated with reuseable containers or even recyclable materials. And a deposit need not even be money; one could leave one's name, address, and Social Security number and be subject to a fine for failure to return the bottle or an equivalent amount of broken glass. The deposit system is just an artful convenience. It is a system of decentralized automatic enforcement. It imposes a penalty that is devoid of ethical significance for any bottles not returned. And because bottles may conveniently be returned to stores that handle bottled goods, and the same trucks that bring fresh drinks can carry empties back where they came from, reuse is an economical byproduct of the enforcement scheme.

Price determination. But how much should the deposit be? At a minimum it should cover the cost of the container, of course; else the consumer is not even paying for the contents. And if, having paid a deposit that covers the replacement cost, consumers husband their bottles and return them faithfully, the problem is solved. If instead they leave them in large numbers at the beach and on the sidewalk, we want a larger deposit to induce a higher rate of return. If we collect a nickel a bottle and it makes no difference, we know that the nuisance of returning empties is equivalent to more than a nickel a bottle for most consumers. Somebody is getting revenue without much being accomplished. We could raise the deposit to $1 a bottle and the return rate might reach 100 percent. The system does not cost people anything in money outlays, because, the cost of wasting bottles being so high, they are not wasting them and paying any money. They are losing only the interest on a few dollars' investment. But we have no measure of the trouble people are going to to preserve their bottles; $1 merely sets an upper limit. (And if we were hoping to get a little money into a cleanup kitty from the unclaimed deposits, we are not getting it.) If $1 seems high enough to be punitive, we can think of it as a penalty rather than a price.

We could even make the deposit $5 per bottle, so that a six-pack would cost as much as a major traffic violation. At that point the deposit would clearly not be a price. It might still be a splendid method of enforcing a ban on littering. Nobody would have to make a citizen's arrest of a litterer, bring the discarded bottle for evidence, and take up a court's time for the imposition of a fine; it would all be handled automatically by the deposit, as long as we didn't insist on criminal records. But at $5 we would surely not be setting the price at which we are indifferent to whether the customer forgoes the deposit for the convenience of wasting his bottle or returns it to get his money back.

One other way of deciding on the deposit is to ask at what price people would be indifferent about whether to return the bottle or not. A possibility is that discarded bottles, at a certain price, will be profitably collected by people, such as some of the homeless or the Boy Scouts, who retrieve them and bring them to the collection stations. If at 15¢ all the bottles show up, we can excuse the people who leave bottles around, because by forfeiting their deposits they have paid for the cleanup. And if the bottles are not all retrieved but we can afford cleanup crews with the unclaimed deposits, again we may not care whether people return their bottles or pay in advance for the cleanup. These possibilities suggest the kind of deposit we might characterize as a price and why, having set a price, we might be content to let everybody decide for himself whether to pay the price and waste the bottle or save the price and return it.

This discussion does not settle how we should deal with the bottle problem; it only indicates what distinguishes a price system from other modes of regulation, including others that entail payments of money.

Specifically, there is no implication here that we have to be ethically neutral about social behavior with beer and soda bottles. Also, there is no a priori assurance that any moderate price would cover the cost of cleanup. Furthermore, we may be attracted to a high deposit if the proceeds cover more than cleanup costs and leave us a balance for other purposes, especially if the people who forfeit deposits are people we do not mind taxing. If cleanup proves impossible, it may be hard to agree on the size of the indemnity to the local community that we would like people to pay in the form of forfeited deposits. And in all of this our evaluation may depend on how the forfeited deposits may legally be spent.

Allocating a fixed supply.   Taxi medallions have counterparts wherever overcrowding is a problem. Taxis may be limited for the benefit of taxi owners, with results not altogether in the interests of their passengers, but the same principle of "marketable rights" has application to congestion or any threatened overuse of some limited capacity or facility. Parking is an example.

With medallions, there is a decision by a central authority on how many cabs might operate, but the question of whose cabs is left to the market. With downtown parking, a central authority may determine how many permits will be issued or how many spaces made available, or exactly where parking will be permitted, and then rather than choose who gets to park or where each person parks, or schedule individuals over the hours of the day or the days of the week, the authorities can let prices take care of those decisions. There are numerous ways. A familiar one is to install meters with rates low enough to keep spaces from going unused but high enough not to attract drivers in numbers much greater than the spaces available. If a uniform meter price leaves outlying spaces unused and centrally located spaces inadequate, higher prices can be set on the meters where spaces are in greater demand. Alternatively, where people regularly park all day every day, windshield stickers can be sold—again at a price not so high that spaces go unused or so low that too many stickers are demanded, leaving favoritism by issuing clerks to determine which drivers get the stickers. (If the stickers are permanent, it is important that a person who no longer needs one, or would rather have the money than the parking privilege, be able to turn his sticker in for cash or to sell it.)

The price of parking does not in this case cover the cost of providing parking, but rather allocates a fixed supply. It ensures that spaces go to those to whom they are worth the most in money. The appeal of the system may therefore depend on what is done with the proceeds. The advantages of the system are the following:

It makes parking more orderly and eliminates congestion.

The costs of searching and waiting—costs that are "paid" by drivers but not received by any authorities—are minimized.

People can make plans and arrive on time.

The system is impersonal; there are no favors and no bureaucracy.

Those who get the spaces pay for them, and those who do not (to whom the spaces were evidently worth less than the money others were willing to pay) can in principle be beneficiaries of whatever is done with the proceeds.

Even the resident of a side street in a town that assigns each resident a parking space on his own street might wish in principle to have a meter installed in his own name so that the space need not go unused when his own car is elsewhere, and so that, if he would rather make other arrangements (such as disposing of his car and using taxis instead) and enjoy the profits from his meter, the space would be more productive.

Thus the price attached to a parking space can be taken as an approximate measure of what some additional spaces would be worth. If the current meter or sticker rate is enough to cover the cost of additional parking, that is a signal that additional parking can be provided at no net cost to the authorities. If parking areas can be sold or leased for more than the net return from meters and stickers, somebody else has a more valuable use for the parking space, and the town is losing money by pricing the parking at less than the land is worth. If permanent parking medallions were issued, and could not be recalled without breach of faith, the arithmetic indicates that the town could cover the cost of buying back enough medallions to retrieve the land from parking and make it available for alternative use.

Discrimination by price. Parking spaces go to the people who can afford them. Whether their parking needs are especially urgent, or driving and parking saves them more money than it saves others, or they are merely wealthier, they get the spaces because they are willing to pay. The apparent discrimination is moderated by the fact that the wealthier the parkers are, the higher the price may go and the more the town can collect. We may nevertheless be tempted to offer spaces free, or at reduced rates, to the poor. A relevant if not decisive consideration should be that because they are poor they would evidently rather have the money than the parking. We might give them parking tokens and expect them to trade them in for cash. If we give them a "property right" that they can enjoy only by driving and parking, they have something less valuable than if they could trade it at a price at which they would rather have the money. There may be good reasons why that could not be done, and why neither the equivalent cash nor the transferable right is feasible; nevertheless, providing parking to someone who would not or could not pay for it is providing something the beneficiary values less than a share in the proceeds from an indiscriminate pricing system.

■

In closing this extended discussion of bottles and parking, which has been intended only to illuminate what is meant by *prices,* I acknowledge that these examples were picked because they are ideal illustrations that epitomize a wide range of activities to which the same principles apply. However, they are not typical. They are easy cases. Automobiles are large, easily recognizable objects; each is a discrete unit; each has an owner of record; cars are never confused with bicycles; they arrive and depart under their own power; tamperproof meters can be bought for a price that makes them a good investment; spaces are locally interchangeable and nobody needs to care which space within a block he occupies; and the money involved is not worth arguing about. Applying the same principle to pets in a public park might not be feasible. Similarly with the bottles. In the abstract, the principle applies to Kleenex, cigarette butts, candy wrappers, and eggshells, but we don't expect it to work for them.

PRICING SYSTEMS

For an economist, markets and prices play a central role. Environmental effects are effects that escape the market. They are outside the price system and "external" to the accounts of the participants. The economist diagnoses environmental problems, therefore, as a failure of the pricing system or the market.

People concerned with information, education, morals, civil law or law enforcement, and norms, traditions, and informal social controls characterize or diagnose environmental problems from their own perspectives. They see the problems as failures of information, of education, of self-control and public-spiritedness, of administration, of social norms, or of the legal system. Each emphasizes the absence of whatever his own profession looks to in the exercise of social control. More than that, each will seek a solution by repairing or extending or creating a price system, an information system, an administrative system, an adjudicatory system, or a system of ethics and morality according to what his own discipline understands best. There is nothing necessarily wrong with that unless each supposes his own perspective to be uniquely correct. They cannot all be right.

Two things can be said confidently about extending the price system as a way of bringing environmental problems under control. One is that there is indubitably a role for prices. Numerous successes can be pointed out. A good part of the development of economic institutions has been bringing what used to be externalities into the market system by the conferring and protection of property rights and the enforcement of contracts, by the availability of better information, and by technological development that facilitates marketing. The second is that some environmental problems are bound to remain beyond the reach of even the most ingenious efforts to create or extend markets. Indeed, there is a presumption that it is going to be difficult to bring additional effects into the market system; if it were easy, it would have already been done.

It is not enough to propose that airlines be charged for the noise aircraft make on takeoff and landing. There has to be a way to measure the noises made by different aircraft and to stipulate what the price should be, what to do with the proceeds, what authority will enforce the price system, what new safety or air-pollution problems may emerge as airlines reduce noise to reduce costs, how the local property values and taxes will change, and how fares and travel will be affected.

There is great variety in the pricing methods that can be and have been used in regulating activities that affect the environment. In recent years, attention has focused on what are usually called *effluent charges* or *emission charges* (largely because of the dominant importance of air and water pollution from stationary sources, partly because of specific proposals that became controversial). Pricing for environmental protection is not wholly or even mainly about emission charges, but they are currently the most familiar, controversial, and important policy alternatives.

Emission charges are furthermore a prototype for examination, despite the risk of reinforcing the misapprehension that they represent everything that pricing for environmental protection is about. Most of the questions about pricing (including the always crucial question "What alternative do you have in mind?") can be discussed in connection with emission charges. Most of the claims that can be made for the advantages of pricing can be illustrated, as well as the weaknesses and objections. So an examination of just what makes pricing mechanisms attractive to some people and unattractive to others, when and where they can be expected to work well or poorly or not at all, and where and when they have advantages over other more centralized and "regulatory" methods will emerge from an examination of the pricing of emissions.

I begin by exploring the different kinds of emission charges—what they are expected to accomplish, how they are imposed and administered, what activities and decisions are intended to be influenced by the charges, how the charges ought to be determined, and what alternative methods of regulation they should be compared with—and by straightening out the language. An *effluent* is something that flows out or flows forth, according to the dictionary, such as the outflow of a sewer, a drainpipe, a storage tank, or a pipeline. In environmental matters, effluents include smoke and gas as well as liquids. The term is readily extended to become synonymous with *emission,* which includes radiation, particulate matter, and even biological organisms and sometimes solid waste. In other words, almost anything that goes down the drain, up the stack, through the walls, or out the window, or that comes out the exhaust pipe, will be called an emission or an effluent. And the generic term *emission* then extends to aircraft noise, electromagnetic radiation, and heat from a cooling tower. Often (but not always—exhaust fumes and engine noise have been mentioned), stationary sources are implied. *Emission* or *effluent* also implies a regular product or byproduct of some process in which the emitted substance is an expected consequence; oil spills and explosions are not generally connoted. These terms exclude things that are carted away in containers or otherwise under control; slag, sludge, garbage, and spent reactor fuel conducted away by train, truck, or conveyor belt, and things safely contained underground or in storage structures, are not referred to as emissions. The image is of something that escapes containment and diffuses into the atmosphere or water or is otherwise broadcast, disseminated, or let loose. *Emission* and *effluent* are generic rather than specific. *Auto emissions,* for example, can refer to everything that escapes from tailpipe or engine or just to the particular exhaust components that are candidates for control. The *effluent* from an anchored fishing boat may be everything flushed into the water or only what is harmful or undesirable. *Smokestack emissions* may mean all the hot gases, or only those that do harm, or only those that have been identified as harmful or targeted for control.

Assume for illustration a charge that is not conceived as a source of revenue or as a penalty for violating some regulation. The charge is intended as a cost to the firm or individual (to simplify the image and the terminology, think of a plant belonging to a business firm) that attaches to one of the "outputs." Firms usually pay for their inputs: materials, fuel, electricity, labor, repair services, and the like. Sometimes they pay taxes on their output. They pay property taxes on fixed installations and they pay fees to operate. An effluent or emission charge is simply another cost that attaches to their production—this one a cost on the amount of some output the firm produces. It is an output, however, to which ordinarily no value attaches, or not enough to make the substance worth recapturing. The output or outflow is usually an unavoidable byproduct.

The alternatives to the charge are to leave the emission unregulated and to regulate it by what are usually called "regulatory standards." The alternative kinds of regulatory standards might be

- a limit on total emissions per day or per year,
- a limit on the emission per unit of legitimate input or output, such as on the sulfur emitted per kilowatt-hour produced, per million BTU of heat used, or per ton of coal burned,

- a prescribed reduction in total emission, or emission per unit, below some traditional level,
- a stipulated change in some input, such as pounds of sulfur per ton of coal or oil consumed, and
- a prescribed change in the mode of combustion or the equipment employed.

These might be varied according to season or wind direction or current air quality, if short-run variation is economical enough to bother with. And the limits may or may not vary with the plant's location; that is, plants located where more people or more crops or more wild animals are affected, or where the people and the crops and the wildlife are more vulnerable, may or may not be regulated differently.

The first thing to ask about a charge system is what the charge is imposed on. A second is what determines the amount of the charge (how many dollars per pound or per cubic foot of something). A third is how the charge will be administered. The object of the charge is to change the quantity, quality, or distribution by time and place of the emission. At the outset we can assume that the desired effects on emissions are basically the same with the charge system as with one of the other kinds of regulation. That is, if we had wanted, with alternative methods of control, to reduce total emissions, to even out emissions over time to prevent peaking of airborne concentrations, to induce relocation of plants downwind or downwater from population centers, or to stimulate new technologies that produced cleaner emissions, those are still central objectives with the charge system. The objectives need not be absolutely identical; there will be things that could be done with the proceeds of a charge system that, though they could be done with budgeted funds under an alternative regulatory regime, would receive different emphasis. But generally we should assume that there is some environmental problem to whose solution the charges and the other regulatory methods are alternative means.

There will be differences in strategy, because in the one case we are dealing with economic markets. An example might be the number of firms. Suppose we are dealing with an industrial location and an emission that has harmful effects over a local area, so that in principle the controls can be administered locally. What difference will it make whether there is one firm, or two, or ten, or a hundred? There could be a single large electric utility, two chemical plants, a dozen firms in the same light industry, or a hundred gasoline stations or laundries. There might be negotiation between the regulating agency and the regulated firms, and individual firms might keep an eye on other firms to get an idea of the rigor with which regulations are being enforced. But suppose a regulating agency were to limit emissions by auctioning permits, each permit allowing some quantity per month. Auctions work very differently according to whether there is a sole buyer, two or three who are both rivals and associates, ten organized in a trade association, or a hundred service stations. A single buyer at an auction places a low bid and takes everything; two or three buyers may collude on low bids, or compete fiercely to put each other out of business, or see an emissions quota as a way of sharing markets and restraining competition in a way the antitrust laws cannot prevent. A hundred service stations may compete and drive the price up to where, at that cost of emitting the substance, further output would be unprofitable.

So the way a charge system works will depend, among other things, on market structure. In general, characteristics of the activity that matter little for other modes of regulation may matter much for charge systems, and vice versa.

For simplicity, imagine a large number of plants (not necessarily identical in what they produce and how they produce it) that all emit a noxious substance. The emissions of each plant are susceptible to measurement, but once in the air the emissions of all the plants become mixed. Damage is not attributable to individual firms, but the emissions of every plant affect the total. How would a charge system work?

This is an easy case. We have an identified culprit (the noxious emission). We can monitor each plant. Only the total of the emissions matters, since the emissions are alike and commingled. All the plants are within a single jurisdiction, the same one in which the victim population resides. Our primary objective is to reduce total emissions, preferably in a manner that treats individual sources "fairly." More accurate, we want to limit the harm the emissions do; but we do that by reducing the emissions.

There are two alternatives to consider in what we know about the "damage function," about the way the severity of the damages relates to the total quantity of the noxious gas. One is that we know how much damage a unit of that noxious substance does, and we can put a money value on that damage. If we can value the damage caused by a pound of the substance without stipulating what the total is to which that pound is added, the damage function must be linear—proportionate to the total quantity. In that case we will probaby want to relate the charge to the damage, perhaps charging each plant for its contribution to the damage. The other possibility is that we begin with an idea of how much of the substance we are willing to allow and then set a charge that keeps total emissions within that limit. A possibility is that damages remain moderate up to a certain concentration and thereafter mount rapidly ("nonlinearly")—perhaps after a certain concentration is reached the atmosphere can no longer be refreshed by wind and rain. Or possibly, without any knowledge of how to assess damage, a target (an aggregate allowed quantity) has simply been set, and we want whatever price will get emissions down within that predetermined limit. The price that goes with that quantity can then be estimated. Permits can be issued at that price, and if the price turns out to be too high or too low to generate that demand for permits, the price can be adjusted up or down.

Alternatively, an auction can dispose of the target number of permits. The auction is merely a way of finding the price that corresponds to that quantity of emissions. Once the price has been found, if conditions do not change abruptly the auction can be dispensed with. Prices can be adjusted up or down when the demand for emission permits exceeds or falls short of the target quantity.

In principle there should be no difference between setting a price and letting demand determine the quantity of emissions and setting a quantity and letting demand determine the price to be paid. If we knew the demand curve—the schedule of prices corresponding to different quantities, or that of quantities corresponding to different prices (which is the same thing)—we would simply pick a price-quantity combination. The difference between the two methods of price setting is significant only when the price-quantity relation is uncertain. At the outset, if one is surer of the correct quantity than of the associated price, the auction-type technique is helpful; if one is surer of the appropriate price than of the quantity that would be allowed, the price can be stipulated and the quantity allowed to emerge. When damages are nonlinear in the total of emissions and rise rapidly beyond some concentration, setting the right quantity (short of the rapid rise in damage) will be the main interest. When damages are proportionate to total emissions, a predetermined limit will usually be of less interest than finding the right level of charges.

Now let us see how the result with a charge system differs from that with the more directly regulatory regime.

In both cases emissions have been reduced. One conspicuous difference is that in one case funds have been collected that are equivalent to the permit price times the remaining quantity of emissions. (And if the price corresponds to an estimate of the damage per pound of emission, the funds are equivalent to the estimated damage.) We will consider in a moment what might usefully be done with those funds. There is also the question of what may legally be done with them—whether they revert to the treasury, are directed by law to particular uses, or go into some environmental-protection budget.

Are emissions in the aggregate reduced the same amount? The answer depends quite simply on whether, if a quantity was determined and the price was allowed to emerge in the market, the quantity was the same that would have been allowed under a regulatory regime. If the basic determination was not of a quantity but of a price related to the estimated damage per pound, and if under the regulatory regime the regulatory standards would not have been arrived at through an implicit calculation of the quantity up to which the economic benefits to producers and consumers would equal or exceed the estimated damages, the quantity may well be different. It may be larger or it may be smaller. And if the regulatory regime would have established not a ceiling on the total amount of emissions but some ratio of allowed emissions per unit of product or per unit of activity or per unit combustion of fuel, we would have to examine and predict the reactions of individual firms under those regulations to arrive at an estimate of what the quantity might have been under the alternative regulatory regime.

Several things will be different. A striking difference will likely be that emissions produced by individual firms will not be the same. Indeed, a key result of the charge system is that it concentrates reductions among the firms best able to reduce emissions, since unit costs are higher for the firms least able to get emissions down.

Another likely difference is that the techniques of abatement or the methods of production that give rise to the emission in the first place may differ. Under the charge system each firm is free to reduce emissions the cheapest way it knows how. Under a regulatory regime the technology for abatement might have been specified.

A related difference in the overall result is that under the charge system less of the result was determined by regulation, more by decision of individual firms.

Will firms like the charge system better than the less flexible regulatory procedure? The answer is in several parts. Some firms may like it better and others not. Much depends on the markets in which firms sell their products, and on whether the firms are in competition with each other. Whether firms prefer charges will depend on the shape of the abatement function—not only how costly it is to reduce emissions by a small amount, but how much the cost per unit abatement rises as emissions are further reduced. Another part of the answer is that it will depend on what is done with the money collected. Finally, it will depend on whether the total of allowed emissions is more or less than would have been allowed under the alternative regime. It is instructive to look at these different parts of the answer.

That some firms will prefer a charge system and some will not is easily demonstrated. Suppose emissions with the charge are half the original quantity and the alternative would have been that every firm would have had to reduce emission by half. Firms will reduce emissions if that is cheaper than paying the price and will pay the price if that is cheaper than reducing emissions. Specifically, each firm can be presumed to have reduced emissions as long as reduction was cheaper than paying the price, and to have settled at a level of abatement at which further reduction would have been more costly than the permission to abate. Since the price charged for emissions is (we are assuming here) uniform among firms, all those emissions will have ceased whose elimination was cheaper than the price. So the aggregate abatement will have been achieved at the lowest possible total cost. Firms for which abatement was less costly will have reduced emissions rather than pay; firms for which abatement was more costly will have paid. Costs will have risen least in the firms able to abate most cheaply— precisely the firms that under a uniform 50 percent reduction would have done it at least cost. Any firm having reduced emissions more than 50 percent will have incurred the costs of reducing by 50 percent and in addition the costs of some further abatement, and will be paying charges only on the remaining emissions. So the cost to that firm will be more than the cost of 50 percent reduction but less than the cost to other firms that found abatement so costly they are paying and emitting at more than half the original rate. Firms that could have abated 50 percent only at much higher costs may be better off than at 50 percent abatement, even though they pay the charge on 100 percent of their emissions.

As mentioned above, the preferences of firms for the pricing technique might depend on what was done with the proceeds. It is easily seen that if the proceeds could be returned in some fashion to the firms or used for their benefit, they will collectively have saved money compared with the no-charge scheme in which each firm had to abate 50 percent. This follows from the fact that abatement costs in total were less than if every firm had had to effect a 50 percent reduction. On average the reduction was 50 percent, but most of the reduction occurred in the firms where reduction was cheaper than average. The total cost, the sum of abatement costs plus the price on remaining emissions, can be either more or less than it would have been under a uniform 50 percent reduction. (If there are many firms for which such a reduction would have been prohibitive, paying the charge may be so much cheaper for those firms that the total for all firms is substantially less than in the other case. On the other hand, if the abatement functions for all firms are sufficiently similar that they all reduced emissions approximately 50 percent, they have all paid about the same abatement costs as under the other regime, and in addition they are paying the charge on the remaining 50 percent.) Thus any excess cost of the pricing scheme over the uniform 50 percent reduction is less than the funds collected (if the costs of administering the system did not eat deeply into the funds).

The money could not simply be refunded, or firms anticipating the refund would treat the charges as zero. But enough money would have been collected in emission charges to make it possible to reduce some non-emission-related tax to which the firms were subject. This would not interfere with the price incentive, and on balance the firms collectively would come out ahead compared with the uniform 50 percent alternative. There is no magic in this; it follows simply from the fact that the pricing system induces abatement by those firms that can accomplish it most cheaply. The firms collectively reduce the cost of abatement, saving money. So it is no surprise that any excess total cost, due to actual payments, is exceeded by the money collected.

The final point was that firms may prefer the pricing scheme or not according as the total reduction in emissions is more or less than it otherwise would have been. There are two important reasons—pointing in opposite directions—why the pricing scheme would lead to a different total abatement. Both reasons are based on the idea that any determination of how much emissions ought to be reduced is bound to depend on some estimate of how costly it will be to reduce them. Whether or not there is an explicit comparison of costs and benefits, any reduced level of emissions is a target for further reduction if cost is no object. Consider the simple "linear" case: If there were some substance that was harmful in proportion to its total quantity, with no "threshold" below which damages were negligible, so that the same amount of damage was averted for every pound eliminated from the atmosphere, and if it could indeed be eliminated at the source at a constant cost (with the final 10 percent of reduction costing no more than the first 10 percent), it is hard to see why any abatement program would stop short of 100 percent. If to begin with it is worth x dollars to eliminate y in damage, and if you can eliminate another y in damage for another x dollars, it is still the same bargain. If instead the first 10 or 20 percent of damage is easily abated but the next 10 or 20 percent is expensive, the third 10 or 20 percent nearly exorbitant, and the final 40 percent astronomical in cost, and if the commodity produced is one that cannot easily be dispensed with, so that consumers would be paying an enormous "pollution tax" in the elevated price of the commodity whose production costs were so increased, there would surely be a balancing somewhere, even if the environmental damages were judged quite severe. Thus implicitly or explicitly the costs of abatement are almost sure to matter.

And the pricing scheme yields information about those costs. Indeed it produces that information free of charge, without the need for regulatory agencies to do engineering or accounting studies. At whatever level of abatement the pricing system leads to, the price will measure the marginal cost of further abatement as seen by the firms. Up to that point abatement has been cheaper than the price, and beyond it would be more expensive. The price is an upper limit to the cost of the abatement already achieved and a lower limit to the cost of any further abatement. Whatever cost the regulatory authorities had in mind (or had calculated), the pricing system will display for them the marginal cost—the going cost for an increment of further abatement—as actually perceived by the firms. This is the nearest thing to the "real" costs that the authorities are likely to get.

Now there are three possibilities. One is that the 50 percent aggregate abatement is achieved at about the cost the authorities had in mind; they consider the abatement already achieved well worth the cost they are imposing on consumers of the products of these firms but further abatement too expensive to impose. A second possibility is that the cost is far higher than they anticipated, 50 percent abatement proving not nearly as achievable economically as they had hoped. The firms' customers will be paying a far higher "abatement tax" in the prices they pay than the authorities intended to impose on them. In this case the authorities may change their abatement target, lowering the price to one at which they think the smaller reduction in emissions is worth the cost. The third possibility is that the 50 percent abatement is achieved at a price far lower than the authorities ever dreamed of. If they had been thinking it would cost $10 a pound to reduce emissions of a substance by 50 percent, and after 50 percent reduction firms are paying only $1 a pound for permits on the other 50 percent, evidently they aimed far short of the abatement that can be achieved at reasonable cost. They should either reduce the supply of permits offered and let the price go up or (what is the same thing) raise the charge per unit emission and see the emissions go down.

The significance of the last point goes well beyond the original question—whether firms should be expected to prefer the price mechanism or the other kinds of regulation. Evidently, if the firms think the regulatory authorities underestimate the costs of abatement and may be about to impose an exorbitantly costly reduction on the firms, the pricing mechanism may get their point across credibly. They could simply challenge the authorities to stipulate the price that the authorities thought was a reasonable estimate at 50 percent reduction, and the firms would then continue their high emissions level only if indeed the abatement costs were higher than the price the authorities had stipulated. If on the other hand the authorities are too pessimistic, or have been cajoled by the firms into believing that abatement is terribly costly, the pricing mechanism is a good way of calling the firms' bluff in the marketplace. The firms might prefer not to reveal in the marketplace their true cost of abatement, living instead with a mandatory 50 percent uniform reduction that they could pretend was about as onerous as they could tolerate.

To conclude this latter point: it would be a mistake to think that the degree of abatement ought in principle to be independent of the choice of regulatory technique. Not only can any given degree of abatement be achieved at a lower aggregate cost by a scheme (such as a pricing scheme) that induces those firms to reduce emissions most that can do it most cheaply; it is equally important to note that the pricing scheme makes manifest the costs of further abatement (and the savings from a relaxation) at the margin. Whenever the direct estimates of abatement costs are uncertain, as they almost always will be, the information produced by a pricing scheme will be directly relevant to setting the environmental target.

THE RATIONALE FOR CHARGING

There are several arguments for putting a price on harmful emissions, and, although they are compatible and reinforce each other, they are quite separate.

The Market Test

As noted above, a price offers an automatic adjustment process—a decentralized decision process—not only inducing the abatement in those particular firms, uses, or production processes where abatement can most economically be carried the furthest, but also providing a measure and a "market test." All abatement that is cheaper than the price will tend to be undertaken. Abatement that is so expensive that paying the price is preferable will be avoided, but only at a cost (paying the price) no less than what any other firm is expending on actual abatement. If the price has been determined at a level that represents the economic worth of abatement (that is, if it measures the economic damages that will be produced or the costs externally inflicted by the emission in question), each firm will undertake whatever abatement saves more damage than it costs, and no abatement will be undertaken that costs more than the damage is worth.

This argument is bound to carry weight if the damage can in principle be estimated and a value assessed for it—a value that can be made commensurate with the economic costs of abatement by attaching a money value per unit of emission. That the damage figure is not known (though it might be known in principle), and the estimates are very uncertain, does not detract from the argument. As long as some estimate or conjecture of the nature and severity of the damage has to underlie any regulatory regime, it makes sense to induce the abatement that can be accomplished at a cost less than the damage, and to avoid abatement that would cost more than avoiding the damage is worth.

There are at least two fundamental problems with the above argument. First, if it is denied in principle that the harm and harmfulness of the emission can be gathered into a damage estimate and expressed as a price per unit of emissions, the argument loses not only its appeal but its basis. This is not the counterargument that what is harmed is "priceless" and that abatement should be unstinting and without regard to cost comparisons; if the damage is infinitely large, a prohibitive price is put on the emissions, and emissions cease—if necessary by cessation of the entire process that gave rise to the emissions. Rather, this counterargument is that the harm goes beyond the damage. It includes attitudes, responsibilities, and the government's philosophy toward the environment. It can include an interest in "criminalizing" certain environmental insults. It may reflect a belief that the real or imagined victims of environmentally transmitted damage, or of harm to the environment itself, will resent and distrust a policy that appears to make emissions optional, to leave them for the marketplace, or to merchandise abatement by getting it done by whoever can do it most cheaply.

A second and altogether different objection to the "market test" is that the costs and damages, even if perfectly measurable in dollars, cannot properly be added together. They cannot be minimized together because they accrue to different people. If my factory is causing a farmer (a wholly unrelated individual, possibly unknown to me) increased costs, reduced productivity, or damages that have to be repaired, at the rate of $1,000 a month, and I can reduce that damage by half at a cost of less than $500 to myself, but reducing damage another 10 percent would cost me substantially more than $100, why should I be obliged to clean up the first 50 percent and not further obligated with respect to the other half of the farmer's damage? True, together we are richer if I abate the first half and stop there. But there is, in the language of economics, a distributional dimension of the problem. This makes it inappropriate to do the arithmetic as though my factory and his farm were both parts of the same enterprise and together the two parts made more money if abatement went just up to the line where costs and benefits were balanced.

At this point the proponent of that market-test argument can retreat a little. Since the virtue of setting a price equivalent to the damage has not been appreciated on distributional grounds, he can still argue that the pricing approach, using a price that is not merely the estimated damage but a higher price if you please, will minimize the cost of whatever level of abatement is decided on by allowing it to be done by all those firms that can abate more economically than they can pay the price. Whatever level of abatement might have been achievable through some other regulatory mode could still be achieved with a price mechanism, but if our sympathy for the victims of the pollution in question is greater than our sympathy for the firms' customers we can induce greater abatement by imposing a higher price. (And of course if we have little sympathy for the victims and much for the people whose cost of living will rise as the costs of abatement show up in the prices they pay, we can tilt the process the other way and set a price lower than the estimated damage.)

Paying the Costs

The second and third arguments for putting a price on emissions relate not to the abatement accomplished, but to the continued charges that are paid for the abatement not accomplished. One of the arguments is simply that firms ought to be required to pay the full costs of what they produce, including the costs they impose on the public. The offending emissions are the "externalities" that in the absence of regulation were not being paid for. If what goes up a firm's smokestack deteriorates the paint on my house, reduces the productivity of my farm, requires me to install air conditioning, or increases my veterinary bill, I am contributing at my own expense to the value of the goods the firm is producing. If the firm rented my house it would pay me, but if it deteriorates my house it does not. If I provide part of my crop as raw material the firm will pay me, but if it reduces my crop by emitting something harmful the cost to me is the same but the firm does not pay. And it ought to pay. Not necessarily to me, but still it ought to pay. That is the argument. As stated, the appeal is ethical rather than economic. It need not have any punitive flavor. The firm may be producing a perfectly good commodity that its customers need, it may be emitting a substance whose harm can be estimated, and it may be willing to pay for what it subtracts from value elsewhere in adding value to whatever it produces. If it does, it need not apologize.

This argument fits almost hand in glove with the market-test argument. One argument is that by paying the price on its continued emissions the firm is complying with the rule that you ought to pay for what you get, where "what you get" includes the benefits of inflicting expenses on the public. The second argument is that paying the price "keeps the firm honest"; the price paid is the guarantee that the firm has not evaded any economically reasonable opportunities to abate the substance. Thus the price (pursuant to one argument) induces abatement at the firm's expense up to where further abatement would cost more than the averted damage is worth, and (pursuant to the other argument) the firm meets its responsibilities by paying for the damage caused by its continuing emissions.

Lest the argument sound too neat, notice that the market-test argument concerns an allocative function that the price performs—getting abatement done where it can be done most economically, and up to where the costs are no longer less than the environmental costs averted —whereas the "pay for what you get" argument is concerned with equity. To illustrate with an extreme case: An activity causes damage, but is so costly to curtail and so essential that no abatement at all is expected. The price is then a pure transfer; it has no effect on behavior. Whether people engaged in the activity should pay is more a casuistic than an economic question. We may even want to find out who they are before we insist they pay just for the principle of the thing.

Disposition of Proceeds

Meanwhile, back at the agency, the money is coming in. Whose money is it? What should be done with it? Is it a pure byproduct of a regulatory scheme, embarrassing to an agency that has no budgetary authority to spend it and perhaps appearing to be a revenue bonus available to meet public needs?

Here is where a third argument for pricing enters. It is not the argument that pricing produces revenue; the goods produced by the emitting firms could just as well have been subjected to an excise tax if we had wanted the purchasers of those commodities to provide revenue to the government. And if we think of the money as punitive damages, we can be pleased to have transferred money from offenders to the government, like the fines collected from traffic violations; but that is not the attitude that goes with pricing in the first place. The argument instead is that these funds, generated from a regulatory mechanism that induces an "economical" level of emissions to continue, are equivalent to the costs or damages estimated to be inflicted by those emissions. They ought to be used to complete the transaction by which the emitting firms pay for what they use and what they do. Paying into a public treasury on account of emissions and paying *for* the emissions by paying to repair, indemnify, or forestall the damage are not the same. And getting the benefits to the victim is every bit as important as getting the money from the firm that produces the damage. That is the argument.

It will be the rare environmental externality that permits us, at no exorbitant administrative expense, to identify all the victims and assess their damages individually. We probably have a crude aggregate estimate of damage, and at the level of an individual victim there may be no reliable way of determining how much of any apparent costs is actually due to the regulated emissions. Still, in principle the distributional objection mentioned above could be mitigated if funds were dedicated to completing that transaction.

How would that be done? The answer depends on how we arrived at our estimate of damage in the first place.

Completing the Transaction

If the damage assessment was the estimated cost of cleanup, removal, repair, and protective measures, so that it is the cost of defending against the emissions rather than allowing them to do their harm, there may be a strong presumption that the funds should be used for exactly that. Specifically, using our earlier example, if we put a 15¢ price on the "emission" of unreturned bottles by requiring a deposit on all bottles, and if the 15¢ represents the estimated cost per bottle of cleaning up roadsides and parks, exactly the same argument that made 15¢ the relevant figure is an argument for using the money to clean up the bottles whose estimated cleanup cost underlies the whole scheme. To the extent that cleanup, repair, and protection are best handled by public authorities, the proceeds of the emissions charge can be used to finance the appropriate programs.

Alternatively, the damage estimate may have reflected the costs imposed on individuals—costs that cannot be averted or repaired economically by public programs. In principle, if the estimate was a good one and if the costs of administration are not too large, funds exist to indemnify the victims for the full costs that were inflicted on them. Whether they protect themselves with air conditioning, reimburse themselves for the losses to their crops, cover the cost of more frequent painting, or take the money as pure financial compensation for some discomfort or privation, they get full restitution if our damage estimate was a good one and lends itself to decomposition into its individual components.

The principle can be made sharp and clear. Whether it can be done in practice is another story. Whether the adjudicatory or assessment process can be carried out fairly and without exorbitant cost and whether the procedure would invite spurious claims and self-inflicted damage (as when people are overinsured against fire or burglary) are bound to be disturbing practical questions about the possibility of completing that transaction. But if (as with all public expenditure or tax programs) the "target efficiency" leaves something to be desired and we do not demand that every individual break even but only that a reasonable attempt be made to provide protection, repair, or compensatory benefits, it may be possible to meet the proposal in spirit if not to the letter.

To recapitulate: There are at least four distinct attractions, separable but compatible, to a charge system. One is to get the abatement allocated among firms so that if some have lower abatement costs than others the cost of any given abatement can be minimized. (This statement can be turned around to read ". . . so that for any given aggregate cost the greatest aggregate abatement can be achieved.") Second, if the price is an approximation of the estimated damage per unit of emission, it offers a market test, revealing the marginal cost of further abatement and inducing the undertaking of abatement where it is no longer less expensive than the costs inflicted by emissions. Third, whoever does the emitting, or whoever purchases the goods and services produced by the emitter, "beneficiary," or "offender," pays the full "social cost" of the goods and services so produced. And fourth, revenue is available that could in principle be used for repair, reparations, and protection, in an amount sufficient to cover the costs inflicted by the emissions if the price has been approximated to those costs (with the "costs" or "damages" augmented by the costs of administering the program).

Focus on Damage

There is a further advantage to pricing that may be enjoyed even if pricing proves to be impracticable or insufficiently superior to be worth substituting if the more direct regulation is in place: It inescapably entails deciding on a price. It focuses attention on the quantitative characteristic of the problem and the proposed solution.

Determining the price is giving an answer to the question "how much?," and exactly what the price attaches to is an answer to "a price on what?"

It is easy to talk in a vague way about putting a price on what goes up an electric utility's chimney, but ultimately the idea has to be reduced to something concrete, like $5 per ton of carbon dioxide, sulfur, or lead, measured at the smokestack or 500 miles downwind, every day or on days when the wind blows from the north, or when the concentration downwind reaches a certain level. And if the price is to be an approximation of the costs and damages inflicted, we not only have to identify the damaging substance but we need to know how to measure the damage—first in the units or quantities in which the damage actually occurs or in the units and quantities of protective or cleanup measure and then in money values commensurate with the price. Inescapably, therefore, a pricing system focuses on the damage, on the economic measure of the damage (or the costs of averting or repairing the damage), and on the actual agent that produces the damage.

To people who are attracted to pricing in the first place, this inescapable focus on the nature and measure of the damage will appear to be merely a virtue implicit in what has already been said. But it has a nontrivial implication: it draws attention to the fact that damages are not proportionate to emissions. Damages associated with emissions may vary substantially from source to source. A price that is uniform per unit of damage will not be uniform per unit of emission. Sources differently located should pay different emission prices for the same substance emitted if a pound of the substance emitted at one location does more damage than a pound emitted at another location.

Why might the emissions differ in the damage they do? One possibility is that low concentrations are harmless, and up to some threshold the damage is negligible. An opposite reason is that beyond some level all the damage is done—the fish are dead, the oysters infectious, or the water undrinkable—and the marginal damage of further emissions is zero. A third possibility is that the emission depends on the weather for the damage it does, being aggravated photochemically or harmlessly rained out of the sky, so that its potency depends on regional climate, local weather, and season of the year. Finally, and most important, the populations and other resources at risk differ from location to location, in number, in value, and in vulnerability.

This brings us to the divisive question of whether we want to discriminate among target populations. If a harmful activity is going to take place somewhere, exposing a certain population to the risk of sickness or death, contributing to the deterioration of their homes or crops or businesses or recreational activities, or entailing defensive costs to individuals or to the firms they work in or the communities they live in, do we want to measure, for the purpose of controlling emissions, the aggregate amount of risk and damage at each location? Or do we want to ignore the fact that aggregate exposure and vulnerability are less for emissions at one location than for emissions at another?

Notice what hinges on this question. If we estimate the costs and damages specific to a particular location and price the offending substance according to the likely damage per unit of emission at each location, we will induce less abatement where exposure and vulnerability are least and more abatement where exposure and vulnerability are large. More than that, because the processes that produce the emission become less costly at one location than at another, any kind of production that is not permanently attached to a particular location (on account of proximity to materials or markets) will have some inducement to relocate where exposure and vulnerability are least. New plants, especially, may be located where the emission price is low, just as plants locate where property taxes, wage rates, or energy costs are low. And the higher the level of emissions per dollar of output, and the higher the cost of abating emissions, the greater will be the inducement to re-locate where the emission price is low.

We are back to that argument that is appealing in the aggregate but poignantly divisive for individuals: There may be fewer people exposed in a particular location because the population is of low density, but each individual feels just as exposed as if he had more neighbors. If two populations are of equal size but one has more people who are especially vulnerable (for example, the elderly), the vulnerable members of the population that is more vulnerable in the aggregate "protect each other" by collectively making it an expensive place to emit the offending substance. And the few elderly or otherwise vulnerable people in the area where the damage that may be done to them is priced low (because they are few) may not appreciate feeling sacrificed for some collective greater good or lesser damage.

Whatever conclusion one reaches about the manifest benefits of discriminatory pricing or the patent unfairness of it, it is an issue that ought to be faced. Pricing schemes require facing it.

Schemes that focus only on the amount of sulfur emitted (irrespective of the target), or on the ambient concentration of a sulfur oxide (irrespective of the exposed populations), deal with a damaging substance but not with the damage. They control the agent but not the effect. Not being concerned with damage, they do not require its identification and measurement.

Pricing schemes, in contrast, require the identification and assessment of damage. They require facing up to questions exactly like this one: Do we want the abatement of noxious substances to be greatest where the exposed and vulnerable population is greatest and least where the exposed and vulnerable population is small, and do we want the emissions to be relocated so that the damage per exposed individual will vary from place to place but the damage for the whole population will be minimized?

For many of us I expect that the answer will be "it depends." If we are dealing with aggregate damage to livestock or forest products, or cleanup costs inflicted on homes and shops, or noise insulation made obligatory in schools and other public buildings, confining the potential damage to small towns and low population densities will seem eminently sensible. However, if we are dealing with carcinogenic or (especially) mutagenic substances, we may be more uneasy about merely maximizing damage abatement. We may even be uneasy about formulating the issue so that we have to face it explicitly.

OTHER PRICING PROCEDURES

There are other pricing mechanisms. To show that charges on the offender are not the only possibility, we can propose the exact reverse: If we have no authority to command that the offending output be attenuated, or to impose a charge or penalty in support of reduction, offering a price may serve the purpose. If we have a damage estimate in dollars per pound of a substance emitted, and we cannot charge that price to the emitting firm, we can pay it that price per pound of emissions abated. One way we need police power, the other way we need purchasing power. The identical price ought to lead to the identical result, with the not-inconsiderable exception that the emitting firm is receiving rather than paying.

If $1 per pound has to be paid on all emissions, abatement will proceed to the point where it ceases to be cheaper per pound than the $1 that can alternatively be paid. But if reimbursement is available at $1 per pound of abatement, it is equally profitable to carry abatement to that same point where the cost per pound of abatement is no longer less than the price.

There are two differences. The obvious one is that the firm's financial position differs by a fixed amount, equal to the original emissions times the price. Compared with no price at all, it is ahead a fraction of that amount if it receives payment for abating, and it is behind by the complementary fraction if it pays on emissions instead. A related difference (possibly a second-order effect) is that in the less profitable situation production costs are higher; thus the retail price will go up and consumers will buy less. All this accords with what we expect when hidden costs are discovered. Costs go up, prices go up, the industry contracts, and the overall reduction in emissions (perhaps to be distinguished from the "abatement," where the latter is thought of as reduced emissions for the given activity rather than reduced activity) depends on the elasticity of the demand for the product and on how large the abatement costs are as a component of total cost.

The second difference is that to pay firms for abatement we need a baseline. There has to be some initial position from which reductions will be counted as abatement. When the firm pays on the basis of actual emissions, the baseline is usually zero and goes unnoticed. (If the emissions on which a price is based are only "excessive" emissions, we need some historical or technological standard; that possibility, which presents an exact counterpart to the present complication, was omitted above.) Administratively this can be a problem. We may not have good base-period data on the firms. Or we may have data from the year or two before the scheme goes into effect; but if the firms anticipate being paid for reducing emissions they may boost emissions during that period. Even if that can be forestalled, there is the question whether each firm should be allowed its own individual base, especially since that gives the more offending firms more room to be rewarded for merely catching up.

A technological norm might be established, but that entails two difficulties. First, firms that emit the same substance are not necessarily producing the same commodities: The same substance may simultaneously be emitted in wood finishing, paint thinning, leather tanning, printing and engraving, and a variety of other activities, making it hard to establish a common normal emission ratio. Second, even though no opprobrium ought to attach to a high level of emissions that was not illegal or improper until an abatement scheme went into effect, the potential windfall gains of the firms that can abate most substantially are not likely to be regarded as altogether legitimate.

The problem generalizes. There are numerous instances in which people could be penalized or charged for a proscribed activity because it is comparatively easy to monitor the level of activity, where rewarding good behavior (if it is merely the absence of disapproved behavior) would be open-ended. Both a fine for littering and a charge on littering may be feasible, but how do you pay picnickers and passing cars for everything they did not leave behind or throw out the window? The conclusion is not that people and firms can never be paid for their abatement; there are instances where it actually works. The point is that there is an inherent asymmetry. There is a crucial baseline parameter to be determined, one that usually is conveniently missing from the more familiar case of charging the emitter.

These considerations are tangential to the question of who ought to pay or be paid—the question whether I have a right to play music or you have a right to quiet, whether I have a right to plow or you have a right to dust-free air downwind, whether I have a right to hunt migratory birds or you have a right to their sanctuary, whether I have a right to do wood finishing or you have a right to be free from the fumes and the fire hazard. Sometimes these Rights (with a capital R) are there to be discovered in the courts or in our consciences; sometimes rights (with a lowercase r) are to be decided by legislatures. There is nothing in principle that tells quite where to draw the line in questions such as whether I should be free to do something unsightly with my house in your neighborhood, whether I should be allowed to breathe freely in a public place if I have a respiratory infection, fishermen allowed to disturb the quiet of a swimming place, infants allowed to cry, or cats to be allowed out if they eat birds. There is much literature on the efficiency or costliness of assigning the rights to the plaintiff or to the defendant when civil suit is the mechanism of control. Here it is enough merely to notice that there is no universal presumption that the ethically correct way to induce a firm to reduce some harmful emission is to command or to entreat, to charge or to reimburse.

In paying for abatement rather than charging for emission we again have the two parts to the transaction and the question whether we wish to complete the transaction. To this point we examined the possibility that the emitter should be paid for emitting less. There is a corresponding question whether the beneficiary should pay for value received. A possibility is that nobody else will pay, and if the beneficiary wants the abatement, all he can do is pay. A price system may then let him pay up to the point where further abatement is not worth the price; and if the price reflects the emitter's costs of abatement, this would be the point at which the emitter and the beneficiary have minimized their joint costs. The earlier discussion considered the possibilities that the costs or the damages inflicted by the emissions would be centrally estimated as a basis for pricing, that the authorities might not know the costs of abatement, that a pricing system would generate information, and that the decentralized adaptation of firms would be an efficient response to the cost characteristics of individual firms. It is often (perhaps typically) the case that, however difficult it is to estimate abatement costs, it is even more difficult to attach a reliable value figure to the costs and damages averted by abatement. Pricing is one way of attempting to cope with that part of the problem too.

In particular cases of purely bilateral damage, in which I am the exclusive source of the emissions that hurt you and you are the only one hurt by my emissions, there may be a certain symmetry in the negotiated outcome no matter who has the initial rights—whether you have the right to be left unhurt (and I must quit or compensate) or I have the right to pursue the activity (and you must acquiesce or reimburse me). If my abatement costs exceed the damage you wish to avoid, in the one case I will pay damages rather than abate; in the other case you will take the damage rather than incur the greater expense of curtailing it. Only if it costs less than it is worth am I likely to avert rather than pay damages or are you likely to pay for relief. The negotiated transfer might be anywhere between those two limits, depending on whether, for example, you have the right to demand only damages or the right to forbid the activity unless I pay your price. (In that case I may pay any price up to the full cost of abatement.) We have here a kind of double market test. The costs on both sides of the transaction play a role in the decision.

The difficulty in the typical case is that my abatement benefits numerous parties downwind, downstream, or by the side of the road. Any beneficiary who refuses to pay his share can be a "free rider," and if nothing is done until everybody pays a share, anyone can insist that he doesn't mind the emissions and nobody should expect him to pay. If you let ragweed grow in your fields and all of your neighbors are prepared to pay the cost of suppressing ragweed, even somebody who suffers acutely from hay fever may pretend to be allergic to something else (even to the proposed pesticide) to be excused from paying his share and even to stake a claim for compensation. (And you may grow ragweed for the profit of being paid to suppress it!)

In the terminology of economics, abatement often has the characteristic of a "public good," something that if produced at all becomes available unstinted to all beneficiaries and cannot readily be withheld to exact payment. But if the water in a pond that had become unfit for swimming is cleaned up at great cost, it may be possible to deny access except to people who pay their share. That still has the problem of gratuitously excluding someone who likes to swim but not quite enough to pay the standard share; unable to document that he likes swimming less than I do, he forgoes it while I pay, and his potential enjoyment goes to waste.

Generally, then, charging beneficiaries is not as promising in practice as in principle it might sound. There is, though, an important case that was hinted at above and will show up in one of the case studies: If an entire area (perhaps a residential area) can be made free of some noxious element and the benefits can be observed as increases in market values (rents and sale prices), it may be possible, if the authority exists, to capture some of the windfalls. If rents double because aircraft noise is eliminated, somebody who does not mind the noise may claim to be unbenefited; but if property values go up he may take his gains and go to live where it is cheaper, converting the quiet into a capital gain. In this case the "public good" problem is still present but the basis for assessing gains may be less elusive.

Fleet Mileage

An unusual and instructive example of a pricing mechanism, this one for both energy conservation and environmental protection, is the fleet-mileage standard established for passenger cars produced in the United States. It is unusual because it appears at first glance to be direct regulation of the most inflexible sort. Each year there is a numerical figure for miles per gallon that the manufacturer must meet or pay a penalty. There is no credit for being ahead of schedule or doing better than the prescribed figure; no carryover, permitting a manufacturer who excels in one year to average out the following year; no falling behind and making it up next year. The penalty is a fine; it is not a "price" that, once paid, entitles the manufacturer to a shortfall in performance.

This case is instructive because embedded in it is an interesting use of the price system. Indeed, the concept on which the fleet-mileage standards are built is a regulatory innovation. (Whether it has potential application other than in automobiles is not certain.) The principle is important. Automobiles are important. And in displaying the rationale for pricing, and showing how pricing can sometimes be embedded in a more administrative scheme, the case is instructive.

The key is the averaging. The manufacturer is not given a mileage standard that every car must meet, or a schedule of mileages for cars of different weight, engine size, or price, or quotas by number or sales value of cars in alternative mileage categories. Rather, the manufacturer is given a mileage figure that all cars produced during the year must together meet on the average. The average is simply the arithmetic mean. By 1985 the average, under 1980 law, will be 27.5 miles per gallon. A manufacturer will be within the requirements if every car meets that figure. He will also be within the requirements if half the cars achieve 30 mpg and the other half at least 25. If two-thirds achieve 30, the remaining third can be as low as 22.5. Cars can get as few as 10 or 15 mpg as long as there are compensatory sales of cars that keep the average up.

Insofar as gasoline mileage is concerned, no individual car buyer is precluded from buying any kind of car. An automobile company can sell anyone a car that gets only 10 mpg on the condition that it simultaneously sells seven cars that get 30, three that get 33.3, or one that gets 45. The snag is that for each of us who would like a car that gets only 10 mpg there may not be somebody who will take a lightweight 45-mpg car, or three who will buy cars getting 33.3, or seven who will buy cars that get 30.

This is where the price system comes in. If the cars that all the customers together would like to buy when cars are priced the way they are normally priced average out at 27.5 mpg in 1985 (and the corresponding lower figures for the years before 1985), the regulation will be redundant. But if customers choose a mix of cars with an average mileage below the specified level, something will have to give. Dealers then will find that they can sell more low-mileage cars that they can get their hands on. They will offer fewer discounts and other customary inducements on those cars. Manufacturers will not, because of the fleet-average requirement, be able to keep up with the demand for the low-mileage cars. They will have to require dealers to take more high-mileage cars than they want, or make it attractive to dealers to sell more of the high-mileage cars than the customers want. In the end, what will keep the customers satisfied and meet the fleet-mileage standard will be price adjustments. To earn the high markups that are possible on low-mileage cars, the manufacturers will have to cut prices to sell the high-mileage cars that are not in sufficient demand.

The result is not much different from that of an excise tax on low-mileage cars to discourage their use (a "weight charge" or "energy utilization" charge) coupled with a negative tax (a subsidy) on energy-saving cars. Whether the purpose is energy conservation, environmental conservation, or both, one can design a combination of taxes on the cars to be discouraged and subsidies (leading to discounts) on the cars to be encouraged, using the taxes to finance the subsidies and breaking even in revenue. The buyers of the low-mileage cars thus pay an enticement to others to buy the high-mileage cars that "justify" the low-mileage cars.

The fleet-mileage standard, imposing only an average on the entire fleet of a given automobile producer, leads to pricing that will look like a combination of a premium (a tax) on cars that are in short supply because of the regulation and a discount (a subsidy) on cars that need to be sold to keep the average up. But it is up to each manufacturer to accomplish all this by adjusting prices on different models and makes and styles, meeting the competition from other automobile firms and from imports, and always selling cars to customers who are subject to no regulation themselves.

How effective the fleet-mileage standards have been is not easy to judge. Gasoline prices rose so much during the period in which the mileage standards were imposed that the market shifted in favor of high-mileage cars. In retrospect, gasoline prices may have done what the mileage standards were intended to do; the mileage standards may thus have been unnecessary. Furthermore, the gasoline prices worked in the same way: High-mileage cars became relatively cheaper over their lifetimes, if not at initial purchase, and low-mileage cars more expensive. (The mileage standards may have induced companies to plan on a higher-mileage fleet, and they may have been somewhat readier than they would have been for the market shifts that occurred.)

Converting Nontransferable Rights

In many areas of regulation, not only the environmental area, rights to participate in some activity or to use some resources evolve over time or are granted in accordance with traditional shares. Water rights and import quotas are examples. The imposition of air-quality standards over a local area, as under the Clean Air Act, has tended rather naturally to treat existing stationary sources in that fashion. Where existing sources together are within the required or implied level of total emissions they have been permitted to continue their individual emissions at traditional levels, not to increase them, while new firms or enlargements of existing firms must be accommodated within whatever room remains for further emissions within the established limits. Once the "excess capacity" is used up, there is no room for further growth and no room for new firms that might produce more and emit less than existing firms.

Proposals have arisen in all the three cases mentioned (California water rights, oil-import permits, and emissions into the air from stationary sources) to commute those specific rights into ownership rights that can be traded, sold, or otherwise transferred or marketed. New or expanding firms could then buy their way into the market, obtaining the water rights or the emission rights from firms to which they had earlier accrued. Firms that could produce more value per unit of emissions would presumably value the emission rights more than some established firms, and a better utilization of the local air capacity could be obtained.

Objections are occasionally raised to the apparent "monetization" or granting of pure wealth where there earlier existed only a traditional right to participate. But what happens is that a valuable right, one whose value may have been unseen because it was never commuted to cash in the market, comes into view. Furthermore, it appears to become worth even more to the firms that elect to sell their traditional rights; otherwise they can always keep them. The new firms whose emissions replace the old emissions are advantaged by being allowed into business, air quality is unimpaired, and the apparent windfall gains have actually been created by enhancing the value of the capacity of the air to absorb emissions up to whatever level was already determined.

The principle is attractive. It already works for taxi medallions, could undoubtedly work for oil-import quotas, and appears feasible for a tangible scarce commodity like water or even some mineral rights. The particular characteristics of local air-quality regulation make practical application more problematic.

Weapons and Warfare

Meteors, Mischief, and War

■ Many people who enjoyed the movie *Dr. Strangelove* know that the movie was stimulated by the novel *Red Alert* by Peter Bryant. Some may be curious how that little 35¢ paperback generated such a memorable motion picture. I can help.

First, how did Peter George—the author's real name—come to write *Red Alert?* He was sitting with two others at a table in the officers' club at an American B-47 base in England in 1957 or 1958 when a bomber took off and roared over the club. (He was a major in the Royal Air Force.) The vibration caused a coffee cup near the table edge to crash to the floor. Somebody said, "That's the way World War III will start." George responded by phoning his publisher, saying that for an advance he'd take three weeks' leave and write the book. The result was *Red Alert,* published in 1958. (He didn't complete it in three weeks!)

Somebody handed me a copy of *Red Alert* as I boarded a plane in Monterey, California; I finished it on the way to Boston. At that time my main interest was the possibility of nuclear warfare, and I was so impressed with the care and imagination that went into the novel that I ordered a number of copies to send to colleagues. (According to correspondence I still retain, I mailed out at least thirty-one copies.)

Douglass Cater was at that time an editor of the monthly *The Reporter.* He visited me to urge me to do an article on "accidental war," and made the suggestion—something that would never have occurred to me—that I introduce the article by reviewing some fictional accounts. I liked the idea and did begin the article with brief reviews of three books, *On the Beach,* by Nevil Shute, *Alas, Babylon,* by Pat Frank, and *Red Alert.*

In the end *The Reporter* decided against my article so I submitted it to the *Bulletin of the Atomic Scientists,* where it appeared as "Meteors, Mischief, and War" in September 1960.

Alastair Buchan, founder and director of the Institute for Strategic Studies in London, had been Washington correspondent for *The Observer* of London. We had become good friends back in 1958, and when he read my 1960 article he proposed that *The Observer* reprint it. *The Observer* was a weekly newspaper, appearing Sundays; the first section was news, the second section was features. My article was the front page of the second section.

Stanley Kubrick was in England working on a movie. He read what I had said about *Red Alert,* got the book, got Peter George's address from the publisher, and offered George a sizable sum to go to the States and work on a screenplay. George accepted happily, and shortly after that he and Kubrick spent a long afternoon in my office with Morton Halperin and me, and then a long evening at my house with William Kaufman, as we tried to fit *Red Alert* into the missile age. In the 1958 book there were, of course, no intercontinental missiles; by the time Kubrick got involved, there were. We tried hard to get to the brink of war, Red-Alert style, without denigrating the loyalty of the air force, and couldn't do it plausibly. Kubrick decided he'd do it as fantasy-comedy.

Various observers have identified Dr. Strangelove—the character, not the movie—with some real people. I think that is a mistake. Peter George told me (personal correspondence), "I think there has been a lot of misjudgment . . . on . . . the character of Dr. Strangelove . . . Strangelove is not really a character at all, he is something out of a nightmare, and to us he represented all those qualities which made Kubrick describe his film as a nightmare comedy."

He also told me, "Two weeks ago the *Sunday Times* here printed an article in which they actually referred to Herman [Kahn] as *the prototype for Dr. Strangelove.* I immediately wrote a refutation, and they were decent enough to print this in full. I sent a copy of their print to Herman, as I felt deeply hurt on his behalf."

The author's full name was Peter Bryan George. His various pen-names included Peter Bryant (for *Red Alert*), Bryan Peters, and I believe another that he would not divulge to me. He died by his own hand in June of 1966. I miss him, and the books he would have written. He did, as Peter George, finish another, *Commander 1* (New York: Delacorte Press, 1965), in which during the next war a nuclear-war theorist with my name, along with Herman Kahn, is presumed dead.

Since the essay is more than forty-five years old, and any preoccupation with superpower "accidental war" today would find the technology of that earlier era old-fashioned, I present only the part that caught Kubrick's eye.

■

INTRODUCTION

If war is too important to leave to the generals, accidental war should not be left to novelists. But for the time being they have it; and while few of them have given a full scenario of how war might come about, they have at least been more explicit in public print than the analysts.

We have had a number of hints, including some vivid ones from Khrushchev and his colleagues, that seagulls or meteors may look like aircraft or missiles on a radar-scope, and that personnel screening in an air force (theirs or ours) may not absolutely eliminate the mischievous psychotic. We have had predictions that petty dictators may soon have the ability to startle us out of our wits with a nuclear explosion somewhere. We have had evidence in the newspapers that a nuclear weapon may drop out of an airplane in peacetime, though not that one can detonate under the circumstances. But while it is easy to imagine how accidents might occur, it is not so easy to trace out how they might lead to war.

LITERARY FLASHBACK

In addition to whimsey inspired by the meteorites that left craters in Arizona and Siberia, we have had several fictional efforts to get a war plausibly started. *On the Beach* has an advantage: we are already in the aftermath before the origin of the war is revealed.[1] The war being taken for granted, its origin can afford to be sketchy and ironic. Still, the sequence of events may illustrate what people have in mind. Apparently the Russians and the Chinese were spoiling for a war, but the initiative came from the Albanians who dropped a bomb on Naples; next was a bomb on Tel Aviv, origin unknown. The Americans and British made gestures at Cairo, which responded with bombs on Washington, which led the Americans to retaliate on Russia. "Somebody had to make a decision, of course, and make it in a matter of minutes. Up at Canberra they think now that he made it wrong" (p. 94.)

China took the occasion to finish off Russia, and both went after each other with radiological weapons. An ironic touch in this sketchy flashback is that the Americans apparently never played a leading role, once hostilities got really started. (The war occurred, incidentally, just about a year from now.) By the time the war was badly out of hand, whoever was making decisions in China and Russia lacked the organization to stop it.

This may be too easy: false alarms, misunderstandings, nth-country problems, and two of the large countries premeditating war anyhow. With all these ingredients—and a little accelerated technology and dramatic license—the reader may assume a horrendous casserole no matter how they are mixed. But even if it is a caricature, the picture of human error and impotence probably epitomizes the popular notion of "accidental war" and the widespread sensation that the machines are taking over.

Alas, Babylon also gets its war started in the Middle East, but the mixture is a little different.[2] In this one deterrence fails because, though we can lick the Russians and we know it, they don't. We also, in this one, have the advantage of "strategic warning"; we know that the Russians are willing to press the issue in the Middle East to the point of general war, but apparently cannot use our forewarning either to attack them first or to persuade them that, their secret having leaked, their chances of success are small. Some interesting dynamics are included: though the Russian decision is prompted by a Middle East crisis, it is affected by their belief that their forces, though superior, are only *temporarily* superior and that the opportunity will be gone if they wait until we catch up. Finally, there is at least one inflammatory "accident," a nuclear air-to-air missile that misses its target and falls on Latakia with vivid results. This novel, too, is mainly about the aftermath of war; it is an imaginative study of civil defense and organization, but getting

214

the war started is incidental. The causation is impressionistic; and the role of "accidents" is only hinted at.

THE BRINK OF WAR

For a detailed scenario of how war might start, or almost start, we have to turn to the paperbacks. One of the niftiest little analyses to come along is *Red Alert*, which explores the possibility that a really sophisticated Strategic Air Command (SAC) general, properly placed, with a few lucky breaks, might get the United States committed to an all-out war with Russia, a war that he believes inevitable but only on highly unfavorable terms unless he can force his country to take the initiative.[3] The sheer ingenuity of the scheme, beautifully analyzed in "realistic" detail, with emphasis on the system rather than on personalities, exceeds in thoughtfulness any nonfiction available on how war might start. The value of the narrative does not lie in the possibility that SAC is so organized that the story could be true; one can suppose that the crucial details have been invented for the sake of the story. What is impressive is how plausible a story can be invented. The author does not frighten us with how loosely SAC might be organized and how easily the system could be subverted; what makes this book good fiction is what makes a good mystery—the author has used his ingenuity to make the problem hard.

The climax, though, is what deserves pondering. The last-minute bargaining by the Russian and American governments, though less plausible than the rest of the book in its details, is a unique examination of the brink of war. As a contribution to the literature on war and peace, *Red Alert* not only demonstrates the occasional superiority of dramatic over logical discourse, but by its example indicts a public discussion that has not got beyond "Prewar Strategy" to Chapter 2, "The Brink of War." If an accident, or a bit of mischief, or a false alarm, or a misunderstanding, can lead to war *but not necessarily*, what makes the difference, if anything, other than luck?

ACCIDENTS OR DECISIONS?

The point is that accidents do not cause war. *Decisions* cause war. Accidents can trigger decisions; and this may be all that anybody meant.

But the distinction needs to be made, because the remedy is not just preventing accidents but constraining decisions.

NOTES

1. Nevil Shute, *On the Beach* (New York: William Morrow and Co., 1957).
2. Pat Frank, *Alas, Babylon* (Philadelphia: J. B. Lippincott Co., 1959).
3. Peter Bryant, *Red Alert* (New York: Ace Books, Inc., 1958).

15

Research by Accident

■ We have been warned, if we have a technology in place that causes problems and needs to be replaced with a new alternative, not to be wholly preoccupied with simply accomplishing, with the new technology, what the old technology did.

The new technology, less familiar than the old, may be different in its comparative applications. If you are too much focused on what the problem is you are trying to solve—doing what the old technology accomplished better and without some of its disadvantages—you can miss opportunities inherent in the new technology. You may also fail to recognize some dangers in the new technology—dangers different from the ones that may have made the old technology obsolete.

I shall illustrate the danger with a historical example, an R&D project that appears to have been utterly obsessed with accomplishing on a heroic scale what had earlier been accomplished on a comparatively diminutive scale: the development of nuclear weapons. Nuclear weapons were conceived, designed, developed, and engineered by physicists, chemists, mathematicians, and engineers, with the intent of building bombs larger by orders of magnitude than any bombs that had ever been built. And "bombs" is what they had in mind, what they envisioned. What bombs traditionally did was to explode and to ignite—to produce overpressure and shock, to crush structures, to tear things and people apart, to start fires.

217

UNANTICIPATED DISCOVERIES IN
THE DEVELOPMENT OF NUCLEAR WEAPONS

The people who designed the atomic weapon were careful in calculating the likely energy yields and in translating the energy yields into ground-level overpressure and thermal radiation according to the altitude of burst. They were not anticipating any weapon effects of military significance except blast and thermal radiation; blast and thermal radiation were what bombs produced. As a result, in my interpretation, there were a number of additional significant weapon effects that were not anticipated, not looked for, not tested for, and discovered only by accident. Literally "accident," in most cases, i.e., an unexpected misadventure.[1]

Indeed, one could propound a "law" of weapon development: if you have a serious safety problem on the test range that is hard to eliminate, you have just discovered a new weapon effect!

The first such effect occurred at Hiroshima. It was "prompt" radiation, neutron radiation that caused immediate or nearly immediate radiation sickness (and was later to prove mutagenic). This effect was not observed by the Americans, who had nobody on the ground; it was a discovery of the Japanese. At the altitude of the bombs of Hiroshima and Nagasaki, neutron radiation would not play a major role: anyone within lethal radius of the neutrons would likely be destroyed in the blast damage or by thermal radiation; but a person distant from collapsible structures, protected by white clothing from thermal radiation, could be vulnerable to radiation sickness and death.

This form of radiation was later elevated into a major weapon effect in the concept of the "neutron bomb," or "enhanced radiation weapon," that, though never deployed, received widespread attention and provoked widespread controversy in 1959–60 and again during the Carter administration. But it was probably unanticipated, because there were no physiologists, or other medical scientists, involved in the atomic bomb development.

The next weapon effect, unanticipated and discovered by "accident," was nuclear fallout. The test of a hydrogen weapon caused a mysterious precipitation to fall on a Japanese fishing vessel, the *Lucky Dragon*. If the Hiroshima neutrons were "prompt radiation," this was "delayed radiation." Once discovered, as a result of this nuclear-test accident, fallout became recognized as a major weapon effect; some military planners considered it, as a weapon of mass retaliation, more potent than blast and radiation, and not dependent on any significant accuracy. (People my age remember vividly the fallout-shelter campaign of 1960–61.) Fallout was what the "infernal device" of the movie *Dr. Strangelove* was going to destroy the world with.

When American weapon designers wanted to measure the effects of high-altitude bursts they chose Johnston Island, well over the horizon to the southwest of Hawaii. After a test a strange thing occurred: Johnston Island lost radio contact with the mainland for many hours. The earth's magnetic field was disturbed. If this could happen to Johnston Island with a single high-altitude burst in peacetime, imagine what could be done to enemy (or own's own) military communications in war! What began as an unexpected test-range nuisance was recognized as a major nuclear-weapon effect. Furthermore, it required understanding and planning: the burst elevations that one might use against military targets were not those likely to produce the radio effect.

A similar thing happened with another high-altitude shot. This time it was radar blackout, shorter lived than radio blackout, but similarly unexpected, similarly potentially potent militarily. At first it was a test-range annoyance; when recognized it became a significant weapon effect. It would have been crucial in attacks confronting antiballistic missile systems.

"Retinal burn" was discovered similarly. Animals were being used to test likely effects on human bodies, especially effects on behavior that might be due to radiation. Some strange behaviors turned out to be due to the fact that many of the rabbits and other creatures had gone blind, some temporarily, some permanently. The flash had burned the retinas of their eyes. But if it could burn rabbit retinas it could burn soldiers' retinas if a nuclear burst—too distant to do them other harm —caught them by surprise looking in the direction of the burst. (An R&D effort was begun to develop safety glasses that would convert from clear to dark quickly enough to protect retinas.)

Still another effect of momentous importance was discovered "by accident" during high-altitude tests at Johnston Island. Electrical equipment that was crucial to monitoring the effects of the blast went out of commission just as the blast went off. This time it clearly couldn't be coincidence. What had just been discovered was "electro-magnetic pulse," a sudden pulse of induced electricity that burned out key components. It appeared potentially capable, once understood and designed for (or against), of destroying entire communications systems, a major weapon effect. (Those who saw the TV movie *The Day After,* some years ago, will remember not only the nuclear fallout but the stalled autos in downtown Kansas City.)

A final effect may be worth mentioning because it might have been discovered by accident in an offshore nuclear test. This is the possibility that if a weapon of appropriate yield were detonated at the right ocean depth and the right distance from shore, with due regard to the configuration of the ocean floor, a massive tidal wave—a tsunami—might be produced that could inundate coastal cities. This effect was thought of, and indeed taken into account, in the planning of underwater tests. I mention it to highlight the role that even amateur imagination can play in the intellectual exploration for technological effects. This effect—a tidal wave generated by a nuclear weapon—was visualized by a diplomat-scholar-novelist more than half a decade before Leo Szilard delivered Einstein's famous letter to President Roosevelt. In *Public Faces,* published in 1933, Harold Nicolson incorporated two technological advances that were to reach fruition only toward the end of World War II, jet (or rocket) engines and atomic bombs.[2] The climax of this extraordinary novel was a British jet-delivered atomic bomb dropped into the Atlantic some three hundred miles off the coast of Charleston (as a weapon test!), which generated a tsunami that hit Charleston and two neighboring cities, killing 90,000 people.

I have told this story of unanticipated technological discovery in detail partly because it is almost monotonously faithful to what we were warned against in my first paragraph—being wholly preoccupied with simply accomplishing, with the sought new technology, what the old technology did—and partly because it involves one of the two most expensive and extensive R&D projects ever undertaken (space technology being the other). But I haven't answered the question why so much of the extraordinary potential of nuclear weapons had to be stumbled on. The question deserves an answer that I can't claim to give. But it looks as if several considerations apply.

One is that people were designing bombs to do more and more, and better and better, what bombs had always done; what *else* nuclear bombs might do that was interesting and useful, or interesting and dangerous, was slow to be appreciated. (When proponents of the Strategic Defense Initiative—"Star Wars"—took center stage, "exotic" weapon effects took front stage, too.)

Second may be that secrecy and curiosity are somewhat incompatible. Only professionals—security-cleared professionals—had access to the technology and to the testing. Later, schoolchildren would design experiments to be performed aboard the shuttle in outer space; no such access was available during nuclear testing. The Harold Nicolsons who might have known just enough not to know any better than to "invent" radio blackout for fictional excitement couldn't get close enough. (And if they did, they might have been denied the security clearance needed for access to their own writings!)

There is a temptation to attribute this blind stumbling onto newer and newer nuclear potentialities to military predilections, military institutions, a military mindset. But the history of postwar civilian nuclear developments does not clearly appear to be qualitatively superior. The first breathless writing about nuclear energy went overboard with electricity "too cheap to meter." That I think we can excuse as simply bad economics and bad technological thinking: somebody forgot that all you get with nuclear energy is hot water. You still have to generate electricity and transmit it. (Free gasoline doesn't mean free automobiles, free roads, free parking . . .)

What the early explorers of nuclear energy noticed was that nuclear generation didn't require any "fuel," anything that had to be "burned." (Nuclear fuel "burns" only metaphorically.) But it was the navy that recognized the more interesting fact that nuclear energy doesn't require any oxygen! (For anthropological reasons we think of "fuel" as what oxidizes, not as either one of two substances that interact to release energy.) Anaerobic generation of energy was something only submariners—and later, space explorers—could appreciate: air was scarcer than diesel fuel under water.

Least appreciated by early enthusiasts for nuclear energy was what is likely, in decades to come, to be valued more than nuclear energy for electric power—radioisotopes. They have revolutionized medical diagnosis and medical treatment; they have revolutionized physiological research, especially neurological research in the brain; their applications in research seem unlimited. Ironically the evolution of nuclear capability went from the gigantic—the megaton fireball and the 1,000 megawatt power plant—to the molecular.

I have picked on the developers of nuclear energy; let me pick, for a while, on myself and some of my colleagues. During the 1970s and early 1980s I participated in something like five different energy studies. Each of these studies involved twenty or thirty people who shared responsibility for the policy conclusions. Each involved economists, technologists, and political scientists; some involved businessmen from energy-producing or energy-using industries. I recently had occasion to go back and look at all these energy studies to see what we had to say about the environment. The first, sponsored by the Ford Foundation and administered by the Mitre Corporation, was a two-year study that resulted in a four-hundred-page book; its subject was nuclear energy.[3] The book contained extensive discussions of reactor safety, nuclear wastes, and weapon proliferation, had eight pages on the health effects of burning coal, and two pages on greenhouse gases.

A second study, administered by Resources for the Future and also financed by the Ford Foundation, produced a book that had six references in the index to carbon dioxide and the greenhouse effect adding up to about ten pages—ten pages out of six hundred![4] We were utterly focused on the "energy crisis"—the oil shortage and the associated inflation. "Greenhouse" hadn't worked its way into the attention of the environmentally concerned scientific community. But I can see no reason why it shouldn't have: enough was known to permit speculation, even analysis of potential consequences. (There was not yet a Harold Nicolson to write the appropriate futuristic novel, or, if there was, this phenomenon hadn't reached his attention.)

In 1979, the Committee for Economic Development published a sixty-two-page booklet that I had written.[5] I had one prefatory paragraph that mentioned environmental health, productivity, and aesthetics, not a word on greenhouse gases. No one ever pointed out my omission of carbon dioxide. No one noticed.

Three years later I participated in a study on energy pricing policy, a joint project of the Committee for Economic Development and the Conservation Foundation. (A co-chairman of the study was William K.

Reilly, president of the Conservation Foundation, who headed the Environmental Protection Agency in the first Bush administration.) We reported on the effect of energy pricing on energy technology, energy conservation, new energy resources, inflation, poverty, employment, income distribution, and economic efficiency in general.[6] We included one sentence on the environment in our seventy-five-page report, and nothing on carbon dioxide. In all these cases the study was oriented toward a "well-defined" issue, a tightly defined issue, a consensually recognized issue, an unambiguous issue. In short, an issue that was badly defined for anticipating what would be perceived to be important in the next decade—or even sooner.[7]

Carbon dioxide I first heard about from an interesting source: a study group at the National Defense University in Washington, D.C., the military services' one-year course for people at the equivalent rank of colonel. The military, of course, had no responsibility for greenhouse policy; the military wanted only to anticipate what climate change might consist of and what difference it might make for military operations. The navy wanted to know whether the Arctic ice cap would exist in the summertime, and how thick it might be, some decades from now; the army remembered the Battle of the Bulge and the decisive influence of fog. For the military there was no "greenhouse problem," only a potential "greenhouse environment," and they were free to exercise imagination.

My first serious acquaintance with the "carbon dioxide problem," as it was then called, was in 1978. The chancellor of Germany had put the issue on the agenda of a "summit" to be held in Venice, and the White House asked the National Academy of Sciences for advice. (I believe the chancellor's motivation may have been that his nuclear energy programs were being attacked by Greens, and he wanted to publicize the perils of coal.) I, utterly innocent of the subject, was made chairman of a committee of twelve and had to educate myself in a hurry. It is pertinent to report here that among the very few people I found who had a broad background in the subject were Jesse Ausubel and Bill Clark, both International Institute for Applied Systems Analysis (IIASA) alumni, and of course Roger Revelle, well known to IIASA. I never, at the time, discovered any other research organization that had done integrated work on the subject. Individuals worked on aspects of the subject at numerous locations; only at IIASA did the topic appear to have organized itself. The National Academy had indeed set up a committee a few years earlier, headed by Jules Charney, to examine the likely "global warming" due to an increase in CO_2. It reported the now classic 3 ± 1.5 C, and that was the end of it.

The subject got a boost at the end of the Carter administration. The synthetic fuels bill that was passed in 1980, out of concern for the high carbon concentration in coal-based gas and liquid, called for a study, again by the National Academy, of the "carbon dioxide problem." A committee, somewhat overlapping my earlier committee, this time chaired by William Nierenberg, studied the subject for two years and issued a book-length report in 1983,[8] a report somewhat at variance with another report released within the same month by the Environmental Protection Agency. Partly, at least, because the two reports differed in their assessments of seriousness and urgency, there was some media attention. Then mostly silence in the United States. Research in aspects of the subject accelerated but with little if any coordination.

It was a few hot summers that propelled the subject into scientific prominence in the United States, and the scientific "community" was not in advance of the general public and the media. In 1995 there were, to take an example, two hundred American economists participating in greenhouse research; fifteen years earlier I think there were two. Some people think the subject is urgent, that a decade matters. Why didn't the subject get, ten or twenty years earlier, the attention it gets now? Was something missing, without which scientific attention could not be mobilized? Money, of course; foundation and government money is available now as it was not some years ago. But what may have been most lacking was imagination. Or perhaps coordination: so many disciplines are involved that scientists engaged in what was potentially "greenhouse research" may not have known there was a greenhouse phenomenon to which their work was pertinent, or, if they did, how to connect with the work of other disciplines remote from their own.

IIASA played a leading role in getting scientific attention, even policy attention, drawn to the greenhouse problem. Might it have done more? What is the next comparable issue that needs an imaginative systems approach to mobilize the world's scientific attention?

NOTES

1. See Cowan and Foray for a taxonomy of research procedures including research by accident. R. Cowan and D. Foray, *The Changing Economics of Technological Learning,* WP-95–39, International Institute for Applied Systems Analysis, Laxenburg, Austria, 1995.

2. H. Nicolson, *Public Faces* (Houghton Mifflin Company, Boston and New York, 1933).

3. S. M. Keeny, Jr., ed., *Nuclear Power: Issues and Choices* (Ballinger Publishing Co., Cambridge, MA, 1977).

4. H. H. Landsberg, ed., *Energy: The Next Twenty Years* (Ballinger Publishing Co., Cambridge, MA, 1979).

5. T. C. Schelling, "Thinking through the Energy Problem" (62-page booklet), Committee for Economic Development, New York, 1979.

6. Committee for Economic Development (CED), *Energy Prices and Public Policy* (75-page report), a Statement by the Research and Policy Committee of the Committee for Economic Development and The Conservation Foundation, New York, July, 1982.

7. See Brooks for development of this argument as a "management attention problem." H. Brooks, *The Problem of Attention Management in Innovation for Sustainability,* WP-95–41, International Institute for Applied Systems Analysis, Laxenburg, Austria, 1995.

8. National Academy of Sciences, Carbon Dioxide Assessment Committee, *Climate Change: Report of the Carbon Dioxide Assessment Committee,* National Academy Press, Washington, DC, 1983.

16

Vietnam: Reflections and Lessons

■ The most salient characteristic of the United States' engagement in Vietnam was that both the Lyndon Johnson and the Richard Nixon administrations saw the initial Viet Cong insurgency and the later full-scale military engagement with North Vietnamese forces as an integral part of the cold war. A senior member of Lyndon Johnson's staff explained to me that the seventeenth parallel was an extension of the Potsdam agreement. We were committed to holding the line at that parallel just as we were committed to hold the line at the Elbe or at the border between Greece and Bulgaria.

Strangely, this conception appeared to entail the view not only that the war was an integral part of the cold war, but also that North Vietnam was an integral part of a monolithic and almost seamless communist bloc. And this was even after the split between China and the Soviet Union had become visible to the outside world as both bitter and probably irreversible.

I doubt whether the North Vietnamese were much concerned with whether they were part of the cold war or not. However willing and eager they were to receive material assistance from the Soviet Union, they were unlikely to think of themselves as any kind of satellite, or even as another Cuba. Their own relations with China were clearly incompatible with any thought of a Moscow–Beijing–Hanoi axis. Any interests they had in Cambodia and other neighboring nations were surely interests of their own, not interests subordinate to those of

Moscow. They could only have shaken their heads in puzzlement if told that the seventeenth parallel created in the 1950s as a national boundary was in any way a spiritual descendant of the conference at Potsdam.

That the North Vietnamese construed the stakes and the issues altogether differently from the way the United States government construed them, especially in identifying the struggle in Vietnam with the cold war, does not itself invalidate an American interpretation at the time that what was a stake at the seventeenth parallel was exactly what was a stake at the thirty-eighth parallel in Korea twenty years earlier. But it does raise the question of whether the United States was *obliged* to see that connection and to respond accordingly. It also prompts the question whether, if indeed the seventeenth parallel acquired the symbolic status of the thirty-eighth parallel, it had already acquired that status at the time Indochina was divided in the 1950s or it had acquired that status as a consequence of the United States' involvement—even as a result of the U.S. government's choice to construe the struggle in Vietnam as part of the cold war.

The issue here is one of expectations and interpretations: whether the United States had to defend its honor, its reputation, and its commitments to allies around the world by defending South Vietnam at whatever cost, is largely a matter of whether Germans and Greeks and South Koreans and Russians and Chinese perceive the struggle in that fashion. If they did, that must be because the United States government manifested and articulated that symbolism and that interpretation just as Ho Chi Minh articulated the struggle as a test of whether a poor Asian socialist country could outlast a rich American capitalist one in a test of military stamina. United States leaders called attention to themselves as responding to a cold war challenge to a seamless boundary surrounding the Soviet bloc.

I belabor the issue because it is a key to the question whether the United States cultivated an unnecessary sense of commitment when it elected to construe the attempts to subvert and invade South Vietnam as part of the Moscow-inspired and Moscow-led cold war. What "escalated" in Vietnam was not only the commitment of resources, the level of violence and the area of involvement, but also the stakes in the contest.

It is important to understand how the stakes can come to be raised so high. I perceive at least two mechanisms that work together. One is *justification,* the other is *deterrence.*

The involvement is justified on grounds that the conflict is not local but worldwide, that the United States must meet its commitments here or have its commitments doubted in other places, that as leader of the free world, the United States has no choice, that this struggle has ramifications for the entire region through a domino process, and has ramifications as far away as Berlin, Greece, and Cuba. The deterrence dimension is the hope of making it clear to the other side that the United States commitment is so immense and so obligatory and so unavoidable that it has no choice but to stick to the end at whatever cost, the hope being that the other side will recognize the fruitlessness of trying to outlast the United States.

The cold war is over, and maybe we need not worry about repeating mistakes that our cold war thinking led us into. But I am not sure that our cold war thinking was peculiar to the cold war. It will almost always be the case when the United States, or an alliance led by the United States contemplates, or engages in, military action, that the action contemplated or engaged in has to be justified; and the justification will almost certainly adduce principles that transcend the concrete local issues. Exalting those principles and dedicating the nation to them will almost certainly enlarge the stakes in the game. And usually also to persuade the opponent that the United States must act unless demands are met or must stay in the contest until some kind of victory is achieved, the United States will have to display and advertise that if it does not rise to the occasion here, other aggressors will be emboldened in other times and places, threatened nations will submit rather than count on American help, and any kind of new world order will lose its infrastructure.

This is a genuine dilemma. The need to find justification in broad principles rather than local interests is genuine and legitimate, and the importance of providing grounds for the belief that the United States and its allies cannot afford to back down should not be minimized. But these two needs are met only at great risk. I can only call attention to the dilemma, I cannot resolve it until I know whether the next occasion is going to be Panmunjom, the seventeenth parallel, Berlin, Cuba, or the Persian Gulf.

A stunning feature of the war in Vietnam was the extraordinary stability of American–Chinese and American–Soviet relations during that entire war. I spent the spring of 1965 in London, reading editorials in the *London Times* and the *Financial Times,* and talking with people in government. The most widespread objection to the bombing of North Vietnam was that the bombing so greatly raised the probability that communist China would intervene; specifically it was almost universally argued that if American aircraft ever went north of Hanoi the Chinese would be impelled to intervene. But the United States regularly had military aircraft within five or ten seconds' flying time of the Chinese border, and I believe there were at least a hundred border crossings recorded in the newspapers, and never a sign that the Chinese would let themselves be provoked into an imprudent military intervention.

It was during that war that American relations with China improved dramatically. The fact that we were in a bitter and expensive war with a Soviet ally that the Soviets were materially supporting seemed to have no influence on Soviet–American relations either. The Soviets obliged by trying to present no embarrassing targets to American aircraft or naval vessels, and both sides were able to pretend that there was no Soviet personnel at North Vietnamese antiaircraft sites.

In the aftermath of the Cuban crisis of 1962 the era of Soviet–American or Soviet–NATO crisis was simply over. The invasion of Czechoslovakia in 1968 temporarily postponed SALT negotiations, but the war in Vietnam did not keep them from resuming. The imperturbability of both China and the Soviet Union during this period is one of the period's most stunning features.

Similarly striking and significant, though not nearly so astonishing, is the role that nuclear weapons did not play. Early in the Korean War the prime minister of Great Britain had flown to Washington to beseech President Truman not to consider using nuclear weapons in Korea. Nobody had to importune Lyndon Johnson not to use such weapons in Vietnam. We had come a long way since 1953, when President Eisenhower approved a policy statement, "In the event of hostilities, the United States will consider nuclear weapons to be as available for use as other munitions."[1] And in 1954, "such weapons must now be treated as in fact having become conventional."[2] And in 1955, "in any combat where these things can be used on strictly military targets and for strictly military purposes, I see no reason why they shouldn't be used just exactly as you would use a bullet or anything else."[3]

Ten years later, in September 1964, Lyndon Johnson said, "Make no mistake. There is no such thing as a conventional nuclear weapon. For nineteen peril-filled years no nation has loosed the atom against another. To do so now is a political decision of the highest order."[4] I confess I do not believe that President Eisenhower really meant what he said, but surely by the 1960s almost nobody expected nuclear weapons to be pertinent unless the war escalated way beyond Vietnam.

It is indeed a tribute to how far nuclear expectations had traveled in that decade that hardly anybody remarked, during Vietnam, on the absence of debate about possible use of nuclear weapons. Of course, there may not have been targets that demanded nuclear attacks. But if nuclear weapons were, in Eisenhower's words, "as available for use as other munitions," we should have heard arguments or reports of arguments about targets, means of delivery, yields, and burst elevations. No, they were simply not available.

Vietnam reminds us of how exceptionally difficult it can be to get out of a war that one would prefer not to continue. There may be very few points, if any, at which a government can turn around and get out, declaring victory (or defeat) but getting out. Is there any way to identify one of those rare moments? The late spring of 1968 may have been one. After the Tet offensive, Washington was full of people who had appeared enthusiasts of the war for several years who were discovering that they had really been against it since even before the Tet offensive. This was a wholly demoralizing setback, particularly to the aspirations and pretensions of military intelligence. It was an easy time to come out and say "I told you so." Maybe it was unfortunate that it turned out to have been enough of a setback for the other side, too, so that nobody could take advantage of the occasion to develop a consensus and go to the president and say it was time to get out.

President Johnson indeed gave President Nixon an opportunity, and Nixon acted wrongly, not necessarily unwisely, but wrongly in the event. I think he recognized the opportunity; but he wanted to do the right thing, and right thing meant nothing precipitous, nothing disgraceful, only getting out "with honor." If you are flying in the clouds and running out of fuel and don't dare to descend for fear the clouds reach the ground, if you ever see an opening, dive! Probably when there is an opportunity to get out of a war one has to grasp it promptly, as President Nixon did not.

The lesson that may need to be learned over and over, a lesson that possibly no one can ever apply, is the extraordinary difficulty of pulling out of a situation in which one has invested heavily. Whatever the reasons why the United States got into Vietnam, the ultimate reason that we were there from late 1965 until the time we finally evacuated was that nobody could persuasively invent a graceful way of getting out. Lyndon Johnson came as close as one might to demonstrating a principle that I have quoted from Ernest May on a number of occasions. That is that "governments" never surrender the wars they fight. New governments have to come in to do the surrendering. Lyndon Johnson let a new government in, and it failed to take advantage.

I do not think the United States government ever seriously studied the option of getting out of Vietnam. The reason I do not think so is not that I have not heard about plans, but that I think planning for that kind of contingency is something that governments are almost constitutionally incapable of—probably all governments and not just governments like the one in the United States. To officially and seriously ask people during Vietnam to make plans to pull the rug out from under those who were over there fighting would be terribly risky—not only with respect to leaks to the enemy, but also leaks to one's own people, and to one's political opponents. To acknowledge withdrawal as a responsible option to study plays into the hands of those who already want to get out and who want an admission in principle that it is a legitimate option, thereby giving them bargaining power.

For that reason, to talk about the need to set up a procedure in which you will always examine that option is to ask the impossible. A leader cannot permit that. Any hint that such an option is being taken seriously could seriously demoralize the military officers responsible for conducting the war. Perhaps such studies can only be done unofficially. Somebody has to volunteer to go off and study the problems saying, "I know that my president could never acquiesce to my doing this at his request; I won't even ask him if he wants it done, because it would be unfair to require the president to give an answer, and his answer would have to be negative."

It occurs to me as I write this [1996] that I may incur disfavor somewhere by even hinting that the United States will ever again need to turn around and get out. But the difficulty of turning around and getting out should go into that calculation of risks that I mentioned earlier, the calculation whether to raise the stakes to justify the action and to create that credible commitment.

Khrushchev in 1960 said that democracies were too soft to fight in wars of national liberation. "Soft" is too simple a diagnosis, but I think a dozen years later we knew what he meant and grudgingly conceded that he had a point. What we didn't know and what he didn't know was that the Soviet Union's kind of socialism and despotism could prove just as soft. He died before Afghanistan could show up his misplaced confidence.

And the Soviet Union didn't even have the cold war to cement its commitment in Afghanistan or to justify it. Vietnam and its many postmortem analyses invite reexamination in the light of the Soviet fiasco in Afghanistan, but I am not the one to provide it.

NOTES

1. McGeorge Bundy, *Danger and Survival: Choices about the Bomb in the First Fifty Years* (New York: Random House, 1988), 246.
2. Ibid., 268.
3. Ibid., 278.
4. *New York Times*, 8 September 1964, 18.

Social Dynamics

17

Social Mechanisms and Social Dynamics

■ Social mechanisms may be contrasted with theories, laws, correlations, and black boxes. There is near consensus on a hierarchy that has "mere" correlations at the bottom, with laws higher up. Laws that are black boxes (i.e., opaque as to how they work) are, even if fully reliable like the law of gravity, less helpful than laws that work transparently. Theories have less status than laws if the laws are well established and the theories not; theories built on established laws, like the theory of planetary motion, are at the summit.

A pervasive question for social phenomena is the role, or the exclusive role, of "methodological individualism," the notion that the ultimate unit of analysis is a rational, or at least a *purposive,* individual. Some believe that any social phenomenon that cannot be reduced to the behavior (choices) of individuals is a black box and therefore unsatisfactory. There is some notion that what is inside a black box must be a social mechanism, or several social mechanisms.

What, though, are social mechanisms, and where do they fit? And are social mechanisms little things, big things, or great big things? Did Keynesian theory constitute a social mechanism; is the arms race a social mechanism; is inflation a social mechanism? Or is giggling such a mechanism, or yawning, or the propagation of gossip? On the relation of social mechanisms to theories, I propose that a theory may comprise many social mechanisms, but also that a social mechanism may comprise many theories. And a particular issue that arises is whether a social mechanism can be purely mathematical. That may depend on what "purely" means, as I shall propose in a moment.

I propose—and I believe I am paraphrasing Peter Hedström and Richard Swedberg in their introductory essay to *Social Mechanisms: An Analytical Approach to Social Theory*—that a social mechanism is a plausible hypothesis, or set of plausible hypotheses, that could be the explanation of some social phenomenon, the explanation being in terms of interactions between individuals and other individuals, or between individuals and some social aggregate. (I interact with an individual if I change lanes when his front bumper approaches within five feet of my rear bumper; I interact with a social aggregate when I adjust my speed to the average speed on the highway.) Alternatively, a social mechanism is an *interpretation*, in terms of individual behavior, of a model that abstractly reproduces the phenomenon that needs explaining.

Let me illustrate by means of a phenomenon that is well described, that follows a recognizable pattern, and that fits a simple curve. According to Marchetti, Meyer, and Ausubel (1996:25), "Literally thousands of examples of the dynamics of populations and other growth processes have been well modeled by the simple logistic. Classic examples include the cumulative growth of a child's vocabulary and the adoption of hybrid corn by Iowa farmers." The authors proceed to show that life expectancy, fertility rates, and infant mortality conform nicely to a logistic pattern over time for virtually every country or region of the world.

The logistic for their purpose is defined as a trajectory of increase or decrease over time in a variable that is subject to upper or lower limits (including zero), with the rate of increase (or decrease) being proportional both to the value of the variable itself and to the difference between the value of the variable and the upper or lower limit. Specifically, if X embarks, from a very small initial value, on a growth trajectory, subject to an upper limit L, the *rate of increase* of X is proportionate to X times $(L - X)$ [i.e., $dX/dt = aX(L - X)$]. The curve is the familiar ogive, sigmoid, or S-curve.

This is not yet a social mechanism, but it invites interpretation. Marchetti et al.'s analysis of population involves some speculative analysis of what individual behavior underlies these fertility and mortality rates. I say they do not yet have a social mechanism not because their interpretations are speculative and far from substantiated but because they are incomplete. If they were complete, I'd say they had presented a social mechanism that *could be* the explanation. Without their speculative interpretation, they have a fascinating black box. Something is going on. Someone might propose a "law" on the basis of enough instances; indeed, if we look at children's vocabularies, Iowa farmers, Finnish and Egyptian fertility, and "thousands of examples," we might formulate a law not limited to population growth. But it would be a law without a mechanism, until we had the mechanism. (And probably, for many of those examples, various mechanisms have been identified, or can be.)

Let me now propose another logistic curve, with an underlying interpretation. A new author publishes a highly successful first novel. Sales data are gathered on a monthly basis. Over the course of three years, sales follow a logistic path, growing exponentially at first, then passing an inflection point, and declining exponentially until the leftover copies are remaindered. We compare that pattern with those of other works of fiction, biography, and history and find a lot of logistic curves, enough so that publishers and bookstores get familiar with the S-curve.

Can we think of a social mechanism that accounts for these dynamics? Of course we can. People read the book, and if they like it, they talk about it, some people more than others; the more people read the book, the more people there are to talk about it. Some of the people they talk to buy the book; if they like it, they talk about it. Talk is proportionate to the number of people who have read the book; if all talk is equally effective, the number talking about it grows exponentially. But there is a limit to the number of people likely to be recruited; eventually most of those who would be interested have already heard of the book, maybe bought it, and when they want to talk about it find that there's hardly anybody left who hasn't already heard about it. If there were initially L potentially interested readers, and N have now read it and want to talk about it, and everybody who has read it meets and talks about it with n out of the L per week, there will be $N \times n \times L$ contacts per week, with $N \times n \times (L - N)$ of them potentially productive, and N will grow logistically.

If we began with the sales data as I described, I would call the process I just described a social mechanism. It may be false—the underlying reason for the shape of the curve may be altogether different—

but it is a mechanism that can account for what we observed. Furthermore, it may be a mechanism we can attempt to verify or disconfirm.

We might call the mechanism I described (but probably not the fertility–mortality mechanism of Marchetti et al.) a "contagion" model. Or a "recruitment" model. We can modify it in several ways. One is to consider only the recent recruits to N to be contagious (i.e., to still talk about the book). In our formula for $dN/dt = Nn(L - N)$, we replace N with the integral of dN/dt from $t - x$ to t, where x is the mean period of contagion. During the early near-exponential growth period, the difference will not much affect the shape of the growth curve, and the final result will have much the same shape. We can also let L change over time in a contagion model if we now interpret it as a disease model and let some of the potential susceptibles learn to take precautions.

The disease analogy is valuable here. A former student of mine, a physician, worked in a public health clinic in Africa for several years, long enough to notice that the demand for free measles vaccinations came in great waves. He grew curious and studied what was going on. At the peak of a measles epidemic, mothers brought their babies over great distances to be vaccinated; the vaccination worked, the epidemic was shortly ended, and all the living babies were immune to measles either from vaccination or from surviving the disease. Then no epidemic could take hold until the stock of nonimmune newborns had reached "critical mass," in which each sick infant could infect, on average, more than one additional infant. Then the disease would begin to take off, but mothers were not motivated to carry their infants long distances until they became acutely aware of neighbors' babies dying of measles. Then the vaccination boomed again. This model included critical mass, the logistic phenomenon, and two "contagions"—the measles contagion, and the contagious transmission of alarm. Its parameters were population density, birthrate, periods of incubation and infectiousness specific to measles, and speed of transmission of alarming information.

The question whether a social mechanism can be purely mathematical, raised earlier, I think I have answered. The S-shaped logistic curve is not a social mechanism, but it can be generated by a social mechanism, and it can be given a specific interpretation as a social mechanism. And I believe that the social mechanism we found underlying our mathematical model (or that we guessed was underlying the model), like most social mechanisms, may suggest other phenomena to which our model is pertinent. It is easy to assimilate our fiction-sales phenomenon to the Iowa farmers' adoption of hybrid corn, but less easy to analogize to the underlying social mechanism for children's vocabulary. And once one sees how the logistic-generating differential equation, $dN/dt = aN(L - N)$, can account for Iowa corn and romantic novels, it is no surprise that "thousands of examples" of logistic-shaped growth processes have been discovered.

Of course, the logistic shape will necessarily be only an approximation to the empirical data, and there may be other differential equations that can generate approximations to the data. The *fact* of a good fit does not alone confirm the conjectured underlying mechanism, and there may be a family of mechanisms of which the contagion model is only one. A sine curve may decently mimic a logistic curve, and if the variable that appears to be exhausting its limit is capable of reversal— unlike the novel, which probably won't come back on the used-book market—we may want to hold judgment until we are sure it is approaching an asymptote and not a wavecrest.

Here is where "pure" mathematics can contribute to the study of social mechanisms. Note that exponential growth itself can reflect a social mechanism; in an infinite population, the $(L - N)$ term never becomes binding, and the logistic curve never reaches that inflection point. We can easily think of social mechanisms that lead to pure exponential growth; having babies is one. Can a simple differential equation generate either exponential growth or sine waves, according to initial conditions or parameter values? How simple can it be?

Ecologists have studied predator–prey relations and found cycles; linear second-order differential equations—derived from a pair of first-order linear equations—are sufficient. Studying the *form* of the equation can suggest what to look for in a social mechanism and can help us to see how the same mechanism might account for either exponential growth or cycles (see the appendix at the end of this chapter).

Before introducing some other social mechanisms, I want to advert to the discussion of what one can do with social mechanisms that one cannot do with "mere correlations," or, perhaps more aptly, "curve fitting." A distinction is often made between *prediction* as the goal of science (and as the "test" of a theory), and *explanation* (i.e., a better understanding of what is going on, a more satisfying place to stop). I think there are at least three other advantages of having a grasp of the social mechanism that lies behind the regularity in behavior.

One is that exceptions to the familiar regularities may be identified with, for example, particular parameter values. An instance is in the contagion model if only those recently infected (recruited) perform the recruitment function. In ordinary exponential growth, $N(t)$ is proportionate to $N(t) - N(t - p)$, with p being here interpreted as the (constant) period that an infected individual remains infectious; the rate of growth is still exponential but slower. (We could also make some allowance for an "incubation" period between infection and infectiousness, which would work in the same direction.) But since ultimately the exponential growth gets damped by the approach to the population limit, it can turn out that a very short period of infectiousness leads to an S-curve that does not approach the population limit. If we compare, say, diseases and find that some show S-curves that peter out and others go on to approach the original limit, knowing something about the mechanism lets us know what to look for—incubation period, period of infectiousness (unlimited with HIV), and perhaps some fraction of the sick quarantined—to explain the differences and verify the mechanism itself.

A second advantage of knowing the mechanism is the possibility of intervention. For example, in the measles case, the number actually sick—not the number that have cumulatively contracted the disease—is probably what the mothers observe. A more rapid growth in N, the number who have already contracted the disease, will be associated with a larger $N(t) - N(t - x)$, the number currently sick. Paradoxically, accelerating the epidemic can accelerate the vaccination rate and reduce the ultimate cumulative number of infants who contract the disease and, of course, the number who die. Other interventions, such as publicity, might be suggested. Since our measles epidemic is only a metaphor for social mechanisms that display the same underlying generative process, there may be varieties of interventions to consider once we have the underlying mechanism and some appreciation of the most influential parameters.

A third advantage is that once we see the mechanism, how it works, and maybe its mathematical shape, we have a kind of template that may fit other phenomena. True, we want to avoid what Robert Solow described as what a person does who gets a new electric drill for

Christmas—go around looking for holes that need to be drilled—but if measles and sales of fiction respond, maybe we can find similar shapes and forms underlying the number of voters supporting Ross Perot during the 1992 election campaign, the number of people who procure microwave ovens, or the number of young people in America who went into science and engineering post-Sputnik. (And we want to beware of concluding too soon that the curve is logistic rather than sinusoidal, or something in between. Once we have a bit of insight into what *might* be the underlying mechanism, we know something about what to look for.)

And it is important to recognize that there often are whole families of social mechanisms, differing from each other significantly, that apply to similar-appearing phenomena, just as there are phenomena that appear similar but reflect wholly different mechanisms. Jon Elster has often called attention to the fact that the eagle, the pterodactyl, and the sparrow have wings, and bats have wings, and flying fish have wings, but the evolutionary mechanisms may unite the pterodactyl, the eagle, and the sparrow but not the bat or the flying fish. Measles, especially its etiology, and flying fish are a far cry from what we might explain as a "social mechanism," but the *models* of the mechanisms may sometimes unite them. In my teaching, I always spend some time on the ordinary household thermostat as a generator of cyclical behavior that helps one to understand what kinds of ingredients in a model—social, mechanical, biological, even psychological—may produce key characteristics of a phenomenon. (Long ago, when I smoked, I found that I kept running out of matches; upon reflection, it seemed that after a match famine I scrounged matches at every chance, to build up a safe inventory, then relaxed and used up all my matches, and had to survive another famine and start scrounging again, somewhat like the mothers responding to the measles cycle. This might qualify as a "psychological mechanism.")

To illustrate what I mean by "families" of mechanisms—what I once called "families of models"—mechanisms that produce similar results, and enjoy similarities but also differences, I shall offer a number of examples of the kind of things often called "self-fulfilling prophecies." A somewhat better term would probably be "self-realizing expectations," with prophecies being only one source of the expectations.

Here are some examples. If people expect a coffee shortage, there will be a coffee shortage. If people believe that only the careless split infinitives, only the careless will split infinitives. If people believe that the only women who smoke on the street are streetwalkers, the only women who smoke on the street will be streetwalkers. If people believe the Harvard department of economics will always attract the best faculty, the Harvard department will always attract the best faculty. If men believe they will be conspicuous without neckties, they will be conspicuous without neckties. If people believe neighbors invariably develop hostility toward each other, neighbors will develop hostility toward each other. If young men believe they needn't learn to cook because the women they marry will have learned how to cook, and if young women believe young men believe that, then young men needn't learn to cook. If people believe it will be hard to get spare parts for Korean-manufactured automobiles, it will be hard to get spare parts for Korean-manufactured automobiles. If scientists, engineers, and international-business people believe that English is bound to become the unique common language of science, engineering, and international business, English will become the language of scientists, engineers, and international-business people. If people believe that nobody with a southern accent can get the party nomination for the U.S. presidency, then nobody with a southern accent can get the nomination. If everybody believes you have to go early to get a seat, you'll have to go early to get a seat. If gunfighters know that when two gunfighters meet on the street they will both draw, and the first to draw will probably kill the other, then when two gunfighters meet they will draw, and the first to draw will probably kill the other. If people believe that only men and women looking for sexual partners go to singles bars, only men and women looking for sexual partners will go to singles bars. If people believe the bank is insolvent, it already is. If people believe that nobody can win a lottery twice, nobody will win a lottery twice. And if people believe that someone recently very popular in social life is on the way out, he or she is on the way out.

These propositions all have, or would have if I eliminated a little variety in the formulation, the same syntactical form. They all invite exploration for underlying mechanisms. Any one of them, I think you will agree, could be true; most of them could also be false. Some of them share a mechanism: coffee shortage, the insolvent bank—we could have mentioned the stock market—and going early to get a seat all look to me like the same principle. A few—the smoking prostitutes, the frequenters of singles bars—look like powerful coercive conventions: women who like to smoke who are not prostitutes will feel the privation when walking at night, and somebody who wants to use the telephone may feel unwelcome or conspicuous in the singles bar. The split infinitive and the necktie appear to be similar; the cooking case could be seen either as a coercive convention or as a socially convenient rule of coordination, since there may be advantages to the division of labor and skills, and in monogamous societies, any other rule specifying which member of a marital pair should learn to cook (e.g., alphabetical) would prove confusing and inefficient. The mechanism behind the inability of the southern accent to get nominated may be twofold: no one wants to waste a vote in the primaries, and no one wants to contribute to the campaign fund of a certain loser; without those votes in the early primaries and without those campaign funds, the case is hopeless.

I'm sure not only that there are thousands of such (possibly true) propositions about self-realizing expectations but that there are, at least, dozens or scores of different mechanisms underlying them. I've never seen a catalogue. If given the opportunity, I'd like to offer a prize to whoever—decided by common consent—provides the richest menu of self-realizing expectations. More than that, I'd like to see the beginning of a catalogue of social mechanisms. And for teaching, I would like to see a catalogue of unexpected or anomalous observed behaviors that test and exercise students' skills in solving the puzzles, conceiving of (potential) social mechanisms.

There has been much discussion of "laws" in the social sciences— what laws are, and how they relate to mechanisms or to correlations. We don't have many recognized laws in my discipline, economics—in recent years, what might earlier have been identified as empirically established "laws" have come to be referred to as "stylized facts." But I want to introduce a kind of law that plays a great role in physics, mechanics, genetics, and chemistry, that plays a great role in demography, that plays an unrecognized role (i.e., unrecognized as "law") in economics, and that, though less pervasive, probably has application to sociology and all the disciplines interested in social mechanisms.

I shall introduce this kind of law by introducing two similar-sounding statements, each of which might qualify as a law, one of which would be a law of behavior of the kind that might be recognized in social theory, and the other a law of the kind to which I want to call attention. Here are the two statements:

1. When the average speed on the Autobahn increases, most drivers will drive a little faster.
2. When most drivers drive a little faster, the average speed on the Autobahn increases.

Alternatively,

1. When the noise level at a reception goes up, most people will speak a little louder.
2. When most people at a reception speak a little louder, the noise level goes up.

In each of these pairs, the first is a proposition about behavior, a falsifiable hypothesis. In each, the second proposition is not about behavior: it follows from the definition of "average speed," or "noise level." There are, especially in economics, less obvious identity relations of this kind, usually arrived at by combining two or more statements that are necessarily, identically, true. The mathematical analogy is the pair

$$aX + bX^2 = Y \quad \text{and} \quad aX + bX^2 = X(a + bX).$$

The first is true only for certain values of X, the second independently of the value of X. In economics, identities of this kind are often called "accounting identities," and they show up in national-income accounting, foreign-transactions accounting, and monetary-system accounting. In demography such an accounting statement would be, for example: In a monogamous society, the number of blacks married to whites is equal to the number of whites married to blacks (as long as we are consistent in the definitions of "whites," "blacks," and "married").

These accounting statements often provide the "feedback loop" in a social mechanism. For example, suppose that the first of the foregoing behavioral statements is found to be approximately true, and that people tend

244   SOCIAL DYNAMICS

1. to each have his or her own preferred average speed, to which he or she would conform if it were the actual average, and
2. when the average speed differs from their preferred average, to drive at a speed midway between their preferred average and the actual average (i.e., they accommodate partway to the actual average). If the average is 65, and one's preferred average is 55, one drives 60; if one's preferred speed is 75, one drives 70.

Suppose now that the average speed on our highway has settled down to where everybody is comfortable (i.e., driving midway between the average and his or her own preferred speed) and the average is 65. Half the people suddenly undergo a change in preference: preferred average for these people goes up by 20 mph. What will happen to the average? Initially, those whose preferred average has increased by 20 mph will drive 10 mph faster. If they were already driving 60, their preferred average must have been 55; now it is 75, and they raise their speed to 70. If they were already driving 75, their preferred average must have been 85; now it is 105, and they will increase their speed to 85. And so on. Since half the drivers raised their speeds by 10 mph, the average must have gone up by 5, to 70.

But it doesn't stop there. Everybody—those whose preferences changed and who raised their speeds, and those who didn't—now experiences an average greater by 5 mph than it used to be, so *all* will raise their speeds by 2.5 mph. And there it goes again: now they all accelerate another 1.25 mph, and so on until the average is 75. Those whose preferences changed are now driving 15 mph faster than before, the rest 5 mph faster.

I imputed an especially simple formula for each driver's chosen speed, linear in the actual and preferred averages; as a result, it turns out that the equilibrium average is simply the average of the preferred speeds. But at least that simple formulation shows the "feedback" effect; those who raise the average pull the others along with them, and pull each other, too. The same mechanism can underlie college grade inflation, restaurant tipping, loudness of dormitory record players, and sometimes legislators' willingness to vote for unpopular measures.

I devoted a chapter entitled "The Inescapable Mathematics of Musical Chairs" to these ineluctable logical propositions in an earlier work (Schelling 1978) and do not want to repeat myself much. But a couple of examples may illustrate. I said, "A fact of some significance is that in a monogamous population the difference between the numbers of unmarried women and unmarried men is the same as the difference between the numbers of women and men" (Schelling 1978:56). I probably should not have said "fact." A fact is usually something that could be true or false and has to be verified; the assertion in that statement follows logically from the definitions of "men," "women," "unmarried," and "monogamous." I added:

> And if we count the women and men over some common age of eligibility for marriage, the percentage difference between the two in a stable population will be the percentage difference in life expectancies at that age. If women live longer or marry earlier there will be more eligible women than men. There will be the same number more of eligible unmarried women than unmarried men. The ratio of unmarried women to unmarried men will be larger, the more people are married. If women begin to marry at seventeen and (as in the United States) have a life expectancy of another sixty years, and men at twenty-one with a life expectancy of fifty, in a stationary population adult women will exceed men in the ratio 60:50. If one-fifth of the men are unmarried, one-third of the women will be. If women marry three years earlier and live seven years longer than men, women will average ten years longer divorced or widowed than men. (Schelling 1978:56)

Some of these (logical) propositions are instantly, or almost instantly, obvious. When Garrison Keillor refers to Lake Woebegone as "where all the children are above average," nobody fails to smile; he could as well say "where all the people give more at Christmas than they receive." It is almost, but not quite, as obvious that if you count all the black neighbors of all the white people in a city, you already know how many white neighbors the black people have. But when there is a great "selling wave" on the stock market, indicated by a decline in average values and heavy turnover, intelligent-sounding people on public radio discuss questions such as where all the money is going that people are taking out of the stock market, apparently unaware that every share sold must have been purchased.

All such logical propositions that I know of are quantitative. They are therefore common in economics, demography, and epidemiology.

(Proportionately more people die in the United States from noninfectious diseases than they did fifty years ago but not because noninfectious diseases have become more deadly.)

Peter Hedström and Richard Swedberg hoped, in organizing the book *Social Mechanisms,* to influence the entire discipline of sociology (and anthropology, political science, and social psychology) to take more interest in social mechanisms, in their discovery and explication, in their typology, in basic mechanisms, and in their variants and offspring. I believe all the authors join in that wish. What we need is to exploit some social mechanisms that will accomplish that. Probably the first step is to achieve critical mass. If we can succeed in that, perhaps we can then look forward to healthy logistic growth.

APPENDIX

Consider two first-order differential equations involving X and Y, each growing or declining as a function of both of their current values (X' denotes the current rate of change of the value of X):

1. $X' = A + BX + CY$
2. $Y' = a + bY + cX$

Differentiating 1, we get:

3. $X'' = BX' + CY'$

Substituting 2 into 3, we get:

4. $X'' = BX' + Ca + CbY + CcX$

If we multiply 1 by b and subtract it from both sides, we eliminate the term in Y, and get:

5. $X'' = (Ca - bA) + (B + b)X' + (Cc - Bb)X.$

The same may be done for Y''; the resulting equation in terms of Y' and Y will have corresponding coefficients (from the symmetry of the coefficients in 5).

If we "solve" this equation, we find five possible modes of behavior:

1. If either of the two coefficients, $(B + b)$ or $(Cc - Bb)$, is positive, X and Y will monotonically grow exponentially.

2. If both are negative, and $(B + b)^2/4 > -(Cc - Bb)$, X and Y will converge monotonically on equilibrium values.
3. If $(Cc - Bb)$ is negative, but $(B + b)^2/4 < -(Cc - Bb)$, X and Y will cyclically (sinusoidally) converge on equilibrium values if $(B + b)$ is negative,
4. will cyclically (sinusoidally) diverge exponentially if $(B + b)$ is positive, and
5. will display a uniform sine curve if $(B + b)$ is zero.

REFERENCES

Marchetti, Cesare, Perrin S. Meyer, and Jesse H. Ausubel. 1996. "Human Population Dynamics Revisited with the Logistic Model: How Much Can Be Modeled and Predicted?" *Technological Forecasting and Social Change*, 52, 1–30.
Schelling, Thomas C. 1978. *Micromotives and Macrobehavior.* New York: W. W. Norton and Company.

18

Dynamic Models of Segregation

PROLOGUE, 2006

■ Sometime in the 1960s I wanted to teach my classes how people's interactions could lead to results that were neither intended nor expected. I had in mind associations or spatial patterns reflecting preferences about whom to associate with in neighborhoods, clubs, classes, or ballparks, or at dining tables. Whether racial or linguistic differences or differences in age or income and wealth were what I had in mind, I'm not sure now. I spent a summer at RAND and took advantage of RAND's library to thumb through a few decades of sociological journals, looking for illustrative material that I could assign to my students. I found nothing I could use, and decided I'd have to work something out for myself.

One afternoon, settling into an airplane seat, I had nothing to read. To amuse myself I experimented with pencil and paper. I made a line of pluses and zeros that I somehow randomized, and postulated that every plus wanted at least half its neighbors to be pluses and similarly with zeros. Those that weren't satisfied would move to where they were satisfied. This was tedious because I had no eraser, but I persuaded myself that the results could prove interesting.

At home I took advantage of my son's coin collection. He had quantities of pennies, both copper and the gray zinc ones we had all used during the war. I spread them out in a line, either in random order or any haphazard way, gave the coppers and the zincs their own preferences about neighbors, and moved the discontents—starting at the left

249

and moving steadily to the right—to where they might inject themselves between two others in the line and be content. The results astonished me. But as I reflected, and as I experimented, the results became plausible and ultimately obvious.

Just to remind you, a line of randomly distributed coppers and zincs that looks like this,

0+000++0+00++00+++0++0++00++00++00++0+0+00+++0++00000+
++000+00++0+0++0,

when each wants at least four out of the eight nearest neighbors to be one's own type, becomes, after two "rounds" of moving:

00000000+++++++++++++++0000000000+++++++++++++++0000
000000000000++++++.

I experimented with different sizes of "neighborhoods"—the six, eight, or ten surrounding coins, different preferences—half like oneself, one-quarter like oneself, and different majority–minority ratios, and got results that fascinated me. A one-dimensional line couldn't take me very far. But in two dimensions it wasn't clear how to intrude a copper or a zinc into the midst of coppers and zincs. I mentioned this problem to Herb Scarf, who suggested I put my pennies on a checkerboard, leaving enough blank spaces to make search and satisfaction possible.

So I made a 16″ × 16″ checkerboard, located zincs and coppers at random with about a fifth of the spaces blank, got my twelve-year-old to sit across from me at the coffee table, and moved discontented zincs and coppers to squares where their demands for like or unlike neighbors were met. We quickly found out it didn't matter much in what order we selected the discontents to move—from middle outward, from out inward, from left to right or diagonally. We kept getting the same kind of results, and the dynamics were intriguing.

I found things I hadn't expected. Usually, once found, these discoveries appeared obvious. If zincs and coppers were majority and minority, or if zincs and coppers had greater and lesser demands for like neighbors, the sizes of eventual clusters and the densities of the different clusters varied accordingly. And when we postulated that zincs and coppers had positive desires for unlike neighbors, especially if they were minority and majority, we got results that appeared weird until we saw what was happening. (The minority, desired as neighbors, had to become "rationed" among the majority.)

I had an interesting experience with computers at that time. I knew nothing about what computers could do, or how they did it, but I knew that RAND had people who did. I approached RAND and asked to be in touch with somebody who could program what I'd been doing. Somebody was put in touch with me. I quickly learned something crucial: programmer and experimenter must work closely, the former understanding what the latter wants, the latter understanding how programs work. But three thousand miles apart, we didn't work that way. For me the results were perplexing. I eventually caught on that I had individuals counting themselves as their own "neighbors," had individuals on edges of the board or in corners miscounting how many neighbors they had, and in other ways had inadequately stipulated exactly how the zincs and coppers were to respond.

I published, along with the "checkerboard" model, a purely analytical model that I called the "bounded neighborhood" model (Schelling 1971); this article is now reprinted in this chapter. That model postulated a finite location that a person was either in or not in, positions within the neighborhood not being of concern. (It could be a model of membership or enrollment or participation, not necessarily location.) I thought the results I got from that model were as interesting as those from the checkerboard, but nobody else appeared to think so. I also explored the nature of a collective "tipping point" with a purely analytical model in a chapter in a book edited by Tony Pascal, *Racial Discrimination in Economic Life,* published about a year later (Pascal 1972). It too got little attention. In that "bounded neighborhood" model it became clear that an important phenomenon can be that a too-tolerant majority can overwhelm a minority and bring about segregation.

I discovered twenty-five years later that I'd been some kind of pioneer. I've never been sure why my little simulation got so much attention after so many years. It must be some limitation of my scientific imagination that I'd no idea I was doing something generic, something with promise beyond my neighborhood application.

I've also had an experience that others may have had, in publishing a much abbreviated version of that model in a book (Schelling 1978), believing that the full treatment in the *Journal of Mathematical Sociol-*

ogy (Schelling 1971) might be more than readers of the book would need. References to my model are usually to the version in the 1978 book, not to the original. I've seen no reference, for example, to the results I got when I postulated a strong preference for neighbors of opposite type. If one is interested in the "neighborhood" effects of differences other than color or race, especially when individuals of one type are much scarcer than individuals of the other type, the "integrationist" preferences become highly plausible. (I put "neighborhood" in quotation marks because residence is not the only possible interpretation.)

Another interesting result that is not in the book version but is in the original—a result that somewhat surprised me until I saw how it worked, and an advantage of doing it manually instead of on a computer—is that if one subjects all the actors to a fairly strict limit on movement, the results are usually that everyone becomes satisfied with less travel and more integration. For example—the linear case is adequate to illustrate—if we impose on all the pluses and zeros a restriction that no one may move more than five spaces, moving to the best available position if satisfaction cannot be achieved within five spaces, the original random line we used above becomes, in one round,

00000+++++000000++++++++000000+++++00000+++++000000
0000+++++++++000.

All except two of the three on the right are satisfied, on average individuals traveled less than half the distance, and the result is much more "integrated." The total number of unlike neighbors in this "restricted travel" version is twice that of the original equilibrium. And in the original, thirty of the seventy individuals ended up with no neighbors at all of opposite type; in this case of restricted movement, only five.

This restricted-movement example is one of several results that may be unanticipated but become obvious with a little experience. Analytically one might say that restricting movement is a substitute for collaboration or anticipation. Unrestricted, and in the absence of collaboration or anticipation, an individual zero will move to the nearest cluster of four or more zeros, passing numerous lonely zeros in what may be a long journey. Sufficiently restricted, the lonely zero may be able only to join the nearest lonely zero, far from satisfactory; but the next lonely zero looking for company can now join the two, making it three, and shortly a fourth will arrive and a fifth. (Increasing the "price" of travel may reduce the "cost" of travel.) By moving, individuals both add and subtract externalities where they leave, and add and subtract where they settle.

A similar principle is observed if the zeros are a minority and the pluses a majority. I remember being so confident that the smaller the minority relative to the majority, the smaller would be the minority clusters, that I wrote this before I tried it. When I tried it, it didn't work. The opposite occurred: the minority clusters became absolutely larger as the minority itself became smaller. What I had originally thought to be so obvious I needn't bother to demonstrate it turned out, upon demonstration, to be just as obviously the opposite.

Now that computers can display all the movement in "real time" there is, I suppose, little advantage in doing this kind of thing manually, but when I was doing it computers could compute but not display, and I often got computer results I could make little sense of until I worked it by hand.

■

INTRODUCTION

People get separated along many lines and in many ways. There is segregation by sex, age, income, language, religion, color, taste, comparative advantage, and the accidents of historical location. Some segregation results from the practices of organizations; some is deliberately organized; and some results from the interplay of individual choices that discriminate. Some of it results from specialized communication systems, like different languages. And some segregation is a corollary of other modes of segregation: residence is correlated with job location and transport.

If blacks exclude whites from their church, or whites exclude blacks, the segregation is organized, and it may be reciprocal or one-sided. If blacks just happen to be Baptists and whites Methodists, the two colors will be segregated Sunday morning whether they intend to be or not. If blacks join a black church because they are more comfortable among their own color, and whites a white church for the same reason, undirected individual choice can lead to segregation. And if the church bulletin board is where people advertise rooms for rent, blacks will rent rooms from blacks and whites from whites because of a communication system that is correlated with churches that are correlated with color.

Some of the same mechanisms segregate college professors. The college may own some housing, from which all but college staff are excluded. Professors choose housing commensurate with their incomes, and houses are clustered by price while professors are clustered by income. Some professors prefer an academic neighborhood; any differential in professorial density will cause them to converge and increase the local density. And house-hunting professors learn about available housing from other professors and their wives or husbands, and the houses they learn about are the ones in neighborhoods where professors already live.

The similarity ends there, and nobody is about to propose a commission to desegregate academics. Professors are not much missed by those they escape from in their residential choices. They are not much noticed by those they live among, and, though proportionately concentrated, are usually a minority in their neighborhood. While indeed they escape classes of people they would not care to live among, they are more conscious of where they do live than of where they don't, and the active choice is more like congregation than segregation, though the result may not be so different.

This chapter is about the kinds of segregation—or separation, or sorting—that can result from discriminatory individual behavior. By "discriminatory" I mean reflecting an awareness, conscious or unconscious, of sex or age or religion or color or whatever the basis of segregation is, an awareness that influences decisions on where to live, whom to sit by, what occupation to join or to avoid, whom to play with or whom to talk to. The essay examines some of the individual incentives, and perceptions of difference, that can lead collectively to segregation. I also examine the extent to which inferences can be drawn, from the phenomenon of collective segregation, about the preferences of individuals, the strengths of those preferences, and the facilities for exercising them.

The ultimate concern is segregation by "color" in the United States. The analysis, though, is so abstract that any twofold distinction could constitute an interpretation—whites and blacks, boys and girls, officers and enlisted men, students and faculty, teenagers and grownups. The only requirement of the analysis is that the distinction be twofold, exhaustive, and recognizable. At least two main processes of segregation are omitted. One is organized action—legal or illegal, coercive or merely exclusionary, subtle or flagrant, open or covert, kindly or malicious, moralistic or pragmatic. The other is the process, largely but not entirely economic, by which the poor get separated from the rich, the less educated from the more educated, the unskilled from the skilled, the poorly dressed from the well dressed, in where they work and live and eat and play, in whom they know and whom they date and whom they go to school with. Evidently color is correlated with income, and income with residence; so even if residential choices were color-blind and unconstrained by organized discrimination, whites and blacks would not be randomly distributed among residences.[1]

This is not to claim that the organized discrimination or the economically induced segregation is less powerful, or less important, or less a matter of social concern, than the segregation that results from individual action. Indeed, aside from the question of which mechanism may account for the greater part of observed separation by color, the organized segregation involves civil rights; and the economically determined segregation raises questions of social equity. On those grounds alone the subject of this chapter might be put in third place. Still, in a matter as important as racial segregation in the United States, even third place deserves attention.

It is not easy, though, to draw the lines separating "individually motivated" segregation, the more organized kind, and the economically induced kind. Habit and tradition are substitutes for organization. Fear of sanctions can coerce behavior whether or not the fear is justified, and whether the sanctions are consensual, conspiratorial, or dictated. Common expectations can lead to concerted behavior. ("Guilt by association," when sanctioned by ostracism, is often self-enforcing.)

The economically induced separation is also intermixed with discrimination. To choose a neighborhood is to choose neighbors. To pick a neighborhood with good schools is to pick a neighborhood of people who appreciate schools (or of people who want to be with the kind of people who appreciate schools). People may furthermore rely, even in making economic choices, on information that is itself color-discriminating; believing that darker-skinned people are on the average poorer than lighter-skinned, one may consciously or unconsciously rely on color as an index of poverty (or, believing that others rely on color as an index, adopt their signals and indices in order to coincide with them). And if the process goes far enough, alienation, strangeness, fear, hostility, and sheer habit can accentuate the tendency toward avoidance. If the sentiment is reciprocated, positive feedback will amplify the segregating tendencies of both groups.

Economic segregation might statistically explain some initial degree of segregation; if that degree were enough to cause color-consciousness, a superstructure of pure discrimination could complete the job. Eliminating the economic differentials entirely might not cause the collapse of the segregated system that it had already generated.

For all these reasons the lines dividing the individually motivated, the collectively enforced, and the economically induced segregation are not clear lines at all. They are furthermore not the only mechanisms of segregation. (Separate or specialized communication systems —especially distinct languages—can have a strong segregating influence that, though interacting with the three processes mentioned, is nevertheless a different mechanism.) Still, they are very different mechanisms and have to be separately understood.

This chapter, then, is about those mechanisms that translate unorganized individual behavior into collective results.

Individual Incentives and Collective Results

Economists are familiar with systems that lead to aggregate results that the individual neither intends nor needs to be aware of, results that sometimes have no recognizable counterpart at the level of the individual. The creation of money by a commercial banking system is one; the way savings decisions cause depressions or inflations is another.

Similarly, biological evolution is responsible for a lot of sorting and separating, but the little creatures that mate and reproduce and forage for food would be amazed to know that they were bringing about separation of species, territorial sorting, or the extinction of species. Among social examples, the coexistence or extinction of second languages is a phenomenon that, though affected by decrees and school curricula, is a massive "free market" activity with results that correspond to no conscious collective choice.

Romance and marriage are exceedingly individual and private activities, at least in the United States, but their genetic consequences are altogether aggregate. The law and the church may constrain us in our choices, and some traditions of segregation are enormously coercive; but outside of royal families there are few marriages that are part of a genetic plan. When a short boy marries a tall girl, or a blond a brunette, it is no part of the individual's purpose to increase genetic randomization or to change some frequency distribution within the population.

In some cases small incentives, almost imperceptible differentials, can lead to strikingly polarized results. Gresham's Law is a good example. Some traditions, furthermore, are sternly self-enforcing: passing to the right of an oncoming car. Some collective actions have almost the appearance of being organized—fads in clothing, dancing, and car styles.

Some of the phenomena of segregation may be similarly complex in relation to the dynamics of individual choice. One might even be tempted to suppose that some "unseen hand" separates people in a manner that, though foreseen and intended by no one, corresponds to some consensus or collective preference or popular will. But in economics we know a great many macro-phenomena, like depression and inflation, that do not reflect any universal desire for lower incomes or higher prices. Similarly with bank failures and market crashes. What goes on in the "hearts and minds" of small savers has little to do with whether or not they cause a depression. The hearts and minds and motives and habits of millions of people who participate in a segregated society may or may not bear close correspondence to the massive results that collectively they can generate.

We also know that people who would not support the government with private donations may vote a system of mandatory taxes to finance public goods. The worth of a new turnpike may depend on keeping traffic below the level of congestion that would just equalize its attractiveness with that of alternative routes. "Freedom of choice" is sometimes nothing more than the lack of enforceable contract. Thus unregulated behavior does not necessarily reflect preferences about its results. People acting individually are often unable to affect the results; they can only affect their own positions within the overall results.

Evolutionary processes may lead to typewriter keyboards, weights and measures and the pitches of screws, systems of coinage, and left-hand or righthand automobile drive that are self-perpetuating in spite of inefficiency until a heroic effort can bring about concerted change. Yet, also, some massive concerted changes can occasionally be brought about by some simple manipulation, as when daylight saving goes into effect or when a round table replaces a rectangular one in a highly stratified conference room.

A special reason for doubting any social efficiency in aggregate segregation is that the range of choice is often so meager. The demographic map of almost any American metropolitan area suggests that it is easy to find residential areas that are all white or nearly so and areas that are all black or nearly so but hard to find localities in which neither whites nor nonwhites are more than, say, three-quarters of the total. And, comparing decennial maps, it is nearly impossible to find an area that, if integrated within that range, will remain integrated long enough for a man to get his house paid for or his children through school. The distribution is so U-shaped that it is virtually a choice of two extremes.

Some Quantitative Constraints

Counting blacks and whites in a residential block or on a baseball team will not tell how they get along. But it tells something, especially if numbers and ratios matter to the people who are moving in or out of the block or being recruited for the team. And with quantitative analysis there are usually a few logical constraints, somewhat analogous to the balance-sheet identities in economics. Being logical constraints, they contain no news unless one just never thought of them before.

The simplest constraint on dichotomous mixing is that, within a given set of boundaries, not both groups (colors, sexes) can enjoy numerical superiority. Within the population as a whole, the numerical ratio is determined at any given time; but locally, in a city or a neighborhood, a church or a school, either blacks or whites can be a majority. But if each insists on being a *local* majority, there is only one mixture that will satisfy them—complete segregation.

Relaxing the condition, if whites want to be at least three-fourths and blacks at least one-third, it won't work. If whites want to be at least two-thirds and blacks no fewer than one-fifth, there is a small range of mixtures that meet the conditions. And not everybody can be in the mixtures if the aggregate ratio is outside the range.

Other constraints have to do with small numbers. A classroom can be mixed but the teacher is one color; mixed marriages can occur only in the ratio of one to one; a three-man team cannot represent both colors equally, and even in a two-man team each member has company exclusively of one color.

In spatial arrangements, like a neighborhood or a hospital ward, everybody is next to somebody. A neighborhood may be 10 percent black or white; but if you have a neighbor on either side, the minimum nonzero percentage of opposite color is fifty. If people draw their boundaries differently we can have everybody in a minority: at dinner, with men and women seated alternately, everyone is outnumbered two to one locally by the opposite sex but can join a three-fifths majority if he extends his horizon to the next person on either side. If blacks occupy one-sixth of the beds in a hospital and there are four beds to a room, at least 40 percent of the whites will be in all-white rooms.

Transitions involve the usual relations among numbers and their derivatives. A college that wants suddenly to have 10 percent of its students black will have to admit 40 percent black freshmen, only to discover that it must then pass three classes before accepting more. Professions, occupations, and residences are constrained by these numerical relations, whether it is color, sex, nationality, age, or degree status that is involved.

Separating Mechanisms

The simple mathematics of ratios and mixtures tells us something about what outcomes are logically possible, but tells us little about the behavior that leads to, or that leads away from, particular outcomes. To understand what kinds of segregation or integration may result from individual choice, we have to look at the processes by which various mixtures and separations are brought about. We have to look at the incentives and the behavior that the incentives motivate, and particularly the way that different individuals comprising the society impinge on each other's choices and react to each other's presence.

There are many different incentives or criteria by which blacks and whites, or boys and girls, become separated. Whites may simply prefer to be among whites and blacks among blacks. Alternatively, whites may merely avoid or escape blacks and blacks avoid or escape whites. Whites may prefer the company of whites, while the blacks don't care.

Whites may prefer to be among whites and blacks also prefer to be among whites, but if the whites can afford to live or to eat or to belong where the blacks cannot afford to follow, separation can occur.

Whites and blacks may not mind each other's presence, may even prefer integration, but may nevertheless wish to avoid minority status. Except for a mixture at exactly 50:50, no mixture will then be self-sustaining because there is none without a minority, and if the minority evacuates, complete segregation occurs. If both blacks and whites can tolerate minority status but there is a limit to how small a minority the members of either color are willing to be—for example, a 25 percent minority—initial mixtures ranging from 25 to 75 percent will survive, but initial mixtures more extreme than that will lose their minority members and become all of one color. And if those who leave move to where they constitute a majority, they will increase the majority there and may cause the other color to evacuate.

Evidently if there are lower limits to the minority status that either color can tolerate, and if complete segregation obtains initially, no individual will move to an area dominated by the other color. Complete segregation is then a stable equilibrium. The concerted movement of blacks into a white area or whites into a black area could achieve some minimum percentage; but in the absence of concert, somebody has to move first and nobody will.

What follows is an abstract exploration of some of the quantitative dynamics of segregating behavior. The first section is a spatial model in which people—actually, not "people" but items or counters or units of some sort—distribute themselves along a line or within an area in accordance with preferences about the composition of their surrounding neighborhoods. In this model there are no objective neighborhood boundaries; everybody defines his neighborhood by reference to his own location. An individual moves if he is not content with the color mixture of his neighborhood, moving to where the color mixture does meet his demands. For simplicity, everyone of a given color has the same preferences regarding the color mixture of his own neighbors.

In the next model space is compartmented. People are either in or out of a common neighborhood; those in it all belong to the same neighborhood irrespective of their particular locations within it. What matters to everybody is the color ratio within the whole neighborhood. In that model we allow variation in the preferences of individuals, some being more tolerant than others, some perhaps having a preference for integration. We look there at the questions, what distribution of preferences or tolerances among the individuals of a given color may be compatible or not compatible with dynamically stable mixtures, what effect the initial conditions and the dynamics of movement will have on the outcome, and what kinds of numerical constraints may alter the results.

In the final section we look at neighborhoods with a limited capacity, like real residential neighborhoods with some fixed number of houses or schools with a limit on pupils.

SPATIAL PROXIMITY MODEL

The results of this section are experimental. They are crude and abstract but have the advantage that anyone can reproduce them using materials that are readily available.

I assume a population exhaustively divided into two groups; everyone's membership is permanent and recognizable. Everybody is assumed to care about the color of the people he lives among and to be able to observe the number of blacks and whites that occupy a piece of territory. Everybody has a particular location at any moment; and everybody is capable of moving if he is dissatisfied with the color mixture where he is. The numbers of blacks and whites, their color preferences, and the sizes of "neighborhoods" will be manipulated.

I am going to put my population into a stylized two-dimensional area. But the general idea is vividly displayed by distributing individuals along a line. There is some fascination in the process as it emerges in the linear model; furthermore, the linear experiment can be replicated by any reader in five minutes; variants can readily be devised, and any reader with a spare half hour can change the hypotheses to suit himself.

Linear Distribution

The line of pluses and zeros in Figure 18.1 corresponds to the odd and even digits in a column of random numbers. It turns out that there are 35 pluses and 35 zeros, and they look reasonably "random." (There is no need to test for oddities and regularities; it is easier to replicate numbers.) We interpret these pluses and zeros to be people spread

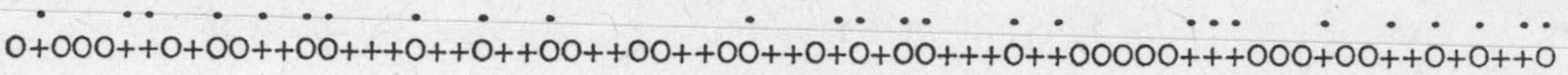

```
 .    ..  .  ...   .  . .  .        .    .. ..   . .       ...   .  . . .  ..
O+OOO++O+OO++OO+++O++O++OO++OO++OO++O+O+OO+++O++OOOOO+++OOO+OO++O+O++O
```

Figure 18.1

out in a line, each concerned about whether his neighbors are pluses or zeros.

We expect the pluses and zeros to be evenly distributed in the large but unevenly in the small. If pluses and zeros are content to live together in a ratio of about 50:50, each finds himself in a satisfactorily mixed neighborhood if he defines his neighborhood as a long-enough stretch of the line. If instead everybody defines "his neighborhood" as his own house and the two neighbors next to him, a quarter of the pluses and zeros are going to be "surrounded" by neighbors of opposite color. Satisfaction depends on how far one's "neighborhood" extends.

Suppose, now, that everybody wants at least half his neighbors to be like himself, and that everyone defines "his neighborhood" to include the four nearest neighbors on either side of him. A plus wants at least four of his eight nearest neighbors to be pluses; a zero wants at least four of his eight nearest neighbors to be zeros. Including himself, this means that he wants a bare majority, five out of the nine. (For those near the end of the line the rule is that, of the four neighbors on the side toward the center plus the one, two, or three outboard neighbors, half must be like oneself.)

I have put a dot over each individual whose neighborhood does not meet his demands. Twelve pluses and 14 zeros are dissatisfied with their neighborhoods. (The expected number is just under 13.)

Now we need a rule about how they move. Let me specify that a dissatisfied member moves to the nearest point that meets his minimum demand—the nearest point at which half his neighbors will be like himself at the time he arrives there. "Nearest" means the point reached by passing the smallest number of neighbors on the way; and he merely intrudes himself between two others when he gets there. We also need an order of moving; arbitrarily let the discontented members move in turn, counting from left to right. The plus second from the left moves first, the plus sixth from the end moves second, and so forth.

Two things happen as they move. Some who were content will become discontent, because like members move out of their neighborhoods or opposite members move in. And some who were discontent become content, as opposite neighbors move away or like neighbors move close. The rule will be that any originally discontented member who is content when his turn comes will not move after all, and anyone who becomes discontent in the process will have his turn after the 26 original discontents have had their innings. The definition of the neighborhood is the four nearest neighbors on either side at the moment one decides to move or to stay; if someone moves in between a man and his next neighbor, the fourth neighbor away ceases to be a neighbor because he is now fifth.

Nobody in this model anticipates the movements of others. When it is his turn to move, he moves if his neighborhood demands are not met where he is and stays if they are, without regard to what he could anticipate if he studied the prospective decisions of others whose turns come later.

Applying these rules, the first discontented man on the left (the plus located second from the end) moves to the right, passing six neighbors, and inserts himself between the zero who was eighth from the end and the plus who was ninth. He now has two pluses among the four neighbors to the left of him and two among the four to the right. The next to move is the plus who used to be fifth from the end; he moves over to the right of the plus that moved first and is followed by the plus who was to his right, who moves over to the right of him. Next the discontented zero moves, and he moves to the left, passing four pluses along the way. (Rightward he would have had to move a greater distance.)

And so forth. The result is the top line of Figure 18.2, containing 8 newly discontent individuals. We now give them their turn; and they rearrange themselves to form the bottom line in Figure 18.2, in which

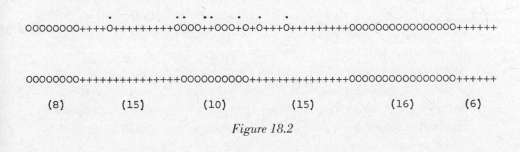

Figure 18.2

everybody is content. (There is no guarantee that two rounds will put everybody in equilibrium. One round may do it, more than two may be required.)

The result is six clusters of like individuals, containing 8, 15, 10, 15, 16, and 6 members respectively, averaging 12 members.

If we count the like and opposite neighbors among the 8 belonging to each of the 70 individuals, we find that 440 out of 540 neighbors are of the same color, or 81.5 percent. Counting himself as the ninth member of his neighborhood, everyone lives in a neighborhood in which his own color predominates by an average ratio somewhat greater than five to one. This resulted from individuals' *seeking* a ratio not less than five to four.

We knew in advance that, if there were an equilibrium, everyone would get to live in a neighborhood at least five-ninths his own color. We knew, or could easily have discovered, that equilibria existed. We could have surmised that our rules of movement would lead to equilibria, because each person's search for others of like color raises the likelihood that people of like color will stay in the place he moves to and those of opposite color will leave it. We got a more striking result.

Notice that regular alternation of pluses and zeros would satisfy everybody with exactly half his neighbors of like color. So would alternating pairs: two zeros, two pluses, two more zeros, and so on. Alternating groups of three or four would not meet the condition; but any groups of five or more in alternation meet it. We got groups of about twelve.

If people, though not wanting to be in the minority, prefer mixed neighborhoods, only 40 of the 70 managed it at all. Thirty have no neighbors of opposite color. Furthermore, those who would like some neighbors of opposite color but are unwilling themselves to be in a neighborhood minority can move nearer to the boundary of their own color group, but will never go beyond the boundary; if everybody wants two or three neighbors of opposite color, there will be turmoil within each group as people continually move to within a couple of spaces of the color boundary; none of this affects the grouping itself.

Another example, taken from another column in the same table of random digits, is presented in Figure 18.3. Initially, out of 72 members, there are 30 discontents; one round of moving leads to the second line in that figure, and again we have six groups and the same resulting neighborhood statistics as in the first case.

```
 ..    .   .   .   .   .    ...       ..    ..   .   .   .  ...    .       .      .  . .    .  . ....
++OOO+OO++O+O++O++O++OOOOO++OOO++OOO++O+++OO+OO+OOOO+OOO+++O+O+++O+OO+O+
```

```
OOOOOOO+++++++++++++OOOOOOOOOOOOOOO+++++++++OOOOOOOOOOOOOOOOOO+++++++++++
```

<table>
<tr><td>(7)</td><td>(14)</td><td>(14)</td><td>(9)</td><td>(17)</td><td>(11)</td></tr>
</table>

Figure 18.3

Some tabletop experimentation suggests that, with everything else the same, different random sequences yield from about five groupings with an average of 14 members to seven or eight groupings with an average of 9 or 10, six being the modal number of groups and 12 the modal size. Similar experimentation suggests that the order of moves makes little difference unless we allow our people to anticipate outcomes and seek either to maximize or to minimize group sizes. (It also appears that the 70 people who fit within the margins of a typewriter are a large enough linear sample if pluses and zeros are about equal in number.)

Variations of the Linear Model

Our model has five elements that are readily varied: neighborhood size, demanded percentage of one's own color, ratio of pluses to zeros in the total population, rules governing movement, and original configuration.

If we reduce neighborhood size, we get the same general pattern of alternating clusters (which we could call "alternating homogeneous neighborhoods" except that they do not correspond to "neighborhoods" as the members define them). Testing with the two random sequences that we have already used, defining the neighborhood as three people on either side of a resident, we find 37 initial discontents in the first case, 5 new discontents after the first round of moving, and an end result of groups with an average size of 7. The second sequence generates 29 discontents, 3 new ones after the first round, with an end result of seven clusters averaging 10 per cluster. Further experiment suggests a mean of 7 or 8 per cluster, or approximately twice the minimum size of cluster that meets the demand (alternating clusters of 4) and with the average person's neighborhood 75 to 80 percent his own color.[2]

To illustrate what happens if we have unequal totals of zeros and pluses, I have eliminated 17 of the 35 zeros in our first sequence (from Figure 18.1), letting a roll of the die determine the fate of each zero. Different rolls of the die will get you different reduced sequences; Figure 18.4 shows the one that I got.

All the zeros are now discontent, and three of the pluses, with neighborhood defined again as the four on either side. Using the familiar rules of movement, all the zeros congregate in the first round, as in Figure 18.5.

Again rolling dice to eliminate about half the zeros from our second sequence (that of Figure 18.3), yielding again a ratio of about 2 pluses for every zero, I found 18 of 20 zeros discontent and 2 of the pluses. After a round of moving there were still 4 discontented members, and after a second round, 2. After the third round, the top line of Figure 18.6 was obtained. Using the same original sequence, but another random deletion, and again another random deletion from the same original, the other two lines of Figure 18.6 were obtained as end results.

As the numerical inequality of majority and minority becomes more

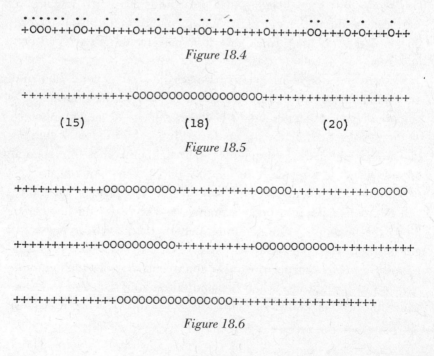

```
 .  . . . . .   . .    .     .     .    .     . .   .      .        .         . .       . . .     .
+000+++00++0+++0++0++0++00++0++++0+++++00+++0+0++0++
```

Figure 18.4

```
+++++++++++++++00000000000000000000+++++++++++++++++
```

(15)   (18)   (20)

Figure 18.5

```
++++++++++++++0000000000+++++++++++++00000+++++++++++00000
```

```
++++++++++++++0000000000+++++++++++++00000000000+++++++++++
```

```
++++++++++++++00000000000000000+++++++++++++++++++
```

Figure 18.6

extreme, one expects the segregation (or "segregatedness") of the majority to become more extreme—there aren't enough of the minority to go around. If pluses outnumber zeros by four to one, even a regular distribution will give pluses an average of but one-fifth neighbors of opposite color. Furthermore, since the minimum size of segregated cluster that will satisfy the minority's demands for one-half neighbors of like color is 5, the minimum clustering among the *majority* that would satisfy the minority is 4×5, or 20.

What is less immediately apparent, but becomes apparent on reflection, is that the minority itself tends to become more segregated from the majority, as its relative size diminishes. That is, the minority clusters become absolutely larger as the minority itself becomes smaller. Or, to put it differently, as the relative size of the minority is diminished, the number (frequency) of minority clusters diminishes more than proportionately.

The reason is not too obscure: as the randomly distributed minority diminishes in proportion to the total population, the likelihood of four or more members of the minority among any eight consecutive individuals diminishes more than proportionately; so the number of potentially stable clusters ("growth nodes") declines relative to the minority population. Since everybody, under our rules of movement, travels to a place where at least four of eight individuals are his own color, they all end up together at places where at least four out of eight originally coincided by chance. Even demanding but three neighbors of like color, a 10 percent minority will form clusters averaging about twice the size of those obtained in Figures 18.2 and 18.3. Demanding half, the mean cluster of a 10 percent minority will contain upward of 100 if the aggregate population is large enough to sustain any growth nodes at all!

Restricted Movement

A related point is interesting. Suppose the minority becomes relatively small, say 20 or 10 percent, still with initial random distribution, and we impose a limit on travel distance. Some, probably many, perhaps all, will become unable to move to where their demands are satisfied. We then modify the rule: if a neighborhood half your own color does not occur within the allowed radius of travel, move to the nearest place where three out of eight occur. The result is that everybody achieves his desired neighborhood, half or more his own color, without traveling as far as if he and the others had been free to travel! The limitation on travel channels them into the smaller, more frequently occurring, potential clusters ("growth nodes"), which proceed to grow into clusters that more than satisfy them.

Thus travel restrictions imposed on individual movement can be a substitute for *concerted* movement. It can also be a substitute for *anticipatory* movement, in which a person stops among three fellows of like color knowing, as he makes it four, that a fifth will soon arrive and stay.

All of this is too abstract and artificial to be a motion picture of whites and blacks or boys and girls choosing houses along a road or even stools along a counter, but it is suggestive of a segregating process and illustrates some of the dynamics that could be present in individually motivated segregation.

Area Distribution

A convenience of the linear model was that, when we moved a person (or a counter) from a spot between two neighbors to a spot between two other neighbors, everybody could just move over to make room or to close up the vacant space, and the linear order was preserved. To do the same in two dimensions is not so easy; we need a rule about who moves over in which direction to make room for the newcomer or to close up a vacated space. A convenient way to meet the problem is to deal with absolute space rather than relative position: divide the area into a fixed number of spaces, leaving some vacant; a person can move only into a vacant space, and when he moves he leaves a space vacant. "Neighborhood" is defined in terms of neighboring spaces.

To be specific: divide the area into squares like a checkerboard (but without any alternating colors) and distribute colored chips at random among the squares, leaving some squares blank. One chip occupies one square, and a "neighborhood" is defined by reference to the surrounding squares; each square on a checkerboard has eight immediate neighbors, so a convenient minimum-sized neighborhood for an individual is his own square plus the eight surrounding; larger "neighborhoods" can be considered by including the twenty-four surrounding squares in a 5 × 5 area, and so on. An actual board, in contrast to a conceptually infinite expanse, has sides and corners; but, then, so probably do most natural areas, and this may be no disadvantage. Along the edge of the board a square has only five neighboring squares, and in a corner but three. The whole area need not itself be square; convenience may dictate some other shape, and if one wants to study the influence of natural boundaries a long and narrow checkerboard six squares wide and twenty long will have a higher proportion of residents on the edge than a square one.

In order that people be able to move there must be some vacant spaces; in order that they have significant choice of where to move there must be quite a few. While it is interesting to study what happens if the supply of vacant spaces is restricted, unless one is actually studying the influence of restricted supply the vacancies need to be a reasonably high proportion of the total. It turns out that 25 to 30 percent vacancies allows fair freedom of movement without making the board too empty.

The rule of movement, then, is that an individual discontent with his own neighborhood moves to the nearest vacant spot that surrounds him with a neighborhood that meets his demands. In most of what I'm going to show you, "neighborhood" has been defined as the eight surrounding squares that, together with one's own square, form a 3×3 square. Color preferences with respect to one's neighborhood can be defined either in absolute terms—the number of one's own color within the eight surrounding squares—or in relative terms—the ratio of neighbors of one's own color to opposite color among the eight surrounding squares. If all squares were occupied, every absolute number would correspond to a ratio; but because one may have anywhere from zero up to eight neighbors, there are eight denominators and therefore eight numerators to specify in describing one's neighborhood demands.

As in the linear model, I make an initial distribution at random. It might make sense to distribute the blank spaces evenly, but I let them be determined at random, too. (It makes some difference.) In some cases I use equal numbers of blacks and whites, in others a ratio of two to one or larger. I then specify for each of the colors what its neighborhood demands are. I specify the rule for moving, which is usually to move to the nearest satisfactory square, with "nearest" measured by the number of squares one traverses horizontally and vertically. And we need a rule to specify the order in which they move; this part is more complicated than in the linear model. In some cases the order of move was determined merely by position on the board, such as working generally from left to right; it is also interesting to see what happens if all of one color completes its moves before the other color moves. It is possible, of course, to test the sensitivity of the results with respect to the order of moves. Because what is reported here has all been done by hand and eye, no exact rule for the order of moves has been adhered to strictly.

As a start, we can use some of the same parameters as in our first linear model: equal numbers of pluses (now denoted by #) and zeros distributed at random among the squares, with a suitable fraction left blank for ease of movement; "neighborhood" defined as the eight surrounding squares; and a universal demand that no fewer than half of one's neighbors be of the same color, the discontent moving to the nearest satisfactory vacant square.

Figure 18.7 shows an initial random distribution. There are 13 rows, 16 columns, 208 squares (for reasons of convenience that I won't go into here). It might seem unnecessary to reproduce an actual picture of randomly distributed pluses and zeros and blank squares; but some of the results are going to be judged impressionistically, and it is worthwhile to get some idea of the kind of picture or pattern that emerges from a random distribution. If one insists on finding "homogeneous neighborhoods" in this random distribution, he can certainly do so. *Randomness* is not *regularity*. If we are going to look at "segregated areas" and try to form an impression of how segregated they are, or an impression of how segregated they *look*, we may want a little practice at drawing neighborhood boundaries in random patterns.

Figure 18.7

SOCIAL DYNAMICS

Patterns, though, can be deceptive, and it is useful to have some measures of segregation or concentration or clustering or sorting. One possible measure is the average proportion of neighbors of like or opposite color. If we count neighbors of like color and opposite color for each of the 138 randomly distributed pluses and zeros in Figure 18.7, we find that zeros on the average have 53 percent of their neighbors of the same color, pluses 46 percent. (The percentages can differ because pluses and zeros can have different numbers of blank neighboring spaces.)

There are, of course, many regular patterns that would yield everybody a set of neighbors half his own color and half the opposite color. Neglecting blank spaces for the moment, a checkerboard pattern will do it; alternate diagonal lines of pluses and zeros will do it; dividing the board into 2 × 2 squares of four cells each, and forming a checkerboard out of these four-cell squares, will also yield everybody four neighbors of like color and four of opposite. And so forth. *Patterning* is evidently related to, but distinct from, any measures of neighborhood homogeneity that we may work out.[3]

Now play the game of solitaire. Identify the discontents—there are 25 pluses and 18 zeros in Figure 18.7 whose neighbors are less than half of like color—and, in some order, move them to where they are content, continuing to move the newly discontent until the entire board is in equilibrium. (There is no guarantee that everybody can find a blank space that suits him, but with the numbers we are using now it usually turns out that he can.) The *particular* outcome will depend very much on the order in which discontented pluses and zeros are moved, the *character* of the outcome not very much. The reader can check this for himself in about ten minutes if he has a roll of pennies, a roll of nickels, and a sheet of paper big enough for 16 columns of one-inch squares.

Working generally from the upper left corner downward and to the right, an equilibrium was achieved as shown in Figure 18.8. Working from the center outward, the same initial distribution led to the equilibrium of Figure 18.9. The "segregation" in Figure 18.8 is too striking to need comment. In Figure 18.9 it is also striking, though more fragmented. The pattern in Figure 18.9 stands out more if we draw some boundaries; this may be cheating a little, in making an apparent pattern stand out, but that is why I first presented it without the bound-

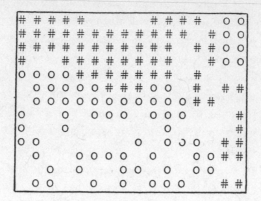

Figure 18.8

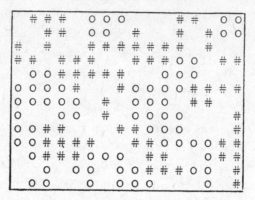

Figure 18.9

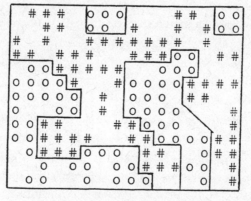

Figure 18.10

SOCIAL DYNAMICS

aries and also why I suggested scrutinizing the random distribution to see that some "segregated patterns" emerged even there. Figure 18.10 is Figure 18.9 with some boundaries drawn in.

Though the patterns are impressionistic, the neighbor count is not. Originally, it will be recalled, the average percentage of like neighbors that the zeros had was 53, and pluses 46. On the average, both colors were virtually at their minimum demands (as they were bound to be with equal numbers in total). But after the discontent have adjusted, and the newly discontent have then adjusted, and so on to equilibrium as in Figure 18.9, zeros on the average have neighbors who are five-sixths zeros, pluses have neighbors who are four-fifths pluses. On the average each zero has five neighbors, of whom (not quite) one is a plus. Including himself, there are thus six people in the average zero's neighborhood, five his own color and one opposite. In the average plus's neighborhood there are about four and a half neighbors, one of whom is a zero; including himself, there are thus five and a half residents of his neighborhood, one of whom is of opposite color.

Another statistic is the percentage of the population that has no neighbors of opposite color at all. In the random distribution of Figure 18.7 the number is 13 (which corresponds exactly to the expected value in an 11×16 matrix with one-third pluses, one-third zeros, and one-third blanks). In Figure 18.9 the number is 54, or approximately 40 percent compared with 10 percent.[4]

The figures are even more lopsided for Figure 18.8, where, counting himself, the average person lives in a neighborhood that is 90 percent his own color (89 for zeros, 91 for pluses), and two-thirds of both colors have no neighbors of opposite color.

Now we can vary some parameters to see what we get. I shall not show any more initial distributions; they all involve the same 13 rows and 16 columns, blank spaces usually equal to about 30 percent of the total, and a random distribution of the two colors. We can vary the ratio of pluses to zeros, the fraction or number of own color that pluses and zeros demand, and in a few cases the size of the "neighborhood." We look, too, at the consequences of an actual preference for integration.

My samples have been too small, so far, to allow serious generalizations, so I shall formulate hypotheses suggested by what I have done. Quantitative measures, of course, refer exclusively to an artificial checkerboard and are unlikely to have any quantitative analogue in the living world. *Comparisons* among them, however, such as the effect of reducing or enlarging the size of a minority, may be capable of some extension to that world.

Intensity of Demand for Like Neighbors

If the two colors are equal in number, if neighborhoods are defined as the eight surrounding squares, and if both colors have the same demands for neighbors like themselves, the segregation that results is slight when the demand is for about one-third of one's neighbors like oneself and striking when the demand is as high as one-half. This result is both impressionistic and quantitative: the results are visually striking in the one case and not in the other, and the resulting ratios of like neighbors to opposite neighbors is upward of four to one for demands of one-half or more, and less than one and one-half for demands of about one-third. See Figure 18.11, in which the demands are for about one-third.[5]

An increase in the demand for like neighbors does three things. First, it increases the number that will be initially discontent. Second, it increases the like-color density that results from each movement: each individual that moves not only *acquires* more neighbors of like color the more he demands, but *becomes* a like neighbor to more neighbors the more he acquires. And, third, the greater the demands the more movement is induced by those that move on the part of those that were originally content. These three effects compound together to

```
  O   O O O O # O   O O O O   O
O   O O   O # # O   O O   O O  
O O # # O O   O # # O     O   O
# # #   O   O O # # O O   O # O
#   # # # #   #     # #       #
  O O #     # #   # O #       #
# O O O #       # O O O #     #
O # # # #   # # # O O   # # # #
O #   # O       O O   O O O   #
O # #   O O # #   O O   O O O  
  O # # # O O # # O O   # O # #
  O O #     # O   # # O # #   #
O O   # #   # #     # #   # #  
```

Figure 18.11

make the resulting segregation a rapidly rising function of demands in the range from about 35 to 50 percent.

When the demands of both colors are for 50 percent, their sum is of course 100 percent. Evidently for neighborhoods with fixed boundaries, no coexistence is possible if the demands of the two colors add up to more than one. In the present model there are not fixed boundaries, so it is possible to have mixed areas with everybody in the majority in his own neighborhood. But the degree of flexibility is not great. Therefore we should expect that demands summing to more than one should result in extreme segregation, as apparently they do.

Unequal Demands

If pluses and zeros are about equal in number but one is more demanding than the other, the more demanding end up with a higher proportion of like neighbors, but not much higher. An illustration is Figure 18.12, in which the zeros (77) and the pluses (72) are about equal in number but the zeros are less demanding. Zeros demand that one out of four or fewer be their own color, two out of five or more; pluses demand two their own color if they have three to five neighbors, three if they have six or seven neighbors, and four out of eight. Zeros end up with a ratio of 2:1 of neighbors their own color; pluses, who are nearly twice as demanding, show the somewhat higher ratio of 2:5.

If one forgets momentarily the logical constraints, there is surprise in this. Shouldn't the more separatist of the two colors get more separated? No, separation is a reciprocal thing: for every white with a black

```
# # # o o o   o o # #   o o o  
# # o   o o o     o # # # o #  
# o     o o   o o # # #   # # #
o o o o     o # # # #     #   #
#     o       # # # # #   # # o
# # o o     o o o o   o       o
# # # # # o       o o o   o   o
# o o # #   o o       o o o o o
# o o # # # # # o   o o o     o
# # o o # # # # o   o o o # o  
# o     # # # # # o # #   # # o
    o o o o o #   # #   #   o  
o o           o   # # #   o o  
```

Figure 18.12

neighbor there is exactly one black with a white neighbor, if "neighbors" are consistently defined. Ratios for the two colors can differ only if pluses have more or fewer pluses as neighbors than zeros have zeros. The ratios differ, that is, only by different mean population densities in the neighborhoods of the two colors. Such a difference does occur but is limited, among other things, by the number of blank spaces on the board. With no blank spaces, the like-neighbor ratios for the two colors would be mathematically constrained to equality if the two colors were equal in number, and for unequal numbers would differ strictly as a function of their numerical ratios. (The percentage of neighbors of opposite color for the majority would be equal to that for the minority multiplied by the numerical ratio of the minority to the majority.)

In Figure 18.12 the pluses are noticeably more compacted than the zeros; the latter are spaced out more. This is a result to be regularly expected—but only after one has learned to expect it.

Unequal Numbers, Equal Demands

If we put one of the two colors in minority status, letting it be outnumbered two to one or four to one, greater segregation occurs than with equal numbers, for any given set of demands on the part of the two colors. When one of the colors numbers only half the other, demands for about one-third neighbors of like color lead to ratios close to two to one for the minority (and, necessarily, still higher for the majority).

Figure 18.13 illustrates this effect. Pluses outnumber zeros about two to one; demands are identical—a minimum of two neighbors of

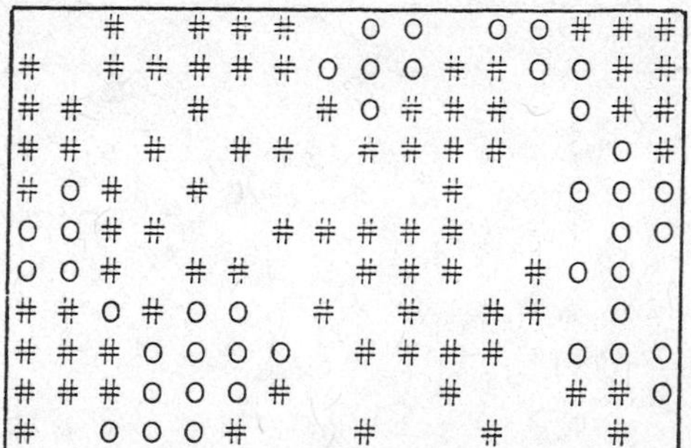

Figure 18.13

like color. The effective "demand" averages about 35 percent. The zeros, whose ratio of like to unlike neighbors in a random distribution is about 1:2, end up with the ratio reversed, 2:1, a fourfold increase in ratio. Pluses went from an initial ratio of 2:1 to a ratio of 4:1.

With extreme color ratios, like five to one or more, the minority tends to display a phenomenon related to its absolute density rather than to its relative density. We observed this earlier in the linear model. The proportion of initially satisfied individuals is so small that nearly everybody in the minority moves. Everybody, furthermore, moves toward whatever cluster of like-colored individuals he can find; and the number of such clusters declines disproportionately as the minority becomes smaller. The result is that the minority forms larger clusters, large enough to cause even a tolerant majority to become locally dissatisfied.

An extreme case of this absolute-number principle is easily envisioned by supposing an area populated initially by one color alone, into which newcomers of opposite color enter one by one. The first is located at random and has no place to go; the best the second can do is to join the first; the third, wherever he lands, if he wants any like neighbors at all, joins the first two, and similarly with the fourth and fifth and all who follow. In the end all the newcomers are together. Each has the choice between joining the only cluster or remaining entirely alone. If the available blank spaces permit them to achieve a significant density, the color initially resident will begin to vacate the locality of the cluster, and the result will be a solid neighborhood of the new color. This result will be independent of the moderateness of the color demands of the newcomers.

The process is illustrated in Figure 18.14, one part of which is an initial random scatter in which the pluses outnumber the zeroes by five to one. Neighborhoods were defined as the 24 surrounding squares. The zeros were given a very moderate demand—an absolute number of but 2 zeros in the entire 24 surrounding squares—and pluses the somewhat immoderate demand that zeros be no more than one-third of the population in the 24 surrounding squares. In the random distribution only a single plus is dissatisfied, the one nearest to the lower right corner. The pattern that results from movement is somewhat sensitive to the precise order of movement imputed to the various dissatisfied zeros, of whom there are 11 out of the 15 individuals. Two results ob-

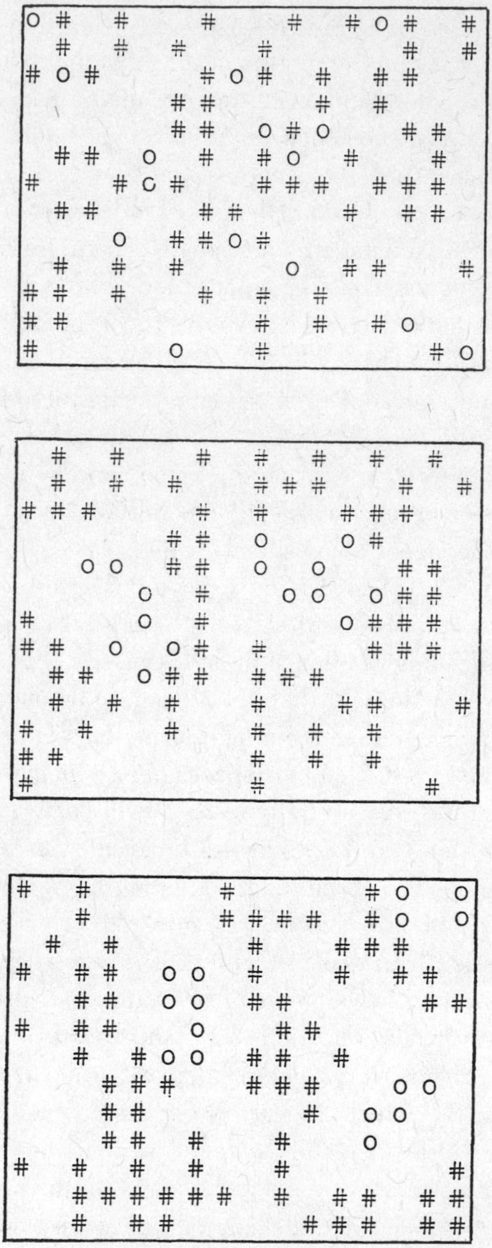

Figure 18.14

SOCIAL DYNAMICS

tained from different moving orders are shown in Figure 18.14. The like-neighbor ratio for zeros can be computed on the basis of either 24 neighboring spaces or, for comparability with earlier results, 8. In the larger neighborhoods, zeros (in the two results) achieve not quite one-half neighbors of like color; computed for the 8-neighbor neighborhoods, they achieve almost three-quarters.

Population Densities

An unexpected result that undoubtedly has ecological significance in some context is in what the sorting does to the population densities of the individual neighborhoods. It will be recalled that with equal numbers of the two colors but different demands, the more demanding color ended with a higher ratio of like to opposite neighbors. This was possible because of a discrepancy in the average number of like neighbors acquired in the process by the two colors. That the more demanding ends up in more homogeneous clusters is mathematically equivalent to the result that the more demanding ends up with more neighbors, in more densely populated neighborhoods. This result was recognized as a mathematical consequence of what appeared to be a discrepancy in the "segregatedness" between the more and the less demanding of the two colors.

Attention was called earlier to Figure 18.12 because pluses had a somewhat higher ratio of like to opposite neighbors than zeros did, a ratio of 2.5 compared with 2.0. The same figure illustrates the density phenomenon. Pluses on the average, in that figure, have 5.35 neighbors, zeros 4.55. Pluses and zeros occupy similar numbers of border positions, so the difference is not due to a discrepancy in the number of neighboring spaces.

Actually the impression one gets in Figure 18.12 is that zeros are even more dispersed, and pluses more compacted, than those numbers suggest. The reason is that many blank spaces are "neighbors" of other blank spaces, yet occur within territories that clearly "belong" to the zeros. Our "neighbor count," computed from the squares adjacent to pluses and zeros, misses this phenomenon. The neighbor count is based on individual neighborhoods, not on any "collective neighborhoods" that we might identify. The pattern in Figure 18.12, however, tempts us to draw territorial boundaries, identifying regions occupied exclusively by zeros and regions occupied exclusively by pluses. When the segregation is quite incomplete, it is by no means easy to do this; and alternative rules for drawing boundaries may lead to quite different results; but in Figure 18.12 the segregation is sufficiently marked to leave little to discretion. We can easily draw neat boundaries that completely separate pluses from zeros, and we can furthermore impute blank spaces almost unambiguously to plus territories and zero territories. If we do this we find the following. Splitting the blank spaces that might plausibly be imputed either to plus territory or to zero territory, the 59 blanks divide into about 14 that we can impute to "plus territory" and about 45 that we can impute to zeros. (Ten ambiguous blanks were divided five each in this calculation.) Including blank spaces "belonging" to them, the 72 pluses occupy territory comprising 86 spaces altogether, and a population density of .83 within that territory. The 77 zeros occupy territory comprising 122 spaces altogether, with a population density of .63. "Zero territory" is 37 percent vacant, "plus territory" only 17 percent.

Figure 18.12 may display the density phenomenon to more than average degree, but it usefully introduces a notion of "collective territory," which appears to be a necessary supplement to the "individual neighborhood" in describing the outcome, even though it enters no one's motivation.

Population densities were then examined for the case of equal demands and unequal numbers, and an equally striking difference in population density showed up. The minority tends to accumulate in denser neighborhoods than the majority. Figure 18.13 displays the greater compactness of the minority. The mean number of neighbors per zero is 6.0, per plus it is just under 5.0. And again one can draw rather unambiguous boundaries dividing pluses from zeros—or "plus territory" from "zero territory"—and find that zero territory has an occupancy rate of about 83 percent, plus territory of about 64 percent. The vacancy rate in plus territory is just over twice that in zero territory. (Four somewhat ambiguous blank spaces, in the fourth column from the righthand side, were allocated two each to plus and zero territory.)

A more extreme result is obtained when one group is both smaller in numbers and more demanding as to neighbors. In Figure 18.15 the ratio of pluses to zeros is almost four to one; pluses demand one plus out of four or fewer neighbors, two out of five or more, while zeros demand two out of five or fewer, three out of six or seven, four out of eight. In

SOCIAL DYNAMICS

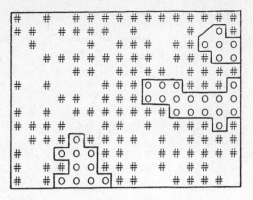

Figure 18.15

addition to rather striking separation of the two colors, there is virtually complete occupancy of "zero territory" amid a quite dispersed
plus population. Pluses average 5.1 neighbors apiece; zeros average
6.8, and, given their locations, 7.0 is the maximum.

This density phenomenon is suggestive but not easily related to residential patterns. Our model not only uses a stylized form of empty
space—uniform squares—but, most important, makes no provision for
other factors that are bound to have a strong influence on residential
density—incomes, family sizes, and the cost of space. (If surfers at a
public beach like to be by themselves but swimmers have an even
stronger incentive to avoid surfboards, our model suggests they will
become separated into groups but the surfers will enjoy more acreage
per capita!)

Size of Neighborhood

Enlarging the area within which a person counts his neighbors attenu-
ates the tendency to segregate, at least for moderate demands and
near-equal numbers of the two colors. This observation may not stand
up when less tolerant demands, and greater differentials in initial
numbers, are put into the larger neighborhoods.

Congregationist Preferences

The reader might try to guess what neighborhood demands generated
the pattern shown in Figure 18.16. The degree of "segregation" com-
pares with that of Figure 18.10. For the two colors together, like neighbors are just over 75 percent; and among the two colors, 38 percent

Dynamic Models of Segregation 281

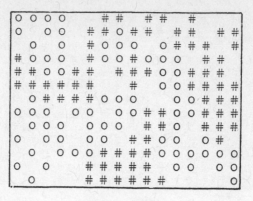

Figure 18.16

have no neighbors of opposite color. Careful inspection would show a few individuals in Figure 18.16 who are more "integrated" than in Figure 18.10.

It might appear that the demanded ratios in Figure 18.16 were slightly—only slightly—less than in Figure 18.10. But in fact there are no demanded ratios in this case. Each individual was assumed to want three neighbors like himself out of eight surrounding spaces (or two out of five, along the edge), and to be indifferent to the presence of the opposite color. That is, opposite neighbors were equivalent to blank spaces in the evaluation of neighborhoods. Everyone's demands leaves room for up to five opposite neighbors out of eight; but in achieving an absolute figure of three out of eight like himself—in "congregating" with his own color—he separates from the others just as if he had demanded majority status.

Integrationist Preferences

The foregoing results all assume that members of both colors have certain minimum demands for neighbors of like color, but no maximum demands. We can experiment with a demand for "integration" either by supposing some preferred ratio, or by supposing that there is an upper as well as lower bound to the fraction of neighbors of like color that one wants. Figure 18.17 shows results from two different "integrationist" preference schedules.

In both cases zeros are just over half the number of pluses. In the left panel there is, for both pluses and zeros, an upper as well as a lower limit to the number of like neighbors demanded: among eight

```
    # O O # # # # # O O O #          # # O     O #     # # # # O O
    # # O O # # O O O O # #          # O O O #     # # O O # O
      # # O # # O O # # #            # # O O O # # # O # # # O
      # # O # O O O O #          # # # # # # # # # O O O # # O O
    # # O # # # O O # #              # # #         # O # O O # # #
    # O # # # # # # # #          # # O #           # # # O O # #
    # # O #     # O O O #        O O O # #     # # O O # # O O #
  # # O # #     # # # O #   # #  O O O O #     # O O O # # O O O
 # # O # #             # #  # # O  # O # # #     # O O # # # O # #
# # O # #             # # # # O O  # # # # #     # # # #   # # # #
# O O #               # O # O # O  # O O # # # # # #
# O # #               # # O # # #  # O O O O O O # #
O # #                 # O # O O O  # O         O O #
```

Figure 18.17

neighbors, at least three and at most six like oneself; among seven, at least three and at most five; among six, at least three and at most four; among five, at least two and at most four; among four, either two or three; among three, either one or two; and one out of two. In the right panel there is a scale of preferences rather than upper and lower limits: out of eight neighbors, five like oneself is the preferred number but, if the board offers no such choice, then four and six are equally preferred as second choice; failing that, three and seven are equally attractive, with two and eight tied for next place, then one and finally none. Similarly with other numbers of neighbors: half for odd numbers, just over half for even, with second and third choices pairing numbers both above and below the preferred number.

Tentative experimentation suggests three phenomena that are not present in the case of purely "separatist" demands:

1. Integration requires more complex patterning than separation; equilibrium is achieved only with a much larger number of moves; and a larger number of individuals move. More individuals may be incapable of being satisfied. And there are problems of the consistency of the integrationist demands, not only of the two colors but of each of them with the overall color ratio in the population.
2. If one of the colors is a minority, the two colors have to pattern themselves in such a way that the minority is "rationed." That is, the patterns have to be "efficient" in the way members of the majority can share minority neighbors. The result may look just as

nonrandom as the segregated results achieved earlier; the patterns are as striking, but they are different patterns. The minority, for example, may be spread out in conspicuous lines rather than clustered in conspicuously convex areas, as in Figure 18.17.

3. The process of moving produces "dead spaces." An area densely settled by either color will be evacuated in its center; neither color will then move into the area, but the boundary is stable because it has contact with the opposite color. The result is that the blank spaces form their own "clusters" in the final equilibrium, giving an appearance quite different from that produced by purely separatist motives.

BOUNDED-NEIGHBORHOOD MODEL

We turn now to a different model, with a changed definition of "neighborhood." Instead of everyone's defining his neighborhood by reference to his own location, there is a common definition of the neighborhood and its boundaries. A person is either inside it or outside it. Everyone is concerned about the color ratio within the neighborhood but not with any configuration of the colors within the neighborhood. "Residence" in this model can therefore just as well, perhaps even better, be interpreted as membership or participation in a job, an office, a university, a church, a voting bloc, a club, a restaurant, or a hospital.

In this model there is one particular bounded area that everybody, black or white, prefers to its alternatives. He will reside in it unless the percentage of residents of opposite color exceeds some limit. Each person, black or white, has his own limit. ("Tolerance," we shall occasionally call it.) If a person's limit is exceeded in this area he will go someplace else—a place, presumably, where his own color predominates or where color does not matter.

"Tolerance," it should be noticed, is a *comparative* measure, and it is specific to this location. Whites who appear, in this location, to be *less tolerant of blacks* than other whites may be merely *more tolerant of the alternative locations.*

The higher the limits, the more blacks and whites would be content to live together in the area. Evidently the upper bounds must be compatible for some blacks and some whites—as percentages they must add to at least 100—or no contented mixture of any whites and blacks is possible. Evidently, too, if nobody can tolerate extreme ratios, an area initially occupied by one color alone would remain so. There may be some number among the other color that, if *concerted* entry were achieved, would remain; but, acting individually, nobody would be the first.

We can experiment with frequency distributions of "tolerance" to see what results they lead to. We cannot discover realistic distributions because they depend on the area in question; and the area in the model is unnamed. What we can do is to look at the *process* by which the area becomes occupied, or remains occupied, by blacks or whites or a mixture of both, and look for some general principles that relate outcomes to the shapes of the curves, the initial positions, and the dynamics of movement.

We assume that all preferences go in the same direction: a person need not care, but if he does his concern takes the form of an *upper limit* to the other color that can occur in this area without his choosing to go elsewhere. There is no lower limit: there are no minority-seeking individuals, nor any who will leave if the area is not suitably integrated. Absolute numbers do not matter, only ratios; there are no economies of scale in being among one's own color. There are no individual positions within the mix: nobody is near the center or near the boundary, nobody has a "next neighbor."

To study the dynamics we shall assume that people both leave and return. (This is restrictive: if the preference for this locality were due merely to the fact that some people were already here and the cost of leaving were high, that cost would not be recovered by returning.) People in the area move out if the ratio is not within their color limit; people outside move in if they see that it meets their requirements.

Information is perfect: everybody knows the color ratio within the area at the moment he makes his choice. People do not, however, know the intentions of others and do not project future turnover.

As to the dynamics of motion, we need not stipulate in advance whether whites move in or out more rapidly than blacks do. Their relative speeds of reaction will sometimes matter, and in our analysis we can watch and see how they matter. We need, though, the somewhat plausible assumption that, as between two whites dissatisfied with the ratio of white to black, the more dissatisfied leaves first—the one with the lesser tolerance. Then, as a result of sorting, the whites within the locality at any given time will all have higher tolerance of blacks than any of the whites outside, and similarly for blacks inside and outside. It is the least tolerant whites that move out first, and the most tolerant that move in first, and similarly for blacks.

Our initial data are represented by a cumulative frequency distribution of "tolerance" of the members of each color group. We can experiment with various hypothetical schedules of tolerance, but for the initial experiment we begin with a straight line.

An Illustrative Straight-Line Distribution of "Tolerance"

For the whites, the horizontal axis measures the number of whites, the vertical axis measures the ratio of blacks to whites representing the upper limits of their tolerances. We can take the total of whites to be 100. Suppose that the median white is willing to live with blacks in equal numbers, so that 50 among our 100 whites will abide a ratio of black to white of 1.0 or greater. The most tolerant white can abide a black–white ratio of two to one, that is, is willing to be in a one-third minority; and the least tolerant white cannot stand the presence of any blacks. The cumulative distribution of tolerances for a white population will then appear as in the top of Figure 18.18. It is a straight line with intercept at a ratio of 2.0 on the vertical axis and intercept on the horizontal axis at the 100 whites who comprise the white population.

Suppose that blacks have an identical distribution of tolerance for whites, the median tolerance being a ratio of one to one, and that the number of blacks is half the number of whites, 50.

It is evident without further analysis that there are at least some whites and some blacks who could contentedly coexist. Fifty of the whites would be willing to live with all the blacks, though not all 50 blacks would be willing to live with 50 whites; but a mixture of 25 blacks and 25 whites, consisting of the more tolerant 25 blacks and 25 of the more tolerant 50 whites, would be content together. There are 10 blacks who could tolerate a ratio of 1.6 to 1, or 16 whites; and any 16 among the 80 or so whites who will tolerate a black–white ratio of 10:16 would be content to join them. To explore all the combinations that might form a contented mix, but especially to study the dynamics of entry and departure, it is useful to translate both our schedules from ratios to absolute numbers, and put them on the same diagram.

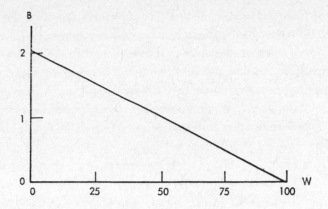

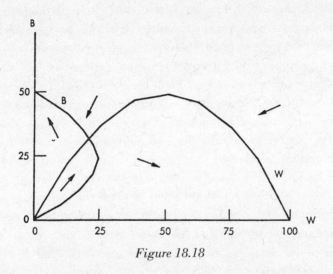

Figure 18.18

Translation of the Schedules

This is done in the bottom of Figure 18.18. The curve labeled W is a translation of the white tolerance schedule. For each number of whites along the horizontal axis the number of blacks whose presence they will tolerate is equal to their own number times the corresponding ratio on the schedule of tolerance. Thus 50 whites can tolerate an equal number of blacks, or 50. Seventy-five can tolerate half their number, 37.5; 25 can tolerate 1.5 times their number, or 37.5. Ninety can tolerate but one-fifth their number, 18; 20 can tolerate 36, and so forth.

Dynamic Models of Segregation 287

In this fashion the straight-line tolerance schedule translates into a parabolic curve showing the absolute numbers that correspond to the limits of tolerance of alternative numbers of whites. (Economists will recognize that the cumulative frequency distribution translates into this absolute-numbers curve in the same way that a demand curve translates into a total revenue curve.) Similar arithmetic converts the blacks' schedule of tolerance into the smaller parabolic dish that opens toward the vertical axis in Figure 18.18.

Static Viability

Any point in Figure 18.18 that lies within both parabolas (the area of overlap) denotes a *statically* viable combination of blacks and whites. There are that many whites who will abide the presence of that many blacks, and there are that many blacks who will abide the presence of that many whites. Any point on the diagram that is beneath the whites' curve but to the right of the blacks' curve represents a mixture of whites and blacks such that all the whites are contented but not all the blacks. Some of the blacks may be content, but not all those present. And a point on the diagram that lies outside both curves—the region to the upper right—denotes a mixture of whites and blacks at which neither all the whites nor all the blacks could be satisfied; some of both colors would be dissatisfied.

Dynamics of Movement

It is the dynamics of motion, though, that determine what color mix will ultimately occupy the area. The simplest dynamics are as follows: if all whites present in the area are content, and some outside would be content if they were inside, the former will stay and the latter will enter; and whites will continue to enter as long as all those present are content and some outside would be content if present. If not all whites present are content, some will leave; they will leave in order of their discontent, so that those remaining are the most tolerant; and when their number in relation to the number of blacks is such that the whites remaining are all content, no more of them leave. A similar rule governs entry and departure of blacks.

We can now plot, for every point on the diagram, the vector of population change within this area. Within the overlapping portion of the two curves, the numbers of blacks and whites present will both be increasing. Within the white curve but outside the black curve, whites will be coming into the area and blacks departing; the direction of motion on the diagram will be toward the lower right, and nothing stops that motion until all blacks have departed and all whites have come in. To the upper left, within the black curve but beyond the white curve, blacks will be entering and whites departing; and the process can terminate only when all the whites have left and all the blacks have come in. Mixtures denoted by points outside both curves, to the upper right, will be characterized by the departure of both colors; and when one of the colors is reduced to where it is within its own curve, continued departure of the other color will improve the ratio for the color within its own curve; those who left will begin to return, and the other color will evacuate completely.

There are only two stable equilibria. One consists of all the blacks and no whites, the other all the whites and no blacks. Which of the two will occur depends on how the process starts and, perhaps, the relative speeds of white and black movement. If initially one color predominates it will move toward complete occupancy. If initially some of both are present, in "statically viable" numbers, relative speeds of black and white entry will determine which of the two eventually turns discontent and evacuates. If both are initially present in large numbers, relative speeds of exit will determine which eventually becomes content with the ratio, reverses movement, and occupies the territory.

There are, then, compatible mixes of the two colors—any mixture denoted by the overlap of the two curves. The difficulty is that any such mixture attracts outsiders, more of one color or both colors, eventually more of just one color, so that one color begins to dominate numerically. A few individuals of the opposite color then leave; as they do, they further reduce the numerical status of those of their own color who stay behind. A few more are dissatisfied, and they leave; the minority becomes even smaller, and cumulatively the process causes evacuation of them all.

Alternative Schedules

This is, of course, not the only result. The outcome depends on the shapes we attribute to the tolerance schedules, and to the sizes of the white and black populations. With steeper straight-line schedules and equal numbers of blacks and whites we can produce a stable mixture with a large number of blacks and whites.

Specifically, suppose that the median white can tolerate a ratio of 2.5 blacks per white, i.e., will inhabit this area even if whites are a minority of 25 to 30 percent. Suppose the most tolerant white can accept a ratio of 5 to 1 and the least tolerant will not stay with any blacks. The tolerance schedule will be a straight line with a vertical intercept at 5.0. If the blacks are equal in number and have an identical distribution of tolerance for the presence of whites, the two schedules will translate into identical parabolas as shown in Figure 18.19.

Here, in addition to the two stable equilibria at 100 blacks and no whites and at 100 whites and no blacks, there is a stable mixture at 80 blacks and 80 whites. In fact, over a wide range of initial conditions it is this mixed equilibrium that will be approached through the movement of blacks and whites. As long as half or more of both colors are present—actually, slightly over 40 percent of both colors—the dynam-

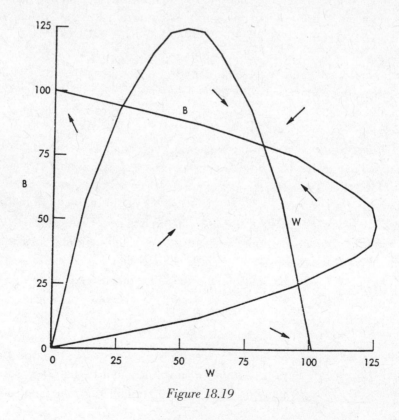

Figure 18.19

ics of entry and departure will lead to the stable mixture of 80 blacks and 80 whites. Even for very small numbers of both colors present, if the initial ratios are within the slopes of the two curves (which allow somewhat more than four to one of either color) and if neither color tends to enter much more rapidly than the other, the two colors will converge on the 80–80 mixture. Still, if the area were initially occupied by either color, it would require the concerted entry of more than 25 percent of the other color to lead to this stable mixture. Thus each of the three equilibria—the all-white, the all-black, and the 80–80 mixture—is stable against fairly large perturbations.

Alternative Numbers

The stable equilibrium generated in Figure 18.19 disappears if the total number of blacks exceeds that of whites or whites exceed blacks by, say, two to one. In that case one curve lies within the other curve, rather than intersecting it, as shown in Figure 18.20. Alternatively,

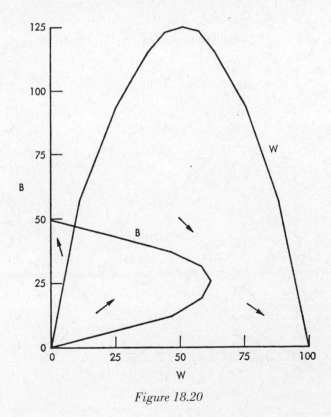

Figure 18.20

leaving total numbers of blacks and whites equal, the stable equilibrium disappears if the straight-line tolerance schedules are made less steep; with the schedules that underlie Figure 18.18, equal numbers result in Figure 18.21. (For straight-line tolerance schedules and equal numbers of the two colors, there is no stable intersection of the two parabolas unless the tolerance schedules have vertical intercepts of 3.0, with median tolerance of 1.5.)

Limiting Numbers

Limiting the numbers allowed to be present can sometimes produce a stable mixture. If the number of whites in the preferred area is limited to 40 and if the most tolerant 40 are always the first to enter and the last to leave, the curves of Figure 18.20 are replaced by those of Figure 18.22, with a stable mixture at 40 whites and a comparable number of blacks.

With the curves of Figure 18.18, however, the numbers of *both* colors would have to be restricted to yield the stable intersection shown in Figure 18.23. If the *total* number present can be restricted, but not the numbers of the two colors separately, we get a kind of neutral equilib-

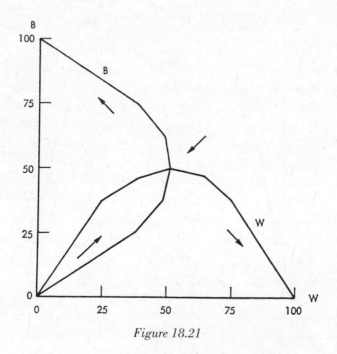

Figure 18.21

　　　　SOCIAL DYNAMICS

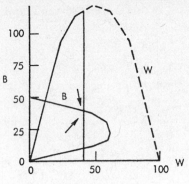

Figure 18.22

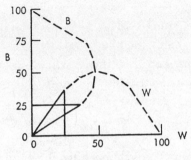

Figure 18.23

rium along the overlapped portion of the 45-degree line shown in Figure 18.24. If there is "turnover" of the population, the mixture may drift toward a higher ratio of whites to blacks or a higher ratio of blacks to whites. If it goes outside the overlapping portion of the two curves to the lower right, the black minority will evacuate.

It is interesting that the limitation on the number of whites that may be present has the same effect in our model as if the whites in excess of that number had no tolerance for any blacks at all. Whether they are excluded, or merely exclude themselves, it is their *absence* that keeps the whites from overwhelming the blacks by their numbers and makes the stable mixture possible.

Varying "Tolerance"

Thus it is not the case that "greater tolerance" increases the likelihood of a stable mixture—at least, not if "greater tolerance" means that within a given population some members are statistically replaced by

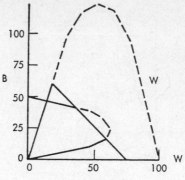

Figure 18.24

others more tolerant. On the contrary, replacing the two-thirds least tolerant whites in Figure 18.22 by even less tolerant whites keeps the whites from overwhelming the blacks by their numbers.

This would not happen if we made *all* whites less tolerant. If we make the tolerance schedule of the whites merely less steep, thus shortening the whites' parabola in Figure 18.22, we do not get our stable intersection of curves. What is required, as we manipulate the tolerance schedule in search of a stable equilibrium, is that at our dividing point of 40 percent or so of the whites the more tolerant whites just within that percentage figure remain as tolerant as they were and the less tolerant just beyond that figure become even less tolerant. (What happens to the very most tolerant and the very least tolerant makes little difference so long as they do not drastically change.) The broken line shown in Figure 18.25 is the kind that will produce the stable mixture when the blacks are outnumbered two to one with the curve of Figure 18.20.

Varieties of Results

Evidently there is a wide variety of shapes of tolerance schedules that we could experiment with and different assumed aggregate ratios of blacks and whites. While there is no room here for a large number of combinations, the method is easy and the reader can pursue by himself the cases that most interest him. There are a few results that deserve to be summarized even though the analysis will not be shown.

1. The only logical restriction on the shape of a "tolerance schedule" is that it slope downward to the right; the only ensuing logical re-

SOCIAL DYNAMICS

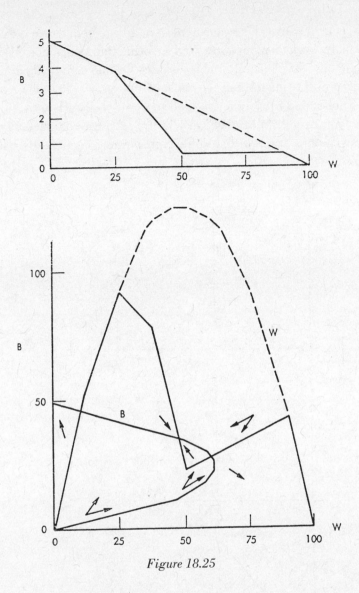

Figure 18.25

striction on the shape of the absolute-numbers curves is that a ray from the origin intersect such a curve only once. Within this restriction it is possible to have curves that provide a single stable equilibrium, two stable equilibria, three or four or even more. The single one may be with one color exclusively present or with both colors present; two stable equilibria may be all-white and all-black, or one mixture and one consisting of a single color, or two mixtures. Three stable equilibria

Dynamic Models of Segregation

can be one mixture plus two extremes, one extreme plus two mixtures, or actually even three mixtures, and so forth. The occurrence of several mixed-color stable equilibria is usually sensitive, though, to small changes in the shapes and positions of the curves. It is the extreme one-color stable equilibria that tend to be least disturbed by shifts in the tolerance schedules or changes in the aggregate numbers; and the occurrence of a *single* mixed stable equilibrium may be fairly immune to shifts in the curves.

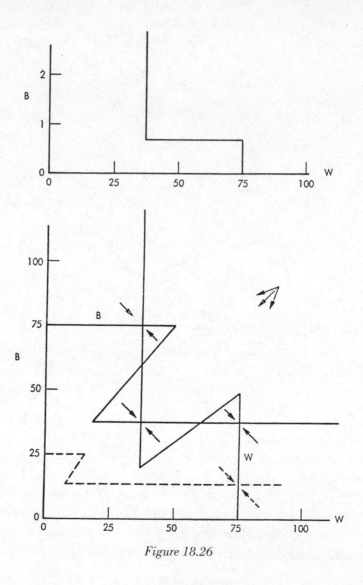

Figure 18.26

Figures 18.26 and 18.27 illustrate a few interesting possibilities. In Figure 18.26 the whites divide into three parts—those that have unlimited tolerance, those that have (the same) limited tolerance, and those that have no tolerance for the presence of blacks. If blacks are equal in number and similarly divided the solid curve for blacks is obtained; there are three stable equilibria, each containing the whites and blacks of unlimited tolerance, one containing them only, and the others containing as well the whites of limited tolerance or, alternatively, the blacks. If blacks are half the number of whites, the dashed

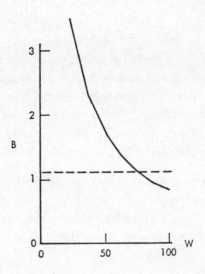

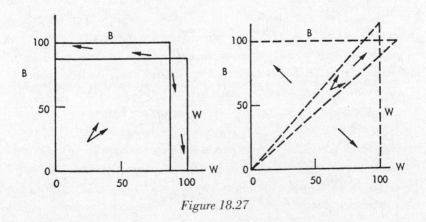

Figure 18.27

Dynamic Models of Segregation   297

line replaces the solid line and there is the single equilibrium. If instead the blacks' curve is the parabola of Figure 18.20, it may intersect the vertical part of the whites' curve to produce a stable mixture, together with another stable all-white equilibrium.

Figure 18.27 illustrates two extreme cases. One tolerance schedule is a rectangular hyperbola, RN = .9, where R is the opposite–own color ratio and N the number, for both blacks and whites in equal numbers. The other is the horizontal line, R = 1.1, all whites having the same tolerance. The latter lies almost entirely within the former and appears much less "tolerant" in the aggregate, but provides a precarious stable equilibrium with all blacks and all whites present—precarious because it is stable only against small perturbations. Evidently a great variety of shapes can be fitted beneath the rectangular hyperbola, being "dominated" by it as far as tolerance is concerned—i.e., being unambiguously less tolerant throughout—yet capable of producing one or more stable mixtures. The rectangular hyperbola for whites is compatible with the black schedule of Figure 18.20 (yielding the parabolic reaction curve) if black numbers are sufficient to make the curve protrude through the "ceiling" at 100 whites.

2. To make possible a stable mixed equilibrium it is sometimes sufficient to limit the number of one color that may be present; it is sometimes necessary to limit the number of both colors that may be present; and if the curves do not overlap at all there is no numbers limitation that will bring about a stable mixture.

3. Limiting the *ratio* of black to white or white to black that may be present, by restricting the further entry of the color that exceeds the limiting ratio, may or may not provide a stable equilibrium according to the shapes and positions of the two curves. Furthermore, limiting the ratio may exclude one or more stable equilibria and thus bring about the particular color combination corresponding to a particular stable equilibrium. Two possibilities are shown in Figures 18.28 and 18.29. The interpretation of the ratio limit, in both these figures, is that when the ratio of white to black is at or beyond its limit, no more whites may enter (though blacks are free to leave, causing the ratio to increase further), and similarly for the limiting ratio of black to white. In Figure 18.28 no stable equilibrium is produced by the ratio limits; the stable equilibria are all-white and all-black but without all the whites or all

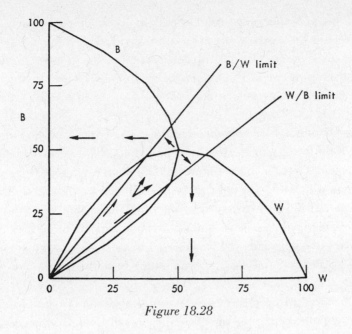

Figure 18.28

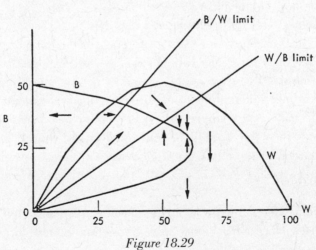

Figure 18.29

the blacks. In Figure 18.29 a stable equilibrium is produced at the white/black upper limit where it intersects the blacks' reaction curve.

4. A limitation on total occupancy can provide a neutral equilibrium that may be wide or narrow according to the shapes of the curves, as in Figure 18.24.

5. If the two colors have similar tolerance schedules for each other, the likelihood of a stable mixed equilibrium is greater, the more nearly equal are the numbers of the two colors. That is, the greater the disparity in total numbers of blacks and whites, the fewer are the tolerance schedules for the two colors that will lead to a stable equilibrium.

6. In general, for a stable mixture, the minority must be the more tolerant of the two groups. Either the mixed equilibrium will be one in which the majority group outnumbers the minority group, or else it will be one in which a larger percentage of the majority absents itself than of the minority. That is to say, if whites outnumber blacks in the aggregate by five to one, a mixed population in the local area requires either that blacks be outnumbered by whites or that four-fifths or more of the whites be incapable of abiding equal numbers of the two colors.

7. If there are only two locations altogether, one of which is preferred by both colors, the alternative to mixed living in the preferred location is not that members of both colors can go elsewhere and live by themselves. The alternative location is bound to be occupied by one of the two colors only, since any difference in the ratios in the two places would make the color with the most adverse ratio in the alternative location doubly motivated to move into the preferred area; and at equal ratios both colors would prefer to move. It turns out that restricting the alternatives to a single area, where not both colors can live segregated, can have the effect (a) of *providing* a mixed equilibrium in the preferred area, or the effect (b) of *destroying* a mixed equilibrium in the preferred area. Plausible shapes of the curves are compatible with either result.

Superimposing on Figure 18.20, for example, the restriction of a single alternative location occupied by all those blacks and whites that do not live in the preferred location, we obtain a mixed stable equilibrium consisting of all the blacks and some of the whites in the preferred area (as well as two stable segregated equilibria). Superimposing the same restriction on Figure 18.19, however, spoils the possibility of a stable mixture and only the two segregated extremes are dynamically stable.

If both blacks and whites are divided in their preferences for the two areas, some of both colors preferring one area, some the other, there may be stable mixtures in both areas, a stable mixture in one with part of one color exclusively in the other, or stable segregated occupancy of the two areas, depending on the shapes of the curves and the initial conditions.

Integrationist Preferences

Surprisingly, the results generated by this analysis do not depend upon each color's having a preference for living separately. They do not even depend on a preference for being in the majority!

For simplicity of exposition it has been supposed that each individual is limited in his "tolerance" for the other color and will go elsewhere, to live among his own color, if the ratio in his preferred place becomes too extreme. And this was indeed the hypothesis under study when the results were originally worked out. The question then presented itself, suppose these blacks and whites actually prefer mixed neighborhoods: what must we do to capture this neighborhood preference in a model of the general sort already developed?

On reflection it appeared that the analysis was already finished and the same model represented both hypotheses. More than that, the same *results* flowed from the two alternative hypotheses.

We postulate a preference for mixed living and simply *reinterpret* the same schedules of tolerance to denote merely the upper limits to the ratios at which people's *preference for integrated residence* is outweighed by their extreme minority status (or by their inadequately majority status).

The same model fits both interpretations. The results are as pertinent to the study of preferences for *integration* as to the study of preferences for *separation*. (The only asymmetry is that we did not postulate a lower limit to the acceptable proportion of opposite color, i.e., an upper limit to the proportion of like color in the neighborhood.)

Policies and Instruments

The analysis is pertinent to the study of the way that *numerical quotas* or *ratio quotas* or *limits on total numbers* may affect the likelihood of a mixed stable equilibrium. It is equally pertinent to the study of the role of *concerted action*. The occurrence of an intersection of the two curves could constitute a stable equilibrium but does not usually guarantee that that equilibrium will result; it usually competes with extreme mono-colored stable equilibria. When there are two or more potential stable equilibria, *initial conditions* and *rates of movement* determine which one will result.

Getting "over the hump" from one stable equilibrium to another often requires either a large perturbation or concerted action. Acting in concert, people can achieve an alternative stable equilibrium. (Blacks and whites cannot both successfully concert in opposition to each other; either color, by concerted action, may overwhelm the other, but not both simultaneously.)

The model as described is limited in the phenomena it can handle because it makes no allowance for *speculative behavior,* for *time lags* in behavior, for *organized action,* or for *misperception.* It also involves a single area rather than many areas simultaneously affected, each of which is one of the "alternatives" that we have in mind when we study another. The model can, however, be enlarged to accommodate some of these enrichments.

TIPPING

The foregoing analysis can be used to explore the phenomenon of "neighborhood tipping." "Tipping" is said to occur when a recognizable new minority enters a neighborhood in sufficient numbers to cause the earlier residents to begin evacuating. The phenomenon has been discussed by Morton Grodzins (1957), who says that "for the vast majority of white Americans a tipping point exists," and cites 20 percent black as a commonly estimated upper limit in some eastern cities. He states as an empirical generalization that, once an urban area begins to swing from mainly white to mainly black, the change is rarely reversed. (This could mean either that tipping is nearly universal and irreversible, or alternatively that tipping, when it occurs, accelerates a process that is inevitable and irreversible anyway.) A study of Chicago (Duncan and Duncan 1957) found no instance between 1940 and 1950 of a mixed neighborhood (25 to 75 percent white) in which succession from white to black occupancy was arrested or reversed.

The "tipping phenomenon" was observed closely by A. J. Mayer (1960) in a well-defined neighborhood of about 700 single-family homes, surrounded by racially mixed neighborhoods. A few houses were sold to blacks in 1955. "The selling of the third house convinced everyone that the neighborhood was destined to become mixed." A year later 40 houses had been sold to blacks; everyone defined the neighborhood as "mixed"; and opinion varied on whether the neighborhood would become completely black. In another two years the percentage had gone above 50 percent, and the end result was no longer questioned.

The same or a similar phenomenon has occasionally been observed for ethnic groups other than blacks, also for clubs, schools, occupations, and apartment buildings, sometimes with males and females rather than ethnic groups, and sometimes with age groups. (An ice cream parlor in Lexington, Massachusetts, "tipped" to a teenage clientele; lady shoppers and mothers of small children ceased coming, and it closed.)

Some crucial characteristics of any model of this alleged phenomenon are whether the neighborhood has a fixed and well-recognized boundary, whether the new entrants (the "minority") are clearly recognizable as a separate group, what the normal rate of turnover is, how many potential entrants there are compared with the size of the neighborhood and at what rate their number increases, what alternative neighborhoods are available for those who evacuate and what alternatives there are for the "minority" that seeks entrance.

This is evidently the kind of process our analysis has been dealing with. Specifically, this is a phenomenon that is alleged to occur in a well-defined neighborhood when something disturbs the original equilibrium at 100 percent white.

Assuming that this is a neighborhood of houses, rather than a blank space available for settlement, there is a rather inflexible capacity limit on the combined total of both colors that can be accommodated. Entry is limited either by the normal turnover of housing or by the rate at which the initial residents can evacuate. There is a primary role of the white population (or initial population, whatever its defining characteristic) that already resides in the area, but an important additional interest in the potential new white entrants who would represent the inflow under normal turnover in the absence of any tipping phenomenon. If the process takes time, the potential population would keep changing in composition, as today's home-hunters settle elsewhere and new ones arise in the general area. We can sometimes assume that whites already resident have somewhat more tolerance than outsiders, relative to their preference for living in this area, simply because it takes a stronger inducement to make a family move out than to make a family merely decide not to move in.

The black population may be small or large relative to the neighborhood. Or it could be small in the short run but cumulatively large with the passage of time.

A number of possibilities are illustrated in Figures 18.30, 18.31, and 18.32. In few if any of these figures is it clear just what we might want to call the "tipping point." There are several points at which something discontinuous happens or some cumulative process begins. Furthermore, it is interesting that *in none of the cases shown does any important discontinuity necessarily occur at the modal or typical toler-*

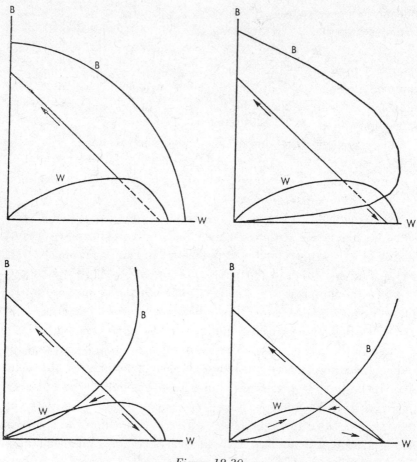

Figure 18.30

SOCIAL DYNAMICS

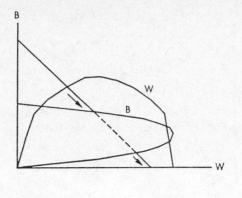

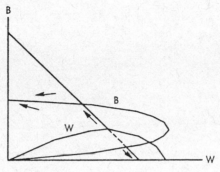

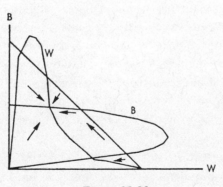

Figure 18.31

ance value. If "most Americans can tolerate about 20 percent blacks in their community," any tipping point or tipping points will tend to occur at quite different percentage figures!

Among the figures shown, an important difference is between those in which the blacks have an "in-tipping" point and those in which they do not. When the black reaction curve encloses the lower righthand

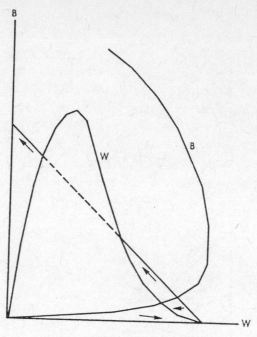

Figure 18.32

point of all-white occupancy, as in the upper left panel of Figure 18.30, there are blacks ready to move in as rapidly as houses become available; when it does not enclose that point, there is an initial all-white stable equilibrium that has to be overcome by some event or process. That process could be concerted entry, erroneous entry by a few, organized introduction of a few, redefinition of the neighborhood boundary so that some who were not inside become "inside," or something of the sort.

A possibility is that the number of blacks willing to live as a small minority in this white neighborhood is not zero but is too small to attract other blacks, but nevertheless reaches a large cumulative total over time, so that a slow process of black entry may gradually bring the black–white ratio up to where more blacks are attracted and, by entering, attract still more, and so on in the cumulative process analyzed earlier. At the point where the black reaction curve cuts the 45-degree line denoting the capacity of the neighborhood, we might say that "tipping-in" has begun. This is the point at which blacks will surge in if houses are available, rather than merely show up from time to time.

Another important difference is between the cases (Figure 18.30) in which there are enough blacks to fill the neighborhood and the cases (Figure 18.31) in which there are not. One possibility is that there are enough blacks seeking entry to cause the whites to evacuate but not enough to fill the neighborhood, so that the neighborhood becomes all black and partly vacant, as in the middle panel of Figure 18.31. Another is that there are not enough blacks to cause all the whites to evacuate, but the whites who remain in the mixed population are too few in number, together with the blacks, to fill the area, as in the lower panel of Figure 18.31, so that a mixed equilibrium occurs with excess capacity. (As the price of housing falls in the face of excess capacity, more blacks may be attracted, but possibly more whites will also.)

Still another case is shown in Figure 18.32. Here the presence of a few blacks will cause whites to evacuate in appreciable numbers but, because the white tolerance schedule becomes inelastic, the white reaction curve becomes steep and cuts the 45-degree line, so that white evacuation ceases and more blacks can move in only as vacancies occur from normal turnover. (If or when the population mix reaches the point where the reaction curve again cuts the 45-degree line, the cumulative process of white evacuation begins again.)

An entering minority may define a subneighborhood as the relevant territory. If blacks are willing to be 30 percent of a subneighborhood of 50 houses, they may "tip in" after the number of black homes reaches 15, even though in a larger neighborhood of 1,000 houses they are only 1.5 percent. An alternative phenomenon is that whites evacuate the subneighborhood because they count the black density locally, on an adjacency basis; in that case we have something like our checkerboard analysis to consult. Evidently the process is limited only by evacuation speeds if no one in the majority can abide a next neighbor from the minority or any significant number across the street or around the corner. The "proximity model" of pluses and zeros may apply in the small, and the "bounded-area model" in the large, as next neighbors react to immediate proximity while more distant ones react to neighborhood proportions.

Speculation has been adduced as an aggravating factor. Whites may respond not to the number or percentage of blacks currently present, but to the anticipated increase in the number. They may, that is, anticipate the process.[6] Evidently if whites believe that the percentage of blacks will become intolerable and are prepared to leave in anticipation once they believe it, the number of blacks required to cause "out-tipping" is not the number that begins a cumulative process in our analysis but rather the number that induces this belief. There will still be a cumulative process: those whites who evacuate in anticipation may enhance the belief of other whites in the inevitability of the process.

Speculative departure, though, requires that there be some penalty on late departure or some premium on early departure. Anticipated financial loss or anticipated delay in the departure could cause people to leave early; otherwise people could wait and see. Such things as lease and ownership arrangements would be relevant here.

The partitioning of territory into well-defined neighborhoods may contribute to a "channeling" process. It may lead blacks to concentrate on one area rather than several; it may lead whites to believe that the blacks will concentrate on one area rather than several. It may lead to experience that tends to confirm the tipping hypothesis, so that if speculative departure is relevant, the beliefs conducive to departure will be reinforced. And it can lead to a concentration of real estate sales activity on a "target neighborhood." If lending and sales agencies have been reluctant to sell houses or lend on them to blacks in all-white neighborhoods, the inhibitions may dissolve upon entry of a few blacks into a particular neighborhood, causing a differential ease of entry and serving as a further signal that black demand, blocked elsewhere, will concentrate on this neighborhood. Thus "neighborhood tipping," in contrast to the domino effect of very local proximity avoidance, depends on comparatively small and well-defined neighborhoods.

An interesting and important question is whether an entire metropolitan area might "tip." There is also the question whether some major nonresidential unit, say the U.S. Army, could tip. City school systems evidently lend themselves to the phenomenon.

The process, if it occurs, is too complex to be treated comprehensively here. But evidently analysis of "tipping" phenomena wherever it occurs—in neighborhoods, jobs, restaurants, universities, or voting blocs—and whether it involves blacks and whites, men and women, French-speaking and English-speaking, officers and enlisted men, young and old, faculty and students, or any other dichotomy, requires explicit attention to the dynamic relationship between individual behavior and collective results. Even to recognize it when it occurs requires knowing what it would look like in relation to the differential motives or decision rules of individuals.[7]

NOTES

This study was sponsored by the RAND Corporation with funds set aside for research in areas of special interest, and was issued as RM-6014-RC in May 1969. The views expressed are not necessarily those of RAND or its sponsors.

1. A comprehensive treatment of socioeconomic differentials between whites and nonwhites, in relation to residential patterns, is in Pascal (1967).

2. A curious property of this six-neighbor neighborhood is that, short of clusters of four or more, the only pattern that meets the demand for half one's neighbors like himself is . . . 00+0++0+00+0++ . . . . Even this one is unstable at the ends: it must run indefinitely in both directions or form a closed curve, else it unravels completely into clusters.

3. Patterning—departure from randomness—will prove to be characteristic of integration, as well as of segregation, if the integration results from choice and not chance.

4. It may be helpful to compare the pattern of pluses and zeros in Figure 18.9 with those of some standard reference pattern, such as rectangular blocks of pluses and zeros on an unbounded checkerboard. The neighbor count of Figure 18.9 turns out to be identical with that obtained if pluses and zeros occur in 7×7 squares of 49 each. (It should be kept in mind that 2×2 squares yield the same neighbor count, one to one, as expected in the random distribution.) Similarly, 3×3 squares are the smallest homogeneous groups in which someone has no neighbors of opposite color, the percentage for 3×3 being 11 percent, almost exactly that expected in a random distribution of the size and shape of Figure 18.7; the 39 percent without neighbors of opposite color in Figure 18.9 correspond to monocolored 5×6 groupings on an unbounded surface (12 out of 30, or 40 percent).

5. Since the number of neighbors is a small integer, the fractions demanded for different numbers of neighbors have to differ. In Figure 18.11, the demands are for one like neighbor out of four or fewer, two out of five neighbors or more. The average number of neighbors in the initial distribution is five and one-half, the average number when equilibrium is reached

is about four and one-half; the average effective preference is therefore in the neighborhood of one-third.

6. In the Russell Woods example, mentioned earlier, the residents certainly expected large numbers of blacks on the basis of the first three or so, and at 40 percent black nearly everybody took an ultimate 100 percent for granted. Just knowing that he is bound to move in a year or two may make a person move at the first convenient opportunity; otherwise only risk of financial loss, or of being "locked in" beyond one's own "static tipping point," would cause speculative evacuation.

7. For further discussion see Schelling (1969). See also Morrill (1965) for a random-movement model that generates, by selective resistance at the boundary, a ghetto-expansion process that can be compared with city maps.

REFERENCES

Duncan, O. D., and Duncan, B. 1957. *The Negro population of Chicago.* Chicago: University of Chicago Press.

Grodzins, M. 1957. Metropolitan segregation. Chicago: University of Chicago Press.

Mayer, A. J. 1960. Russell Woods: Change without conflict. In N. Glazer (ed.), *Studies in housing and minority groups.* Berkeley: University of California Press, 1960.

Morrill, R. L. 1965. The Negro ghetto: Problems and alternatives. *The Geographical Review,* 55, 339–361.

Pascal, A. H. 1967. The economics of housing segregation. RM-5510-RC, RAND Corporation, Santa Monica, California, November.

Schelling, T. C. 1969. Neighborhood tipping. Harvard Institute of Economic Research Discussion Paper No. 100, Harvard University, Cambridge, Mass., December.

Schelling, Thomas C. 1971. Dynamic models of segregation. *Journal of Mathematical Sociology* 1 (abbreviated version appeared as "Models of Segregation," *American Economic Review* 59, no. 2, May 1969).

—— 1972. A process of residential segregation: Neighborhood tipping. In *Racial discrimination in economic life,* ed. Anthony H. Pascal. Lexington, Mass.: D. C. Heath.

—— 1978. *Micromotives and macrobehavior.* New York: W. W. Norton.

Decisions of the Highest Order

19

The Legacy of Hiroshima

■ It is more than sixty years since the first—and the last—nuclear weapons were used in warfare. These six decades of nonuse are a stunning achievement, and probably involve some stunning good luck.

There has never been any doubt about the military effectiveness of nuclear weapons or their potential for terror. A large part of the credit for their not having been used must be due to the "taboo" that U.S. Secretary of State John Foster Dulles perceived to have attached itself to these weapons as early as 1953, a taboo that the secretary deplored.

The weapons remain under a curse, a now much heavier curse than the one that bothered Dulles in the early 1950s. These weapons are unique, and a large part of their uniqueness derives from their being perceived as unique. We call most of the others "conventional," and that word has two distinct senses. One is "ordinary, familiar, traditional," a word that can be applied to food, clothing, or housing. The more interesting sense of "conventional" is something that arises as if by compact, by agreement, by convention. It is simply an established convention that nuclear weapons are different.

True, their fantastic scale of destruction dwarfs conventional weapons. But as early as the end of the Eisenhower administration, nuclear weapons could be made smaller in explosive yield than the largest conventional explosives. There were military planners to whom "little" nuclear weapons appeared untainted by the taboo that they thought ought properly to attach only to weapons of a size associated with Hiro-

313

shima or Bikini. But by then nuclear weapons had become a breed apart; size was no excuse from the curse.

This attitude, or convention, or tradition that took root and grew over these past six decades is an asset to be treasured. It is not guaranteed to survive; and some possessors or potential possessors of nuclear weapons may not share the convention. How to preserve this inhibition, what kinds of policies or activities may threaten it, how the inhibition may be broken or dissolved, and what institutional arrangements may support or weaken it deserves serious attention. How the inhibition arose, whether it was inevitable, whether it was the result of careful design, whether luck was involved, and whether we should assess it as robust or vulnerable in the coming decades is worth examining. Preserving this tradition, and if possible helping to extend it to other countries that may yet acquire nuclear weapons, is as important as extending the Nuclear Non-Proliferation Treaty, again being renegotiated in 2005.

The first occasion when these weapons might have been used was early in the Korean War. Americans and South Koreans had retreated to a perimeter around the southern coastal city of Pusan and appeared in danger of being unable either to hold out or to evacuate. The nuclear-weapons issue arose in public discussion in this country and in the British parliament. Prime Minister Clement Atlee flew to Washington to beseech President Truman not to use nuclear weapons in Korea. The visit and its purpose were both public and publicized. The House of Commons, considering itself to have been a partner in the enterprise that produced nuclear weapons, considered it legitimate that Britain have a voice in the American decision.

The successful landing at Inchon mooted the question whether nuclear weapons might have been used if the situation in the Pusan perimeter had become desperate enough. But at least the question of nuclear use had come up, and the outcome was in the negative.

There may be more than enough reasons to explain the nonuse at that time in Korea. But I do not recall that an important consideration, for the U.S. government or the U.S. public, was apprehension of the consequences of demonstrating that nuclear weapons were "usable" and of thereby preempting the possibility of cultivating a tradition of nonuse.

Nuclear weapons again went unused in the disaster brought by the entry of Chinese armies into the Korean conflict, and were still unused during the bloody war of attrition that accompanied the Panmunjom negotiations. Whether the weapons would have been used, and where and how they might have been used, had the war ground on for many more months, and what the subsequent history would have been had they been used in North Korea or in China at that time is of course speculative. Whether the threat of nuclear weapons, presumably to be used against China rather than on the battlefield, influenced the truce negotiations remains unclear.

McGeorge Bundy's 1988 book *Danger and Survival: Choices about the Bomb in the First Fifty Years* documents the fascinating story of Dwight Eisenhower and Dulles and nuclear weapons. At the meeting of the National Security Council on February 11, 1953, just weeks after Eisenhower's inauguration, "Secretary Dulles discussed the moral problem in the inhibitions on the use of the A-bomb . . . It was his opinion that we should break down this false distinction" (Bundy, 241). I do not know of any analysis of that time of government actions that might have tended to break down the distinction or what actions or inactions would have preserved and strengthened it. But evidently the secretary believed, and may have taken for granted that the entire National Security Council believed, that the restraints were real even if the distinction was false, and that the restraint was not to be welcomed.

Again on October 7, 1953, Dulles: "Somehow or other we must manage to remove the taboo from the use of these weapons" (Bundy, 249). Just a few weeks later the president approved, in a Basic National Security Policy document, the statement "In the event of hostilities, the United States will consider nuclear weapons to be as available for use as other munitions" (246). This statement surely has to be read as more rhetorical than factual. Taboos are not easily dispelled by pronouncing them extinct, even in the mind of one who does the pronouncing. Six months later, at a restricted NATO meeting, the U.S. position was that nuclear weapons "must now be treated as in fact having become conventional" (268). Again, saying so cannot make it so; tacit conventions are sometimes harder to destroy than explicit ones, existing in potentially recalcitrant minds rather than on destructible paper.

According to Bundy, the last public statement in this progress of nuclear weapons toward conventional status occurred during the Quemoy crisis. On March 12, 1955, Eisenhower said, in answer to a question, "In any combat where these things can be used on strictly military targets and for strictly military purposes, I see no reason why they shouldn't be used just exactly as you would use a bullet or anything else" (278). Bundy's judgment, which I share, is that this again was more an exhortation than a policy decision.

Was Ike really ready to use nuclear weapons to defend Quemoy, or Taiwan itself? It turned out he didn't have to. The conspicuous shipment of nuclear artillery to Taiwan was surely intended as a threat. Bluffing would have been risky from Dulles's point of view; leaving nuclear weapons unused while the Chinese conquered Taiwan would have engraved the taboo in granite. At the same time, Quemoy may have appeared to Dulles as a superb opportunity to dispel the taboo. Using short-range nuclear weapons in a purely defensive mode, solely against offensive troops, especially at sea or on beachheads devoid of civilians, might have been something that Eisenhower would have been willing to authorize and that European allies would have approved, and nuclear weapons might have proved that they could be used "just exactly as you would use a bullet or anything else." The Chinese did not offer the opportunity.

On the status of nuclear weapons, the Kennedy and Johnson administrations were a sharp contrast to the Eisenhower. There was also a change in roles within the Cabinet. Hardly anybody born after World War II remembers the name of Eisenhower's secretary of defense. But most who have studied any American history know the name of John Foster Dulles. A bit of research with Bundy's book shows the contrast. In Bundy's index there are thirty-one references to Dulles, two to Charles Wilson. Under John F. Kennedy and Lyndon Johnson the score is reversed: forty-two references to McNamara, twelve to Dean Rusk.

The antinuclear movement in the Kennedy administration was led from the Pentagon, and in 1962 Secretary of Defense McNamara began his campaign—his and President Kennedy's—to reduce reliance on nuclear defense in Europe by building expensive conventional forces in NATO. During the next couple of years McNamara became associated with the idea that nuclear weapons were not "usable" at all in the sense that Eisenhower and Dulles had intended. Undoubtedly the traumatic October of 1962 contributed to the revulsion against nuclear weapons on the part of some of Kennedy's key advisers and Kennedy himself.

The contrast between the Eisenhower and the Kennedy-Johnson attitudes toward nuclear weapons is beautifully summarized in a statement of Lyndon Johnson's in September 1964. "Make no mistake. There is no such thing as a conventional nuclear weapon. For nineteen peril-filled years no nation has loosed the atom against another. To do so now is a political decision of the highest order" (*New York Times*, September 8, 1964, 18).

That statement disposed of the notion that nuclear weapons were to be judged by their military effectiveness. It disposed of Dulles's "false distinction": "A political decision of the highest order" compared with "as available for use as other munitions."

I am particularly impressed by the "nineteen peril-filled years." Johnson implied that for nineteen years the United States had resisted the temptation to do what Dulles had wanted the United States to be free to do where nuclear weapons were concerned. He implied that the United States, or collectively the United States and other nuclear weapon states, had an investment, accumulated over nineteen years, in the nonuse of nuclear weapons; and those nineteen years of quarantine for nuclear weapons were part of what would make any decision to use those weapons a political one of the highest order.

It is worth a pause here to consider just what might be the literal meaning of "no such thing as a conventional nuclear weapon." Specifically, why couldn't a nuclear bomb no larger than the largest blockbuster of World War II, or a nuclear depth charge of modest explosive power for use against submarines far at sea, or nuclear land mines to halt advancing tanks or to cause landslides in mountain passes be considered conventional? What could be so awful about using three "small" atomic bombs to save the besieged French at Dien Bien Phu, as was discussed at the time? What would be so wrong about using nuclear coastal artillery against a communist Chinese invasion flotilla in the Gulf of Taiwan?

This question has received two answers, one mainly instinctive, the other somewhat analytical, but both resting on a belief, or a feeling—a feeling somewhat beyond reach by analysis—that nuclear weapons are simply different, and generically different. The more intuitive response can probably best be formulated, "If you have to ask that question you wouldn't understand the answer." The generic character of everything nuclear was simply—as logicians might call it—a primitive, an axiom; and analysis was as unnecessary as it was futile.

The other, more analytical, response took its argument from legal reasoning, diplomacy, bargaining theory, and theory of training and discipline, including self-discipline. This argument emphasized bright lines, slippery slopes, well-defined boundaries, and the stuff of which traditions and implicit conventions are made. (The analogy to "one little drink" for a recovering alcoholic was sometimes heard.) But both lines of argument arrived at the same conclusion: nuclear weapons, once introduced into combat, could not, or probably would not, be contained, confined, limited.

Sometimes the argument was explicit that no matter how small the weapons initially used, the size of the weapons would ineluctably escalate, there being no natural stopping place. Sometimes the argument was that the military needed to be disciplined, and once they were allowed any weapons it would be impossible to stop their escalation.

The "neutron bomb" is illustrative. This is a bomb, or potential bomb, that, because it is very small and because of the materials with which it is constructed, emits "prompt neutrons" that can be lethal at a distance at which blast and thermal radiation are comparatively moderate. As advertised, the neutron bomb kills people without great damage to structures. The issue of producing and deploying this kind of weapon arose during the Carter administration, evoking an antinuclear reaction that caused it to be left on the drawing board. But the same bomb—at least, the same idea—had been the subject of even more intense debate fifteen years earlier, and it was there that the argument was honed that was ready to be used again in the 1970s. The argument was simple; and it was surely valid, whether or not it deserved to be decisive. It was that it was important not to blur the distinction—the firebreak, as it was called—between nuclear and conventional weapons; and either because of the neutron bomb's low yield or because of its "benign" kind of lethality it was feared, and it was argued, that there would be a strong temptation to use this weapon where nuclear weapons were otherwise not allowed, and that the use of this weapon would erode the threshold, blur the firebreak, and pave the way by incremental steps for nuclear escalation.

The argument is not altogether different from that against so-called peaceful nuclear explosions (PNEs). The decisive argument against PNEs was that they would accustom the world to nuclear explosions, undermining the belief that nuclear explosions were inherently evil and reducing the inhibitions on nuclear weapons. The prospect of blasting new riverbeds in northern Russia, or a bypass canal for the waters of the Nile, or harbors in developing countries generated concern about "legitimizing" nuclear explosions.

A revealing demonstration of this antipathy was in the universal rejection by American arms controllers and energy-policy analysts of the prospect of an ecologically clean source of electrical energy, proposed in the 1970s, that would have detonated tiny thermonuclear bombs in underground caverns to generate steam. I have seen this idea unanimously dismissed without argument, as if the objections were too obvious to require articulation. As far as I could tell the objection was always that even "good" thermonuclear explosions were bad and should be kept that way. (I can imagine President Eisenhower: "In any energy crisis where these things can be used on strictly civilian sites for strictly civilian purposes I see no reason why they shouldn't be used just exactly as you would use a barrel of oil or anything else." And Dulles: "Somehow or other we must manage to remove the taboo from the use of these clean thermonuclear energy sources.")

But it is important not to think that nuclear weapons alone have this character of being generically different, independently of quantity or size. Gas was not used in World War II. The Eisenhower-Dulles argument could have applied to gas: "In any combat where these gases can be used on strictly military targets and for strictly military purposes, I see no reason why they shouldn't be used just exactly as you would use a bullet or anything else." But as supreme commander of the Allied Expeditionary Forces, General Eisenhower, as far as we know, never proposed any such policy. Maybe if, at the time, he had been put through the exercise he would have convinced himself, not that gas should never be used but that gas was at least different from bullets, and decisions on its use raised new strategic issues. And ten years later he might have recalled that line of thinking when, I think reluctantly, he let his secretary of state urge doing for nuclear weapons what Eisenhower apparently never thought of doing for gas in the European theater.

Some other things have this all-or-none quality in warfare. Nationality is one. The Chinese did not visibly intervene in the Korean War until it was time to intervene in force. American military advisers have always been cautioned to avoid appearing to engage in anything that could be construed as combat, the notion being that such contamination could not be contained. There was some consideration of American intervention in Indochina at the time of Dien Bien Phu, but not on the ground; and in the air it was thought that reconnaissance would count less as "intervention" than would bombing. There is typically the notion that to provide equipment is much less participatory than to provide military manpower; we arm the Israelis and provide ammunition even in wartime, but sending so much as a company of American infantry would be perceived as a greater act of military participation than $5 billion worth of fuel, ammunition, and spare parts.

I mention all this to suggest that there are perceptual and symbolic phenomena that persist and recur and that help to make the nuclear phenomenon less puzzling. And I find it remarkable how these perceptual constraints and inhibitions cross cultural boundaries. During the Chinese phase of the Korean War the United States never bombed airbases in China; the "rules" were that Chinese bombing sorties originated from North Korea, and to abide by the rules Chinese aircraft originating in Manchuria touched wheels down at North Korean airstrips on the way to bombing their American targets. That reminds us that national territory is like nationality: crossing the Yalu River between China and North Korea, on the ground or in the air, is a qualitative discontinuity. Had General Douglas MacArthur succeeded in conquering all of North Korea, even he could not have proposed that penetrating just "a little bit" into China proper wouldn't have mattered much because it was only a little bit.

Still, these qualitative all-or-none kinds of thresholds are often susceptible to undermining. A Dulles who wishes the taboo were not there not only may attempt to get around it when it is important, but may apply ingenuity to dissolving the barrier on occasions when it may not matter much, in anticipation of later opportunities when the barrier would be a genuine embarrassment. Bundy suggests that in discussing the possibility of atomic bombs in defense of Dien Bien Phu Dulles and Admiral Arthur W. Radford, the chairman of the Joint Chiefs of Staff, had in mind not only the local value in Indochina but also the use of Dien Bien Phu in "making the use of atomic bombs internationally acceptable," a goal that Dulles and Radford shared.

The aversion to nuclear weapons—one might even say the abhorrence of them—can grow in strength and become locked into military doctrine even without being fully appreciated, or even acknowledged. The Kennedy administration launched an aggressive campaign for conventional defenses in Europe on the grounds that nuclear weapons certainly should not be used, and probably would not be used, in the event of a war in Europe. Throughout the 1960s the official Soviet line was to deny the possibility of a non-nuclear engagement in Europe. Yet the Soviets spent great amounts of money developing non-nuclear capabilities in Europe, especially aircraft capable of delivering conventional bombs. This expensive capability would have been utterly useless in the event of any war that was bound to become nuclear. It reflects a tacit Soviet acknowledgment that both sides might be capable of non-nuclear war and that both sides had an interest, worth a lot of money, in keeping war non-nuclear—keeping it non-nuclear by having the capability of fighting a non-nuclear war.

Arms control is so often identified with limitations on the possession or deployment of weapons that it is often overlooked that this reciprocated investment in non-nuclear capability was a remarkable instance of unacknowledged but reciprocated arms control. It is not only potential restraint in the use of nuclear weapons; it is investment in a configuration of weapons to make them capable of non-nuclear combat. It reminds us that the inhibitions on "first use" may be powerful without declarations, even powerful while one party refuses to recognize its own participation for what it is.

With the possible exception of the antiballistic missile treaty, this conventional buildup in Europe was the most important East–West arms understanding until the demise of the Soviet Union. It was genuine arms control, even if inexplicit, even if denied—as real as if the two sides had signed a treaty obliging them, in the interest of fending off nuclear war, to put large amounts of treasure and manpower into conventional forces. The investment in restraints on the use of nuclear weapons was real as well as symbolic.

That the Soviets had absorbed this nuclear inhibition was dramatically demonstrated during their protracted campaign in Afghanistan. I never read or heard public discussion about the possibility that the Soviet Union might shatter the tradition of nonuse to avoid a costly and humiliating defeat in that primitive country. The inhibitions on the use of nuclear weapons are such common knowledge, the attitude is so confidently shared, that not only would the use of nuclear weapons in Afghanistan have been almost universally deplored, it wouldn't even have been thought of.

But part of that may be because President Johnson's nineteen-year nuclear silence had stretched into a fourth and then a fifth decade, and everyone in positions of responsibility was aware that this unbroken tradition was a treasure we held in common. We have to ask, could that tradition, once broken, have mended itself? Had Truman used nuclear weapons during the Chinese onslaught in Korea, would Nixon have been as impressed in 1970 by the twenty-five-year hiatus as Johnson was by the nineteen-year one in 1964? Had Nixon used nuclear weapons, even ever so sparingly, in Vietnam, would the Soviets have eschewed their use in Afghanistan, and Margaret Thatcher in the Falklands? Had Nixon used nuclear weapons in 1969 or 1970, would the Israelis have resisted the temptation to use them against the Egyptian beachheads north of the Suez Canal in 1973?

The answer surely is that we do not know. One possibility is that the horror of Hiroshima and Nagasaki would have repeated itself and the curse would have descended again with even more weight. The other possibility is that, the long silence broken, nuclear weapons would have emerged as militarily effective instruments and, especially used unilaterally against an adversary who had none, a blessing that might have reduced casualties on both sides of the war as some think the bomb on Hiroshima did. Much might have depended on the care with which weapons were confined to military targets or used in demonstrably "defensive" modes.

We were spared from temptation in the Gulf in 1991. Iraq was known to possess, and to have been willing to use, "unconventional" weapons—chemicals. Had chemical weapons been used with devastating effect on U.S. forces, the issue of appropriate response would have posed the nuclear question. I am confident that had the president, in that circumstance, deemed it essential to escalate from conventional weapons, battlefield nuclear weapons would have been the military choice. Nuclear weapons are what the army, navy, and air force are trained and equipped to use; their effects in different kinds of weather and terrain are well understood. The military profession traditionally despises poison. There would have been strong temptation to respond with the kind of unconventional weapon they knew best how to use. To have done so would have ended the forty-five peril-filled years. We can hope no president has to face such a "political decision of the highest order." I've no doubt any president would recognize that this was the kind of decision he was facing.

I have devoted this much attention to where we are and how we got here regarding the status of nuclear weapons in the belief that the development of that status is as important as the development of nuclear arsenals has been. The nonproliferation effort, concerned with the development, production, and deployment of nuclear weapons, has been more successful than most authorities can claim to have anticipated; the accumulating weight of tradition against nuclear use I consider no less impressive and no less valuable. We depend on nonproliferation efforts to restrain the production and deployment of weapons by more and more countries; we may depend even more on universally shared inhibitions against nuclear use. Preserving those inhibitions and extending them, if we know how, to cultures and national interests that may not currently share those inhibitions will be a crucial part of our nuclear policy.

I quote from an editorial that Alvin M. Weinberg, the distinguished nuclear physicist, wrote on the fortieth anniversary of Hiroshima and Nagasaki in the *Bulletin of the Atomic Scientists*. After saying that he had always been convinced that both American and Japanese lives were saved by the use of the bomb in Japan, he gives another reason for his belief that Hiroshima (but not Nagasaki) was fortunate. "Are we witnessing a gradual sanctification of Hiroshima—that is, the elevation of the Hiroshima event to the status of a profoundly mystical event, an event ultimately of the same religious force as biblical events? I cannot prove it, but I am convinced that the 40th Anniversary of Hiroshima, with its vast outpouring of concern, its huge demonstrations, its wide media coverage, bears resemblance to the observance of major religious holidays . . . This sanctification of Hiroshima is one of the most hopeful developments of the nuclear era."

A crucial question is whether the antinuclear instinct so exquisitely expressed by Weinberg is confined to "Western" culture. I believe the

The Legacy of Hiroshima   323

set of attitudes and expectations about nuclear weapons is more recognizably widespread among the people and the elites of the developed countries; and as we look to North Korea, Iran, or others as potential wielders of nuclear weapons, we cannot be sure that they inherit this tradition with any great force. But it is reassuring that in the same way we had no assurance that the leadership of the Soviet Union would inherit the same tradition or participate in cultivating that tradition. Not many of us in the 1950s would have thought that were the Soviet Union to engage in war, and lose a war, in Afghanistan it would behave there as if nuclear weapons did not exist.

We can be grateful to the Soviets for behaving that way in Afghanistan, adding one more to the list of bloody wars in which nuclear weapons were not used. Forty years ago we might have thought that the Soviet leadership would be immune to the spirit of Hiroshima as expressed by Weinberg, immune to the popular revulsion that John Foster Dulles did not share, immune to the overhang of all those peril-filled years that awed President Johnson. In any attempt to extrapolate Western nuclear attitudes toward the areas of the world where nuclear proliferation begins to frighten us, the remarkable conformity of Soviet and Western ideology is a reassuring point of departure.

An immediate question is whether we can expect Indian and Pakistani leaders to be adequately in awe of the nuclear weapons they now both possess. There are two helpful possibilities. One is that they share the inhibition—appreciate the taboo—that I have been discussing. The other is that they will recognize, as the United States and the Soviet Union did, that the prospect of nuclear retaliation made any initiation of nuclear war nearly unthinkable.

The instances of nonuse of nuclear weapons that I have discussed were, in every case, possible use against a nonpossessor. The nonuse between the United States and the Soviet Union was differently motivated: the prospect of nuclear retaliation made any initiation appear unwise except in the worst imaginable military emergency, and that kind of military emergency never offered the temptation. The experience of the U.S.–USSR confrontation may impress the Indians and Pakistanis; the greatest risk is that one or the other may confront the kind of military emergency that invites some limited experiment with the weapons, and there is no history to tell us, or them, what happens next.

I know of no argument in favor of the Comprehensive Test Ban

Treaty (CTBT), which the Senate rejected in 1999, more powerful than the potential of that treaty to enhance the nearly universal revulsion against nuclear weapons. The symbolic effect of 180 or more nations ratifying the CTBT, which is nominally only about testing, should add enormously to the convention that nuclear weapons are not to be used and that any nation that does use nuclear weapons will be judged the violator of the legacy of Hiroshima. I never heard that argument made on either side of the debate over the treaty. When the treaty is again before the Senate, as I hope it will be, this major potential benefit should not go unrecognized.

Most recently there is the concern that Iran and North Korea may acquire, or may already have acquired, some modest number of nuclear warheads. (Libya appears to have withdrawn from contention.) Great diplomatic skill and international cooperation will be required to suppress or discourage their interest in acquiring such weapons. Equally great skill, or greater, will be required to create or enhance the expectations and institutions that inhibit their use.

Credits

1. "Strategies of Commitment." This essay consolidates four prior publications: "Promises," *Negotiation Journal* (April 1989): 113–118; "Commitment," *The New Palgrave Dictionary of Economics and the Law,* ed. Peter Newman (London: Macmillan, 1998), 295–300, reproduced with permission of Palgrave Macmillan; "Commitment: Deliberate vs. Involuntary," from *Evolution and the Capacity for Commitment,* ed. Randolph M. Nesse, © 2001 Russell Sage Foundation, 112 East 64th Street, New York, NY 10021, reprinted with permission; and, as appendix: "Altruism, Meanness, and Other Potentially Strategic Behaviors," *American Economic Review* 68 (May 1978): 228–230.

2. "What Makes Greenhouse Sense?" *Indiana Law Review* 38, no. 3 (2005): 581–593. Portions previously published in *Foreign Affairs* 2 (May/June 2002), 2–9, with a small segment from "Some Economics of Global Warming," *American Economic Review* 82, no. 1 (March 1992): 1–4.

3. "The Economic Diplomacy of Geoengineering," *Climatic Change* 33, no. 3 (July 1996): 303–307, © 1996 Kluwer Academic Publishers, with kind permission of Springer Science and Business Media. This essay was first delivered as a talk at a meeting of the American Association for the Advancement of Science in January 1996.

4. "Intergenerational and International Discounting," *Risk Analysis: An International Journal* 20, no. 6 (December 2000): 833–839, © 2000 Society for Risk Analysis. An earlier, more technical version was "Intergenerational Discounting," *Energy Policy* 23, no. 4/5 (1995): 395–401, © Elsevier Science Ltd.

5. "Self-Command in Practice, in Policy, and in a Theory of Rational Choice," *AEA Papers and Proceedings* 74, no. 2 (May 1984): 1–11. This essay was first delivered as the Richard T. Ely Lecture.

6. "Coping Rationally with Lapses from Rationality," *Eastern Economic Journal* 22, no. 3 (Summer 1996): 251–269. This essay was first delivered as the Presidential Address at the 1996 meeting of the Eastern Economic Association in Boston.

7. "Against Backsliding," from *Development, Democracy, and the Art of Trespassing: Essays in Honor of Albert O. Hirschman,* ed. Alejandro Foxley et al. (Notre Dame, Ind.: University of Notre Dame Press, 1986), 233–238.

8. "Addictive Drugs: The Cigarette Experience," *Science* 255 (January 24, 1992): 430–433.

9. "Life, Liberty, or the Pursuit of Happiness," from *Challenge to Leadership: Economic and Social Issues for the Next Decade,* ed. Isabel V. Sawhill (Washington, D.C.: Urban Institute Press, 1988), 253–277.

10. "Should Numbers Determine Whom to Save?" has not been previously published.

11. "What Do Economists Know?" *American Economist* 39, no. 1 (Spring 1995): 20–22.

12. "Why Does Economics Only Help with Easy Problems?" from *Economic Science and Practice: The Roles of Academic Economists and Policymakers,* ed. Peter A. G. van Bergeijk et al. (Cheltenham, UK: Edward Elgar Publishing, 1997), 135–146.

13. "Prices as Regulatory Instruments," from *Incentives for Environmental Protection,* ed. Thomas Schelling (Cambridge: MIT Press, 1983), 1–40.

14. "Meteors, Mischief, and War," *Bulletin of the Atomic Scientists* 16, no. 7 (September 1960): 292–300 (excerpt, 292–293). The prologue has not been previously published.

15. "Research by Accident," reprinted from *Technological Forecasting and Social Change* 53, no. 1, 15–20, © 1996 with permission from Elsevier.

16. "Vietnam: Reflections and Lessons," *Asian Journal of Political Science* 4, no. 2 (December 1996): 103–107. This paper was originally a lecture delivered in August 1996 at the Master of Public Policy Programme of the National University of Singapore, while the author was the Lee Kuan Yew Distinguished Visitor there.

17. "Social Mechanisms and Social Dynamics," from *Social Mechanisms: An Analytical Approach to Social Theory,* ed. Peter Hedström and Richard Swedberg (New York: Cambridge University Press, 1998), 32–44.

18. "Dynamic Models of Segregation," *Journal of Mathematical Sociology* 1 (1971): 143–186, © Gordon and Breach Science Publishers. Prologue: adapted from "Some Fun, Thirty-Five Years Ago," in *Agent-Based Computational Economics*, ed. Kenneth Judd and Leigh Tesfatsion, vol. 2 of *Handbook of Computational Economics*, Handbook in Economics series (Amsterdam: North-Holland, 2006), © Elsevier.

19. "The Legacy of Hiroshima," *Philosophy and Public Policy* 20, no. 2/3 (Summer 2000), 9–13. An earlier version of this article appeared in *The Key Reporter*, the quarterly publication of the Phi Beta Kappa Society, vol. 65, no. 3 (Spring 2000).

Index

2, 15–17; relationship to threats, 2–9; role of personal traits in, 17–21; relationship to genetics, 19, 20–21; being committed vs. becoming committed, 19–20; in Kyoto Protocol, 30–31, 40–41, 43–44; in WTO, 38, 40; in NATO, 38–40; to actions vs. commitment to results, 40–41; of United States in Vietnam, 227–228; as deterrent, 228, 232; justification of, 228, 232

Committee for Economic Development, 222–223

Comprehensive Test Ban Treaty, 324–325

Compulsive behaviors, 93–94

Concern for Dying, 135

Conrad, Joseph: *The Secret Agent*, 17–18

Conservation Foundation, 222–223

Contraceptive education, 127, 128

Control of the Arms Race, The, 161–162

Council on Foreign Relations, 161

Credibility: in bargaining tactics, 2; of threats, 2, 3, 4, 7; of commitment, 2, 3, 4, 7, 9–15, 17–21, 228, 232; of bluffs, 3; of promises, 9–15; of blackmailers, 12; relationship to character traits, 17–21

Cuban missile crisis, 5–6, 7, 229, 316–317

Czechoslovakia, 229

Day After, The, 220

Daydreaming, 97–98

Death: right to die, 128, 129–139; and medical technology, 129; living wills, 129, 131, 135–136; definitions of, 130. *See also* Euthanasia; Suicide

Delaney Amendment, 163

Democracy, 171; secret ballots, 15; and government promises, 17

Depression (psychology), 68, 86–87

Developing countries: diseases in, 34, 35–36; agriculture in, 34, 36; vs. developed countries, 34, 43–44, 55–57, 324; climate in, 34–36, 56, 58; carbon emissions in, 37, 43; and Kyoto Protocol, 43–44; benefits of greenhouse gas abatement for, 55–58; gross domestic product (GDP) in, 56–57; direct investments in, 57–58

Dien Bien Phu, 317, 320–321

Discount rates: relationship to pure time preference, 51, 52–54; relationship to marginal utility, 51, 54–58

Diseases: and climate, 34; malaria, 35; measles, 35

Drowsiness, 85–86

Dr. Strangelove: doomsday machine in, 2–3, 219; and George's *Red Alert*, 211–213

Dulles, John Foster, views on nuclear weapons, 313, 315, 316, 317, 319, 320–321, 324

Duncan, O. D., and B., 302

Economics: truths in, 147–151, 243, 244–247, 257, 258; vs. physical sciences, 149–150; relationship to public policies, 152–164; health economists, 156–158; and values, 156–158, 169, 193–194; theory of externalities, 168–169; public goods in, 203–204, 257; laws in, 243, 244, 257; unintended/unexpected aggregate results in, 249, 256, 257

Einstein, Albert, 220

Eisenhower, Dwight, views on nuclear weapons, 229–330, 315–316, 319

Electric Power Research Institute, 45

Electric utilities, 167–168, 171

El Niño, 27, 46

Elster, Jon, 71, 79n2, 241

Embarrassment, 95–97; Goffman on, 96

Energy crisis of 1970s, 41

Energy pricing policy, 222–223

Energy: The Next Twenty Years, 29–30, 222

Environmental policy: afforestation, 47–48, 49–50; regarding toxic waste sites, 52, 162, 166–167; and cost-benefit analysis, 162–163, 164; costs imposed by, 162–163, 164, 167–168; and attitudes toward pollution, 163, 164, 192; regarding carcinogens, 163, 199–200; regarding electric utilities, 167–168, 171; distributional issues regarding,

Environmental policy *(continued)*
168; regarding endangered species,
169; role of values in, 169; social controls as, 169–179; bottle bills, 171,
174–177, 179, 195–196; role of prices
in, 179–207; regulatory standards vs.
emission/effluent charges, 181, 182–
184, 186–191; emission/effluent
charges, 181–204; role of damage determination in, 184–186, 192–193,
195–196, 197–200, 202–203; and
technology for abatement, 186–187,
201

Ethnic minorities, 127. *See also* Segregation

Euphoria, 87, 119

European Payments Union, 17

Euthanasia, 128; as assisted suicide, 66,
132–136, 139; as active, 131, 132–
133, 134–135, 139n2; as passive, 131–
132; in the Netherlands, 133, 138;
public attitudes toward active euthanasia, 134–135, 139n2

Evolution, biological, 19, 21, 91–92, 241,
256–257

Explanation vs. prediction in science,
239–241

Externalities, 166–180, 193, 195; social
controls regarding, 169–179

Faking, 21. *See also* Bluffs

Falkland Islands, 322

Fankhauser, Samuel, 51

Fantasy, 97–98

Fear, 88–90, 97; phobias, 68, 92–93

Federal Food, Drug and Cosmetic Act:
Delaney Amendment to, 163

Fees and charges, 170; emission/effluent
charges, 163, 181–204; bottle deposits,
171, 174–177, 179, 195–196; options
offered by, 172, 173, 192; vs. fines and
penalties, 172–173, 195, 204; vs.
taxes, 173, 182, 195; vs. paying firms
for emissions abatement, 200–204

Fines and penalties, 171; vs. fees and
charges, 172–173, 195, 204; vs. taxes,
173

Flat tax, 155

Fleet mileage, 204–206

Fletcher, Joseph, 137–138

Forbes, Steve, 155

Ford Foundation, 222

Forgetfulness, 98–99

"Framework Convention on Climate
Change," 30

Frank, Pat: *Alas, Babylon,* 212, 214–
215

Free rider problem, 108, 203

Fried, Charles, 14

Fuchs, Victor, 155, 156–158

Gains from trade, 151

Geoengineering, 42–43, 45–50; defined,
46–47; international negotiations regarding, 48–50

George, Peter Bryan: *Red Alert,* 211–213,
215

Germany, 40, 223

Gertner, Robert H., 7

Global warming, 27–44, 223–224; relationship to greenhouse effect, 27–29;
science relating to, 27–29, 32–33; and
Kyoto Protocol, 30–31, 32, 40–41, 43–
44; technologies relating to, 31–32; impact of, 33–36; and developing countries, 34–36; and rationing of carbon
emissions, 36–38; and geoengineering,
42–43, 45–50

Goffman, E., on embarrassment, 96

Greenhouse effect, 27–29, 222–224; and
geoengineering, 42–43, 45–50. *See
also* Carbon dioxide; Methane

Greenhouse gas abatement: discounting
benefits of, 51–58; vs. hazardous-waste
cleanup, 52; as redistribution of income, 53–54, 58; benefits for developing countries vs. developed countries,
55–56, 57

Gresham's Law, 257

Grodzins, Morton, 302

Gross domestic product (GDP), in developing vs. developed countries, 56–57

Groupthink, 112–113

Guarantees, 12–13

Gulf Stream, 41

Gun control, 127, 154

Halperin, Morton, 212; *Strategy and Arms Control,* 162
Harris, Louis, 139n2
Harvard Center for International Affairs, 161
Harvard-MIT Seminar on Arms Control of 1960, 162
Hastings Center Report, The, 135
Hazardous waste, 166–167, 172; Superfund program, 52; toxic waste sites, 52, 162, 163
Health care: in developing countries, 34, 35–36; Fuchs on, 155, 156–158; public policies regarding, 155, 156–158; positive/value-free vs. policy-value questions regarding, 156–158
Hedström, Peter: *Social Mechanisms,* 236, 247
Herrnstein, Richard, and C. Murray: *The Bell Curve,* 153
Hiroshima, 218, 322, 323, 324
Hirschman, Albert, 107, 108
Hitchcock, Alfred, 11; *Vertigo,* 92
Ho Chi Minh, 227
Hodgson, Ray, 79n3
Homer, on Menelaos-Antilochos race, 6
Hostages, 10–11
Hughes, Howard, 92
Hurricanes, 50

Iceland, 38
IIASA. *See* International Institute for Applied Systems Analysis
Iliad, Menelaos-Antilochos race in, 6
India, 43, 44, 324
Indonesia, 43
Informer, The, Jeppo in, 87
Insomnia, 86, 97
Institute for Strategic Studies, 162
Insurance companies, 15
Intergovernmental Panel on Climate Change (IPCC), 27, 29
International Institute for Applied Systems Analysis (IIASA), 223–224
International Institute for Strategic Studies, 161
International negotiations: bargaining tactics in, 17; regarding carbon dioxide

emissions, 30–31, 32, 36–38, 39, 40–41, 43–44, 49; within WTO, 38, 40; within NATO, 38–40; regarding geoengineering, 48–50
IPCC. *See* Intergovernmental Panel on Climate Change
Iran, 324, 325
Iraq, Persian Gulf War of 1991, 322–323
Israel: relations with United States, 320; Yom Kippur War, 322
Italy, 38, 40

Janis, Irving, on groupthink, 112–113
Japan, 43–44, 55
Johnson, Lyndon: academics in administration of, 161; and Vietnam War, 226, 229, 230–231; views on nuclear weapons, 229, 230, 316, 317, 322, 324

Kahn, Herman, 212, 213
Kaufman, William, 212
Keillor, Garrison, on the children of Lake Woebegone, 246
Kennedy administration: Cuban missile crisis, 5–6, 7, 229, 316–317; academics in, 159–160, 161, 162; John F. Kennedy's views on use of nuclear weapons, 316–317, 321
Keynes, John Maynard, 235
Khrushchev, Nikita, 213, 232
Kissinger, Henry, 160
Kitto, H. D. F., 14
Koppett, L., 88–89
Korean War, 227, 229, 314–315, 320, 322
Kreps, David M., 7
Kubrick, Stanley, 212
Kyoto Protocol, 30–31, 32, 40–41, 43–44

Labor-management relations: threats to strike, 2, 3–4; Boulwarism, 16
Law: suits, 2, 6, 14–15, 166, 170, 171; three-strikes-and-you're-out laws, 8, 154; regarding corporations, 14–15; regarding contracts, 14–15, 65–66, 180; mechanics lien laws, 15; and anticipatory self-commands, 65–67; regarding

316, 317, 319, 320–321; vs. conventional weapons, 229–230, 313–314, 315–319, 321–322; taboo against use of, 229–230, 313–325; battlefield nuclear weapons, 313–314, 316, 317, 322–323; Nuclear Non-Proliferation Treaty, 314; vs. peaceful nuclear explosions (PNEs), 319; vs. chemical weapons, 319, 322–323; Comprehensive Test Ban Treaty, 324–325

Nunn, R. Gregory: *Habit Control in a Day*, 79n3, 94

Oceans: El Niño, 27, 46; influence on climate, 27–28, 32, 46, 49; absorption of carbon dioxide by, 31, 46, 49; Gulf Stream, 41; and West Antarctic Ice Sheet, 41–42

OECD. *See* Organization for European Cooperation and Development

O'Leary, K. Daniel, 79n3

Oman, C. W. C., 19

On the Beach, 212, 213–214

Organization for European Cooperation and Development (OECD), 38

Organization for European Economic Co-operation (OEEC), 38–39

Ozone, stratospheric, 46

Pain, anticipatory self-command regarding, 63–65, 74, 76–78, 80nn6,7, 88

Pakistan, 324

Panic, 90

Pareto optimality/improvements, 73, 151

Parking meters, 171, 177–179

Pascal, A. H., 251, 309n1

Peaceful nuclear explosions (PNEs), 319

Pearce, David W., 16

Performative utterances, 9–10

Persian Gulf War of 1991, 322–323

Peters, Bryan. *See* George, Peter Bryan

Phelps, Edmund, 71

Phobias, 68, 92–93. *See also* Fear

Picker, Randal C., 7

Pollak, Robert, 71

Pornography, 127

Potsdam agreement, 226, 227

Preventive detention, 127

Prices: price wars, 7; price controls, 17; of abortion, 153; determination of, 171, 173–174, 175–177, 184, 185–186, 197–200; determined by auctions, 171, 184, 185–186; as measures, 173–174, 189–190, 191–193, 196; scarcity value reflected by, 174; of taxi medallions, 174, 177, 207; discrimination by, 178–179, 199; role in environmental policy, 179–207; emission/effluent charges, 181–204; of gasoline, 206; energy pricing policy, 222–223

Pricing systems, 166, 179–207; regulatory standards vs. emission/effluent charges, 162–166, 181, 182–184, 186–191; bottle deposits, 171, 174–177, 179, 195–196; parking meters, 171, 177–179; role of fees and charges in, 172–173; as social controls, 172–179; decentralized decisions in, 173–179; determination of prices in, 175–177, 191; discrimination in, 178–179; emission/effluent charges, 181–204; damage determination in, 184–186, 192–193, 195–196, 197–200, 202–203; funds collected in, 186, 187, 188–189, 194–196, 197; emissions abatement induced by, 187–189, 191–193, 194, 196; as requiring firms to pay full costs of emissions, 193–194, 195, 196–197; paying firms for emissions abatement, 200–204; fleet mileage, 204–206

Princess Bride, The, 9

Prisoners' Dilemma, 108

Productivity and climate, 34, 56

Promises: relationship to commitment, 2; vs. threats, 2, 7–9, 10, 11, 13, 14; as unwelcome, 7; role of performative utterances/speech acts in, 9–10, 12; credibility of, 9–15; and hostages, 10–11; by eunuchs, 11; defined, 11–12; of veracity, 12; guarantees, 12–13; two-tiered promises, 12–13; conditionality of, 13; breaking of, 13–14; false promises, 14; secret ballots, 15; by governments, 17

Property rights, 171, 180

Public Faces, 220, 221, 222

Public goods, 203–204, 257

Public policies, 152–164; regarding the environment, 52, 162–164; regarding government budgets, 107, 111, 155–156; regarding abortion, 152–153; regarding race relations, 153; relationship to socioeconomic status, 153, 158; regarding crime and punishment, 154; regarding illegal drugs, 154; regarding health care, 155, 156–158, 161; regarding defense, 158–162

Quemoy crisis, 316

Quinlan, Karen Ann, 129

Race: and public policies, 153; relationship to socioeconomic status, 153, 255–256. *See also* Segregation

Radford, Arthur W., 320–321

Radioisotopes, 221–222

Rage and temper, 90–91

RAND Corporation, 158–159, 249, 251

Rationality: and pain, 63–65, 74, 76–78, 80nn6,7, 88, 92; rational consumer model and self-command, 67–72; and addiction, 69, 82–83, 93–94, 99, 100–105; lapses in, 82–105; and apparent changes in preference, 83–84; and sleep/drowsiness, 85–86; and depression, 86–87; and euphoria, 87; and alcohol consumption, 87–88, 90; and fear, 88–90, 92–93, 94, 97; during extremes of motivation, 88–92; relationship to voluntariness, 89, 99–100; and panic, 90; and rage/temper, 90–91; and thirst, 91–92, 102; and phobias, 92–93; and compulsive behaviors, 93–94; and television watching, 94; and nervous interaction, 94–97; and giggling, 95; and embarrassment, 95–97; and daydreaming/fantasy, 97–98; and absentmindedness/forgetfulness, 98–99; and temptations, 99–104; rules for determining who gets saved, 140–143. *See also* Self-command, anticipatory

Rawls, John, on the veil of ignorance, 142

Red Alert, 211–213

Redistribution of income, 53–54, 58

Reilly, William K., 222–223

Resources for the Future, 222

Revelle, Roger, 223

Reynolds, R. J. (RJR), 121

Rights: right to be sued, 14–15; right to sue, 14–15; as inalienable, 65–66, 112, 131; right to bear arms, 127, 137; conflict between, 127–128; of parents, 127–128; right to abortion, 128; right to die, 128, 129–139, 139n2; of the comatose, 130; of the incompetent, 130–131; right to unassisted suicide, 133, 136; relationship to obligations, 138–139; trading of emission rights, 171; property rights, 171, 180; determination of, 201–202; under Clean Air Act, 206, 207; to emit from stationary sources, 206, 207; import quotas, 206, 207; water rights, 206, 207; transferable vs. nontransferable, 206–207; mineral rights, 207

Rio conference of 1992: "Framework Convention on Climate Change," 30; Kyoto Protocol, 30–31, 32, 40–41, 43–44

Roosevelt, Franklin D., 220

Rules for determining who gets saved, 140–143; and self-interest, 141; and desert, 141–142; and veil of ignorance, 142; relationship to appropriate behavior, 143

Rusk, Dean, 316

Russia, and Kyoto Protocol, 30

Sales taxes, 148

Scarf, Herb, 250

Schiavo, Terri, 129

Science, 29

Scitovsky, Tibor, 79n2

Scowcroft, Brent, 160

Scripps Institute of Oceanography, 45

S-curves, 236–237, 238–239

Searle, John R., on speech acts, 9

Secret Agent, 17–18

Segregation, 249–310; spatial proximity model of, 249–251, 252–253, 260, 261–284, 307; and tolerant majorities, 250–251, 252; neighborhood tipping,

251, 302–309, 310n6; bounded neighborhood model of, 251–252, 260–261, 284–302, 307; role of communication systems in, 253, 256; role of organizations in, 253–254, 255, 256; role of individual choices in, 253–254, 255–256; role of economic conditions in, 255–256; and integrationist preferences, 282–284, 301

Self-command, anticipatory, 63–80, 79nn2,3,4, 80n5; and pain, 63–65, 74, 76–78, 80nn6,7, 88; and obstetrical anesthesia, 63–65, 74, 88; defined, 64; role of second parties, 64–65; two-selves analogy regarding, 65, 66, 70, 71–78, 83; and suicide, 65, 66, 75–76, 80n6; legal issues regarding, 65–67; relationship to model of rational consumer, 67–72; and cigarette smoking, 72, 82–83, 93–94, 99, 100–105; and utility comparisons, 73–74, 76–78, 80nn6,7; self-blackmail, 79n4; and television watching, 94; and forgetfulness, 98–99; and eating, 99; as collective self-binding, 108–110, 111–112

Self-fulfilling prophecies, 241–243
Sen, Amartya, 79n2
Sex education, 127, 128
Shefrin, H. M., 79n2
Shorr, Daniel, 21
Shute, Nevil: *On the Beach*, 212, 213–214
Singapore, malaria in Malaysia vs., 35
Sleep, 85, 86, 97
Smith, Adam, on self-command, 67
Smokestack emissions, 182, 193
Social controls, 169–179; self-controls, 170; law suits as, 170, 171; tax incentives/penalties, 170, 171; prohibitions, 170–171; regulations, 170–171; overt controls, 170–172; imprisonment, 171; fines and penalties, 171, 172–173; bottle deposits, 171, 174–177, 179, 195–196; parking meters, 171, 177–179; market creation, 171, 180; subsidies, 171, 205–206; carcass deposits, 171–172; pricing systems as, 172–179. *See*

also Fees and charges; Fines and penalties
Social goals, 127, 128–129
Social mechanisms: relationship to theories, 235–236; defined, 236; relationship to mathematics, 236, 238–241, 247–248; as interpretation in terms of individual behavior, 236–239; as explanations vs. predictions, 238–241; families of, 241–243; and self-fulfilling prophecies, 241–243; and accounting identities, 243–247
Socioeconomic status: relationship to cigarette smoking, 115, 116, 122, 123; relationship to attitudes regarding euthanasia, 135; relationship to public policies, 153, 158; relationship to race, 153, 255–256
Solow, Robert, 240–241
South Korea, 43. *See also* Korean War
Soviet Union: nuclear strategy against, 2–3; Cuban missile crisis, 5–6, 7, 229, 316–317; relations with United States, 5–6, 7, 229, 316–317, 321, 324; relations with China, 226; relations with North Vietnam, 226–227; Czechoslovakia invaded by, 229; Afghanistan invaded by, 232, 321–322, 324
Spatial proximity model of segregation, 249–251, 252–253, 260, 261–284, 307
Speech acts, 9–10
Steiner, George, 72
Stigler, George, 79n2
Strategic behavior, 21–23
Strategic Defense Initiative/"Star Wars," 221
Strategy and Arms Control, 162
Strikes, labor, 2, 3–4
Strotz, Robert, 71
Suicide: ambivalence regarding, 65, 66, 75–76, 80n6; anticipatory self-command regarding, 65, 66, 75–76, 80n6; legal issues regarding, 66; as assisted, 66, 132–136, 139; in the Netherlands, 133; public attitudes toward, 133, 134–136, 139n2; in France, 134; in United Kingdom, 134; in United States, 134; by drugs, 134, 137; and institutional-

Suicide *(continued)*
ized persons, 136–137; by gunshot,
137–138
Sulfur aerosols, 32, 42, 47, 48, 49
Superfund program, 52
Suspense, and addiction, 104, 105
Swedberg, Richard: *Social Mechanisms*,
236, 247
Szilard, Leo, 220

Tailgating, 5
Taiwan, 8–9, 316, 317
Taxes: sales taxes, 148; flat tax, 155;
green taxes, 164; tax incentives, 170,
171; vs. fines and penalties, 173; vs.
fees and charges, 173, 182, 195; excise
taxes, 205–206; public goods financed
by, 257
Taxi medallions, 174, 177, 207
Temptations, 66, 86, 99–105, 109. *See
also* Addiction
Terrorism, 29
Thaler, Richard, 79n2
Tharp, Roland, 79n3
Thatcher, Margaret, 322
Thirst, 91–92, 102
Threats: to resign, 2; credibility of, 2, 3,
4, 7; to strike, 2, 3–4; to sue, 2, 6; conditionality of, 2, 6–7; vs. promises, 2,
7–9, 10, 11, 13, 14; defined, 2, 8; to
use nuclear weapons, 2–3; doomsday
machine in *Dr. Strangelove*, 2–3, 219;
relationship to commitment, 2–9; po-
tency of, 3; vs. warnings, 3, 7, 8; as
bluffs, 3, 14, 316; as probabilistic, 4–7;
tailgating, 5; as welcome, 7–9
Time preferences, 51, 52–54, 71
Toxic waste sites, 52, 162, 163, 166–167
Trivia, 113
Truman, Harry S., 229, 314, 322
Truths: in economics, 147–151, 243–247;
and definitions, 148; accounting identities, 148–151, 243–247
Turkey, 38

United Kingdom, 38, 134, 314, 322
United Nations, budget of, 43, 49

United States: Kennedy administration,
5–6, 7, 153, 159–160, 161, 162, 229,
316–317, 321; Cuban missile crisis, 5–
6, 7, 229, 316–317; relations with Soviet Union, 5–6, 7, 229, 316–317, 321,
324; relations with China, 8–9, 229,
315, 316, 317, 320; relations with Taiwan, 8–9, 316, 317; National Labor
Relations Board, 16; Marshall Plan,
17, 38, 39, 40; Congress of, 17, 43,
110, 111, 163, 325; George W. Bush
administration, 30; and Kyoto Protocol,
30–31, 32, 43–44; agriculture in, 34;
climate and production for markets in,
34; and NATO, 38–40; Superfund program, 52; balanced-budget amendment
to Constitution, 107, 111, 155; Vietnam War, 108, 226–232; First Amendment, 110; Federal Trade Commission,
121; gun control in, 127, 154; individual liberty in, 127–130; Clinton administration, 130, 160; attitudes toward
physician-assisted suicide in, 134–
136, 139n2; stock market in 1994,
148; private savings rate in, 149; abortion financing in, 152–153; defense
policy in, 158–162; Carter administration, 160, 218, 224, 318; George H. W.
Bush administration, 160, 223; Nixon
administration, 160, 226, 230–231,
322; fleet mileage in, 204–206; Johnson administration, 226, 229, 230–231,
316, 317, 322, 324; Truman administration, 229, 314, 322; Eisenhower administration, 229–330, 313, 315–316,
317, 319, 320–321, 324; relations with
United Kingdom, 314; relations with
Israel, 320; relations with Iraq, 322–
323
U.S. Central Intelligence Agency, 160
U.S. Department of Defense, 159–160,
161, 162
U.S. Department of Energy, 162
U.S. Department of Transportation,
121
U.S. Environmental Protection Agency,
162, 163, 223, 224